SALT & LIGHT

SALT & LIGHT

A Christian Response to Current Issues

DAVID J. GYERTSON

EDITOR

WORD PUBLISHING
Dallas·London·Vancouver·Melbourne

SALT AND LIGHT: A CHRISTIAN RESPONSE TO CURRENT ISSUES

All Scripture quotations, unless otherwise noted, are taken from the *Holy
Bible: New International Version* (North American Edition), copyright ©
1973, 1978, 1984 by the International Bible Society. Used by permission of
Zondervan Bible Publishers. Verses marked NKJV are from the *Holy Bible,
New King James Version*, copyright © 1982 by Thomas Nelson, Inc. Verses
marked PHILLIPS are from the *New Testament in Modern English* by J. B.
Phillips, rev. ed. published by the Macmillan Company, copyright © 1958,
1960, 1972. Verses marked TLB are from *The Living Bible*, copyright ©
1971 by Tyndale House Publishers, Wheaton, Illinois.

Library of Congress Cataloging-in-Publication Data

Salt and light : a Christian response to current issues / David J. Gyertson,
    editor.
    p.   cm.
    ISBN 0–8499–3499–0
    1. Church and social problems—Christianity.   2. Church and social
problems—United States.   1. Gyertson, David J., 1946– .
HN35.S25   1993
261.8'3—dc20   92–36199
                                                                    CIP

34569 LB 98765432

Printed in the United States of America

You are the salt of the earth. But if the salt loses its saltiness, how can it be made salty again? It is no longer good for anything, except to be thrown out and trampled by men.

You are the light of the world. A city on a hill cannot be hidden. Neither do people light a lamp and put it under a bowl. Instead they put it on its stand, and it gives light to everyone in the house. In the same way, let your light shine before men, that they may see your good deeds and praise your Father in heaven.

Matthew 5:13–16

Jesus Christ

The Sermon on the Mount

Contents

Acknowledgments

Grateful acknowledgment is made for permission to reprint the following articles:

"The Visible World," by Pat Robertson from The Secret Kingdom, copyright © 1992 by Word, Inc., Dallas, Tex. Used by permission.

"The Devil's Gauntlet," reprinted as *The Devil's Gauntlet*, by Os Guinness, copyright © 1989 by Os Guinness. Used by permission of InterVarsity Press, P.O. Box 1400, Downers Grove, Ill. 60515.

"The Foundations for Faith and Freedom" and "The Destruction of Faith and Freedom," excerpted from *A Christian Manifesto*, of Francis A. Shaeffer, copyright © 1981. Used by permission of Good News Publishers/Crossway Books, Wheaton, Ill.

"Meeting Secular Humanism," by J. I. Packer and Thomas Howard from *Christianity: The True Humanism*, copyright © 1985 by Word, Inc., Dallas, Texas. Used by permission.

"Snapshots of Faith in Action," excerpted from *Turning Point: A Christian Worldview Declaration* by Herbert W. Schlossberg and Marvin Olasky, copyright © 1987. Used by permission of Good News Publishers/Crossway Books, Wheaton, Ill.

"The Way Forward," from *When Choice Becomes God*, by F. LaGard Smith. Copyright © 1990 by F. LaGard Smith. Published by Harvest House Publishers, Eugene, Oreg. 97402. Used by permission.

"Euthanasia and the Right to Die," from "Euthanasia" in *The Right to Live; the Right to Die*, by C. Everett Koop. Wheaton, Ill.: Tyndale House Publishers, 1976, pp. 88–117. All rights reserved. Reprinted by permission of the publisher.

Introduction

The Salt and Light Mandate

*T*he turning point in my life came through a salvation encounter with the Creator God, who revealed himself to me through his only Son Jesus Christ. However, the real **purpose** for and **power** of that redemption came when I realized through the systematic study of Scripture that his truth was not just for the personal needs of a troubled runaway, but the **life source** for the problems and critical issues that have plagued people and society from the beginning of time.

It was in that revelation where the seeds for a lifestyle and worldview of "living by the Book" were born. Years later a lifelong dream was realized when the Christian Broadcasting Network gave me the privilege of developing a comprehensive approach to the study of the Scriptures by that very name. Today *Living By The Book* is helping thousands apply God's unchanging Word to twentieth-century life.

During my tenure as general editor of *Living By The Book,* I hosted daily a nationwide call-in talk show for the CBN Radio Network called *On-The-Line* and periodically co-hosted the television broadcast of "The 700 Club with Pat Robertson." Through these "classrooms of the air" I was challenged by the lives and thought of men like Tony Campolo, C. Everett Koop, Donald Wildmon, Gary Bauer, George Grant, William Dannemeyer, William Bennett, and Charles Colson.

In my career as a college educator and president of Regent University, much of my pro-active Christian thinking—my theology of Christians in society—has been shaped by the writings of Francis Schaeffer, Os Guiness, J. I. Packer, and Marvin Olasky. My fifteen years of working with Pat Robertson, founder of the Christian Broadcasting Network, has been a refiner's fire, challenging me to realize that right thinking—orthodoxy—is irrelevant if not accompanied by the orthopraxy of right living.

Each of these "Gamaliels" has forced me to think and live beyond my theological comfort zones and fellowship preferences. They have driven me back to the Magna Carta of the Christian faith—Jesus' Sermon on the Mount—which constantly reminds his disciples of their mission in society.

The hallmark of Jesus' teaching was his ability to take the foundational principles of God's kingdom, which had been complicated and confused by centuries of analytical debate, and make them applicable to the current day and the common man. In the first twelve verses of Matthew 5, Jesus presents the **character revolution** necessary to prepare reliable and responsible agents of Christ in culture.

Believers, whose work and witness will survive the test of eternity, now have their heads and hands transformed by a poorness of spirit that humbly identifies with the griefs and joys of a searching world. They pursue both positions and possessions for the greatest good. They are a people of justice, purity, mercy, and forgiveness, who know that these eternal qualities, enabled through Christ's abiding Spirit, are necessary to guarantee the vitality and to preserve the integrity of our salt and light mission.

The "salt and light" lifestyle commanded by our Lord in Matthew 5:13–16, the verses immediately following the Beatitudes, is one of those classic good news/bad news paradoxes. As Christians engage in the challenging task of living in a fallen world, we are viewed by some as a preserving chemical, essential not only to hindering decay but also to sustaining life and bringing accented flavors into a tasteless society. To others our saltiness awakens an awareness of thirst that can only be satisfied in the living waters of Christ. And for others we become the sting in the open wounds of those fearing or even despising the presence of such an aggravating and intrusive substance.

As revealers of light, the followers of Christ illumine darkened pathways, helping to answer life's perplexing questions of meaning, purpose, and destiny. For others we become the dawning of a new day that dispels paralyzing fears. But others, whose deeds are done in darkness, flee such exposure or seek to quench it through denial, disparagement, and outright persecution.

The saltiness of our savor and the brightness of our light is ultimately a character issue. We can **know** what is right and even be trained to **do** what is right, but in the kingdom of Christ that has never been sufficient. Our thoughts and work must issue from the pure motives of the "circumcised" heart.

Our salt and light role in a fallen society has never been a simple one. From the first century, the faithful followers of Christ have wrestled with methods and motives as they have sought to be the Lord's vessels of both personal and social redemption. It is, however, an essential one if the fullness of God's plan for humanity and creation is to be achieved.

Not since the days of the early church or the times of the great Reformers like Luther, Calvin, and Wesley have Christians been more aware of the need to make the principles of faith and the teachings of Scripture relevant to everyday life. With the collapse of atheistic ideologies and the bankruptcy of values-neutral thinking, America and the world are once again ready for a fresh revelation and application of "the way, the truth, and the life." Historically, the best thought and action of Western civilization has demonstrated that only this Christ-centered worldview gives permanent meaning to human existence and provides a reliable hope for the human dilemma.

Pro-active Christians are once more moving into the classrooms, the courtrooms, and the boardrooms of our nation. The challenge we face is to enter these arenas and to successfully engage these with opposing points of view in ways that neither compromise our message nor negate our witness. The battlegrounds include the sanctity of life, personal and religious rights, sexuality, ethics, justice, free speech, and secular humanism. Such current issues are as immediate and relevant as the headlines of today's newspapers and tomorrow's uncertainties.

I felt that a text was needed that responsibly addressed the hard issues of our day from a conservative, scriptural perspective—one that would both inform and inspire, challenging people, in the words of Quaker philosopher Elton Trueblood, to the lifestyle of the "tough mind and tender heart." This book does just that: equipping disciples to be prepared for and committed to our Lord's "in the world but not of it" challenge.

Modern-day Christianity has produced many biblically centered thinkers who have written on the critical issues that must be confronted if the lifelines of contemporary society are to be preserved and extended. These contemporary Mars Hill apologists are challenging us to shake off the old heresies that separated God from everyday public life and to respond to the pressing issues in areas beyond our traditional Christian comfort zones.

The following selections from the writings of some who have effectively taken up this mandate in our day represent only a taste, a glimmer, of the rich Christian thinking that is addressing our current social, political, educational, and cultural challenges. These brief articles in no way fully represent the depth or completeness of each writer's thinking on these matters nor articulate the totality of the biblical view. It is my desire that, at the very least, they will motivate you to dig deeper, to think more critically, to work more effectively, and to pray more consistently about committing yourself to becoming our Lord's "salt and light" in a thirsting and searching society.

Special thanks are due the *Living By The Book* editorial and production staff for their assistance in preparing this volume, especially to Skip Horton for editing the essays and to Mark Wilson, the general editor, for his oversight of the project.

If you are interested in obtaining the entire "Current Issues By The Book" course, for which *Salt and Light* is the textbook, write: *Living By The Book*, The Christian Broadcasting Network, 700 CBN Center, Virginia Beach, VA 23463–0001.

David J. Gyertson, Ph.D.

DAVID J. GYERTSON, Ph.D., is the president of Regent University, Virginia Beach, Virginia, and the designer and executive editor of the *Living By The Book* discipleship curriculum produced by the Christian Broadcasting Network.

1

The Modern Crisis

Pat Robertson

*T*he modern world is in crisis. Many people have the feeling that unless drastic changes are made quickly in the way this country is being run, the United States may not last out the century as the number-one superpower. We are moving rapidly into a state of social, intellectual, economic, and moral decline. Anywhere you look today you can see the evidence of looming disaster; you can hear urgent cries for change. Where can we turn for stability in our life? Is there anything or anyone to help us? The world as we know it is in chaos.

It is clearer each day that the world is hurtling toward some type of catastrophe. The upheavals in Eastern Europe and problems with the political process in the United States are ongoing concerns. The federal budget deficit is out of control, and the worldwide debate over ecology and the environment is escalating as never before. Anyone can see that our problems are only getting worse, and the people of America and the entire world are reaching the point of desperation. Some people are apparently willing to try solutions that are not well thought out or well reasoned, just to make a change.

PAT ROBERTSON is founder and chairman of the Christian Broadcasting Network, chancellor of Regent University, president of United States Media Corporation, chairman of The Family Channel, and president of Operation Blessing. He is host of the daily television program "The 700 Club" and the author of such bestsellers as *The Secret Kingdom* and *The New World Order*.

Recently we saw what could happen when, in similar circumstances, a new president came into power virtually overnight in Peru and took drastic measures to restore order and balance in his country. The reformer, President Alberto Fujimori, effectively abandoned the democratic process. He could see that the system had grown corrupt, crime was out of control, and the entire nation was seemingly in peril, so he simply took matters into his own hands and the people went along with it. That is a potentially dangerous precedent. Yet, despite his dramatic action, months later terrorists were bombing the utilities of Lima, the capital city of Peru.

In this country we need only pause to consider what happened in the spring of 1992 in South Central Los Angeles. As a result of the unpopular jury decision in the Rodney King case, angry protesters took part in riots that cost more than forty lives and more than $1.5 billion in property damages. There is unrest and bitterness in the black community and a splintering of society. There is a deepening decline in moral values. What have we left to build upon? Everywhere people are crying out for something better.

In my book, *The New World Order*, I surveyed the conditions driving the world toward chaos. We don't hear as much about the government's world order agenda these days, but the conditions are still there, and, if anything, they are intensifying. Looking at the economic trends of the 1990s, it is clear that the exponential compounding of debt has taken us to the brink of economic collapse. Today there is a very real possibility of a money crisis to be followed by ruinous inflation.

During 1991 and '92 I was invited to go to Zaire and develop agricultural and economic programs to help aid that faltering economy. Zaire is an example of a rich, productive economy that collapsed under decades of mismanagement. Today anyone can see the results of the breakdown there. The currency has inflated from one zaire-to-three dollars to eight hundred thousand zaires-to-one dollar.

Nothing works properly. Airlines fly erratically; telephone service is not available; the roads are impassable; the hospitals have no medicine. Once an exporter of food, there is now not enough food for the people. Seventy percent of the people are unemployed. Forty percent of them have AIDS. There is catastrophe everywhere. Conditions for Zaire and other nations of Africa have plunged precipitously in the past ten years.

Rich and Poor

In many parts of the world there is a heightened sense of uncertainty amid what seems to be incredible prosperity. The wealthy are very wealthy; those with access to capital have never had it so good. The wealth available to them is simply staggering. The statistics in various news magazines indicate that the percentage of wealth controlled by the top 1 percent of the population continues to grow while the bottom 63 percent of wage earners have experienced only marginal growth in income over the past decade.

Of course the economic structure is not totally frozen: Some people have been able to move from middle-income levels into the upper-income brackets—there is still some economic mobility—but there is no question that the total share of wealth to those in the upper-income categories has grown more rapidly than the other segments of society.

Over the past ten years CBN News has tracked the social and moral conditions of this nation, and the reports I have seen are shocking. The educational crisis is appalling. This country is becoming a nation of illiterates. We have also done story after story on crime, addiction, divorce, the collapse of the family, and other issues, and the situation is not getting any better. We don't see any signs in this country that things are improving.

Ironically, in the former Soviet Union moral conditions are no worse and potentially much better than here. At least there is a genuine hunger for moral and spiritual values, and that is the absolutely essential first step to recovery. It is ironic that while America is moving away from the heritage which made us great, the former Communist nations are seeking after God.

The key words in any description of our plight are economy, energy, crime, poverty, morality, education, hunger, and pollution. Volumes are written on each. And each carries the same deterioration theme—deterioration and danger. The great cosmic clock appears to be winding down.

All about us we see "fear in a handful of dust," in Eliot's words, as man stares horror-stricken at,

A heap of broken images, where the sun beats,
And the dead tree gives no shelter, the cricket no relief,
And the dry stone no sound of water.[1]

Even starker are the images from the book of Isaiah in which the Old Testament prophet speaks of the darkness that descends upon a people when they have been disobedient to the will of God. Isaiah wrote:

> We grope for the wall like the blind,
> And we grope as if we had no eyes;
> We stumble at noonday as at twilight;
> We are as dead men in desolate places.
> We all growl like bears,
> And moan sadly like doves;
> We look for justice, but there is none;
> For salvation, but it is far from us.
> For our transgressions are multiplied before You,
> And our sins testify against us;
> For our transgressions are with us,
> And as for our iniquities, we know them.[2]

Just as Isaiah predicted, the world is crying out for solutions to problems that are too big for us. Our governments are on the verge of collapse; our finances are in desperate condition; the environment is polluted; millions die of starvation in Third World nations where the population is skyrocketing and industry is collapsing. Underlying fear is covered by a thin veneer of affluence. "'There is no peace,' / Says my God, 'for the wicked.'"[3]

Our condition is not difficult to understand. We need only trace a few strands of the hangman's noose that seems poised over our heads, beginning with the most immediately destructive, the threat of nuclear holocaust.

The Age of Terror

Let us go back to 1940. Three physicists—Enrico Fermi, Leo Szilard, and Eugene Wigner—working in a makeshift laboratory in a handball court under the grandstand at the University of Chicago, split the atom and thereby confirmed the theoretical formula of Albert Einstein: $E = mc^2$. The split, or fission, caused a multiplication of energy in the order of 6 million-to-one.

At last man had found a source of cheap and abundant energy for the world forever. A new industrial revolution was at hand. Age-old territorial disputes would end. Wars would cease. The poor could be warmed, sheltered, fed. No nation need be without.

History records a different outcome. The work of those three deeply religious men evolved into an age of terror, not an age of abundance. There was Hiroshima. Then Nagasaki.

That was only the beginning. Physicists quickly perfected nuclear fusion and a release of energy of 50 million-to-one. Utilizing hydrogen, a fuel as abundant as the waters of the seas, this process held promise as the energy source of the millennium. There need be no fossil fuel shortage, no air pollution, no fabulously wealthy OPEC oil cartel, and no desperately poor Third World.

The utopia did not come. Instead we have hydrogen bombs rated in millions of tons of TNT. The superpower nations, during the fifties and sixties, built arsenals capable of destroying all life on earth. A balance of terror developed between the United States and the Soviet Union bearing the terrifying acronym MAD—Mutual Assured Destruction.

Then came the seventies. The United States, wearied by its struggle in Southeast Asia, gradually dismantled its military capability, delaying the start of weapons systems commensurate with advanced technology. The Soviet Union, meanwhile, pushed its flagging economy to the breaking point to build the most awesome array of weapons ever assembled by a nation in peacetime.

Instead of balance, the world of the 1980s was faced with an imbalance of terror in favor of a malevolent dictatorship bent on world domination. Ultimately it was the inherent weaknesses of the Soviet system which brought that giant colossus to its knees. Its economy was in such terrible decay after years of godless socialism, collapse was inevitable. Even though I had predicted the collapse of the Soviet Union as early as 1969, it was stunning to see that event fulfilled in 1989 and 1990.

Today it is clear that Marxism was a failure from the very beginning. Its leadership was corrupt. The people lacked incentive to work; moral decay destroyed the sanctity of the family. Faith in God was prohibited, thus the souls of the people grew pale and desperate. Some kind of change had to come about.

Today Russia and the Commonwealth of Independent States (CIS) are looking to the West for help. Having endured a long string of upsets, complicated by hunger, a shocking coup attempt, and general disarray, the leaders of these fifteen former Communist nations are more open-minded now than ever. But we should never forget that the majority of the former Soviet nuclear capability is still intact, and the possibility of a hardline pro-Communist coup is very real indeed.

And nuclear weapons have found their way to Iraq and Iran. Nuclear and chemical technology rests with the madman Saddam Hussein. Mohamar Qaddafi of Libya and Syrian President Hafez al Assad are still very real threats to peace. The nations controlling Middle East oil are often ruthless, as we witnessed in the Iraqi invasion of Kuwait and the events of Operation Desert Storm in the spring of 1991. Despite the apparent peace in the Middle East, our age still retains the potential to touch off World War III. "Age of terror" is an apt description.

The Struggle for Energy

Intertwined with the age of terror is the concern for sufficient energy to satisfy the mushrooming demands of our planet. Scientists believe the demand for energy may be as ominous as the nuclear threat, despite the deceptive ebb and flow in short-range supply and demand.

In 1950 there were 2.51 billion people in the world. By 1980 the figure soared to 4.41 billion. The demand for everything from food to factories skyrocketed. Today we have a worldwide population of nearly 6 billion people, and unless interrupted by drastic changes or some terrible catastrophe, by 2010 the population will exceed 8 billion men, women, and children. With a birthrate of 100 million per year and a death rate of 50 million, the population of the world is growing with unbelievable speed.

But nothing exploded like the demand for energy. In 1950 the world used the equivalent of 2.66 billion metric tons of coal. In 1980 consumption was 9.5 billion metric tons. Today the world consumes the equivalent of 14.5 billion metric tons of coal, and the demand continues to grow.

In thirty years the population had not quite doubled; yet energy use had more than tripled. We were running wild with everything that required fuel.

This massive growth presented a simple truth as the decade of the eighties got under way: The planet does not contain enough nonrenewable and renewable sources of energy to supply indefinitely the basic needs and growing aspirations of a world population that continues to explode.

It seems clear that if some sort of solution is not forthcoming, we face the following perilous prospects:

• Those possessing dwindling energy sources will extract ever-increasing prices. This trend will hold true in the long run, even when temporary conditions cause occasional price drops that give the world a false sense of security. If recent patterns continue, the cost of energy will place such insupportable burdens on worldwide industry and financial markets that money supplies will be imprudently increased. This could set off hyperinflation and lead to worldwide financial collapse.

• To prolong high-energy lifestyles, the developed nations may use military force to seize dwindling resources. The war in the Persian Gulf was after all not so much an exercise to support the rights of the oppressed as it was a move to protect our continued access to Middle East oil.

• As oil import costs continue to mount, industrially developed nations will show more and more strain as they try to maintain a balance of trade. Aggressive financial actions, including punitive trade measures, seem certain and will heighten world tension.

• The prognosis is even worse for the weaker nations. They simply do not have the money to buy oil and pay interest on their huge debts at the same time. Many face bankruptcy already. Such default by any of several nations can cause suffering internally and global economic confusion externally. It could trigger a worldwide bank collapse, for example, unless the United States is willing to bail out the country in trouble.

• America's cities pose a unique danger that has wide-ranging potential, traceable in large part to energy consumption and high costs. The mammoth office buildings, shopping centers, and apartment houses of New York, Detroit, Chicago, Cleveland, Boston, Philadelphia, and other cities are energy gluttons. The rising operating costs have been staggering. Compounding this financial burden is the fact that the physical plants of these cities—the sewers, water lines, and other underground support utilities, plus the roads, bridges, and other systems above ground—have far exceeded their life expectancies. The cities don't have the money for proper maintenance and replacement. Time bombs are ticking away both above and below ground. Should they begin to explode, the cities will be brought to their knees. The social and economic consequences nationally and globally will be staggering.

• Imprudent substitution of hazardous, untested energy sources in the face of diminishing traditional sources could present the world with intolerable environmental problems affecting all of life. Yet rigid regulation could inhibit exploration, discovery, and creativity needed to overcome shortages. The dilemma breeds deep strife.

• The reluctance and/or inability of car manufacturers to respond to worldwide energy problems threw a major portion of American industry into a tailspin that threatened the wider economy. By the early eighties, foreign car manufacturers, led by the Japanese, had seized 28 percent of U.S. domestic auto business. Today, including foreign transplant operations, that figure has grown to 30 percent. Many major American industries, in fact, have been badly hurt in recent years by foreign competition and trade practices. Anger and discontent are mounting, with a crescendo of protectionist threats all around us.

The struggle for energy and the manifold ramifications of that struggle have propelled the world to the brink of upheaval. Even the tiniest of international movements has the potential for escalation.

Economic Disaster

Picking up another related thread, we learned that the lesser-developed nations of the world owed more than $500 billion to banks and wealthier nations early in 1981. Annual interest on those loans approached $100 billion, which was $35 billion more than the total debt of those nations only eight years earlier. Now, by 1992, just the Latin American nations have a combined debt of $442.7 billion. Tragically, they are being forced to borrow simply to pay their interest charges. A number of loans are being refinanced so the nations do not appear to be in default.

During this period, Poland was in the news as its people suffered the penalty of reaching for freedom from Soviet-led repression. That country's disastrous financial condition is typical of many other countries of the world. In 1982 it owed $24 billion of the total $89 billion owed to the West by Russia and the Eastern Bloc countries. By 1987, Poland's debt had soared to more than $40 billion. An agreement by foreign creditors arranged by the Paris Club in 1991 to write off nearly half that amount has given them some leverage, but current debt remains at more than $25 billion, and today the hopes of the Polish people for democracy and privatization remain in doubt.

It seems certain, with so many countries in a condition like Poland's, that one day a scene similar to the following will be played out.

A sweaty-palmed finance minister from Russia or Brazil or Poland will sit in a room in Switzerland or Germany or France and be told by several dignified bankers that his country's loans are in default. No more money is available. When word leaks out, the canny finance minister from oil-rich Kuwait, Abu Dhabi, Saudi Arabia, Iraq, or Libya could quietly withdraw his country's deposits from the banks in question. When word of this withdrawal is circulated, a wild scramble to get cash out of weakening banks could result.

Major institutions could fall like dominoes overnight. Eurodollar certificates of deposit could be wiped out, along with other large domestic certificates. Broad-based money market funds could lose virtually all their bank assets. There would very possibly have to be a nationwide freeze on bank withdrawals in this country to prevent a collapse of the banking system. Bonds, stocks, gold, silver, and jewels would fall like stones. Trade and commerce could be brought to a standstill.

Only a multinational effort to print a trillion or more dollars could stave off fiscal disaster. And this rescue would merely accelerate post-World War I, German-style hyperinflation, followed eventually by a worse crash.

In 1974–75 the world economy lurched, and several big banks and real estate operations failed, but the system held together. In 1980 it lurched again. That time silver crashed and the bond market lost $300 billion. Many financial institutions became technically insolvent as the market value of their bond and mortgage portfolios plunged in the wake of a 21 percent prime interest rate. One major bank failed and Chrysler became a government ward, but the system survived.

It lurched again with the savings and loan collapse, but was saved by a $500 billion federal bailout. Despite high profits, banks and insurance companies have neither restored liquidity as they did after the mid-seventies problem, nor have their portfolios improved as much as desired. Nonbank businesses are still illiquid and overextended despite recent dramatic drops in short-term interest rates.

Furthermore, the U.S. government continues to borrow to cover budget deficits. The federal deficit is a record $400 billion and the direct debt is a mind-boggling $4 trillion. Inflation, although dipping at least temporarily, can still come alive quickly. It seems built into the system at every level. Prices do not actually fall; their rate of increase merely slows.

Questions are inevitable. Are major business and financial institutions, as well as individuals, bound for bankruptcy? Will this trigger the sort of doomsday scenario described above?

A Tailspin in Morality

As the nineties unfold, nothing portrays our world crisis more clearly than man's internal and moral condition. The unmistakable scent of what the Bible calls the antichrist spirit is in the air. It was present at the Tower of Babel and at Sodom and Gomorrah. It was present in the French Revolution and in Nazi Germany. And it is present in Europe and the United States today. The signs of this spirit are clear. They emerge in this fashion: A significant minority, then an actual majority, of the people in a society begin to throw off the restraints of history, then the restraints of written law, then accepted standards of morality, then established religion, and, finally, God himself.

As the rebellion gains momentum, the participants grow bolder. Those practices that once were considered shameful and unlawful move into the open. Soon the practitioners are aggressive, militant. As each societal standard falls, another comes under attack. The pressure is relentless. Established institutions crumble. Ultimately the struggle that began as a cry for freedom of expression grows into an all-out war against the rights of advocates of traditional morality. The latter are hated, reviled, isolated, and then persecuted.

Honor, decency, honesty, self-control, sexual restraint, family values, and sacrifice are replaced by gluttony, sensuality, bizarre sexual practices, cruelty, profligacy, dishonesty, delinquency, drunkenness, drug-induced euphoria, fraud, waste, debauched currency, and rampant inflation.

The people then search for a deity that will both permit and personify their basest desires. At Babel it was a tower—man's attempt to glorify himself. In ancient Mediterranean cultures, like those of Sodom and Gomorrah, it was a god or goddess of sex. In France, it was the goddess of reason; in Germany, Hitler and the Nazi party; in Europe and especially in the United States, the god of central government under the religion of secular humanism.

The pattern is always the same. So is the result. No society falling under the grip of the antichrist spirit has survived. First comes a period of lawlessness and virtual anarchy, then an economic collapse followed by a reign of terror. Then comes a strong dictator who plunders society for his personal aggrandizement; he dreams of a worldwide empire and storms into war. Eventually come defeat and collapse.

In some cases God intervenes directly to destroy the antichrist society before it reaches full flower. In others, the society destroys itself. Sometimes a righteous nation takes action; in others the task is performed by stronger barbarians. But always there is destruction.

In the United States, trends, also reflected in other countries, are well defined:

• Organized crime is the largest industry in the land. With gross revenues of $150 billion, the profits of crime eclipse the profits of the American oil or auto industries, producing power and influence that compromise and corrupt the fabric of society. The impact of illegal drug use, as only one example, is staggering. In 1981 cocaine grossed $35 billion and marijuana $24 billion, establishing that Americans spent more on those two illegal drugs than they contributed to all charities, education, and religion combined. By 1991, there were 6.3 million users of cocaine in the United States and 19.5 million users of marijuana, and national spending on drugs continues to climb.

• The sexual revolution has snaked its way into the schools, the homes, and virtually all of society. Traditional standards regarding nudity, fornication, adultery, homosexuality, incest, and sadomasochism have been under fierce attack and many are crumbling. Educators deluded by humanism are offering sex education without moral standards to children; some courses appear to advocate masturbation, premarital sex, and homosexuality. Motion pictures, television, and the publishing industry pour the excesses of unbridled gratification into communities and homes.

• From this rampant hedonism has emerged permission to minimize the inconvenient side effects of sexual pleasure. The Supreme Court ruled that the thing conceived through sexual relations between two humans is not itself a human and therefore may be destroyed prior to the fourth month of pregnancy. The killing of unborn infants through abortion has thus proceeded at the rate of 1.5 million a year.

• At the same time, family life has been battered. In the decade of the seventies, the number of couples living together outside of marriage doubled, and divorce reached a rate of one for every two marriages. But data were not crystallized for the marred lives of children caught in the breakup of families, for the suicides of young and old unable to survive the trauma of sudden rootlessness, for the wasted lives of despair.

Financial morality has been corrupted as the government, exalted by humanist philosophy, has become god and provider. In 1941 the population of the United States was 133.7 million; government spending was $13.6 billion. Forty years later the population had grown by 72 percent, to 229.3 million; federal spending had grown by 4,762 percent, to $661.2 billion. By 1992 the population had grown to 250 million, an increase of 92 percent over 1940, yet the spending of the federal government had grown an astounding $1.5 trillion, an increase of 10,929 percent over 1940. We have already touched on the result: federal debt nearing $4 trillion, ever-increasing inflation, and domestic and world economies in danger of collapse.

• As self-restraint and regard for God rapidly diminish under the assault of secular humanism, a new rule of law has been emerging. Judges are less inclined to make decisions based on the Bible, the Constitution, natural laws, or precedent. Instead, they often impose as a rule of law whatever seems sociologically expedient or whatever reflects the prevailing sentiment of the ruling elite. As Justice Charles Evans Hughes declared early in the century, "The Constitution is what the judges say it is," pointing to a trend in which a government based on men's opinions would supersede a government based on laws. Lawlessness has thus come a long way.

Revolt Against God

Underlying all the threads we have examined as integral to the deepening crisis coming upon the world—and we have examined only a fraction of them—is one that transcends all others. It is the increased disregard for the Creator of the world.

Shortly after the turn of the century, a false view of reality began to take hold in America. Although its name did not become well known immediately, humanism spread into all aspects of life and became the dominant philosophical view about the time of World War II. Today millions of people openly embrace it, and many millions more follow along under its influence.

Francis A. Schaeffer, the Christian philosopher-theologian, described humanism's influence this way:

> . . . the humanist world view includes many thousands of adherents and today controls the consensus in society, much of the media, much of what is taught in our schools, and much of the arbitrary law being produced by the various departments of government.
>
> The term humanism used in this wider, more prevalent way means Man beginning from himself, with no knowledge except what he himself can discover and no standards outside of himself. In this view Man is the measure of all things, as the Enlightenment expressed it. . . .
>
> Since [the humanists'] concept of Man is mistaken, their concept of society and of law is mistaken, and they have no sufficient base for either society or law. They have reduced Man to even less than his natural finiteness by seeing him only as a complex arrangement of molecules, made complex by blind chance. Instead of seeing him as something great who is significant even in his sinning, they see Man in his essence only as an intrinsically competitive animal, that has no other basic operating principle than natural selection brought about by the strongest, the fittest, ending on top. And they see Man as acting in this way both individually and collectively as society.[4]

Thus, for a vast number of people, God has been removed from the center of things, and man has taken His place. All things exist for man and his pleasure.

In a church-state dialogue sponsored in 1981 by the Virginia Council of Churches, a professor of humanistic studies summed up the direction of American leadership most clearly: "We must throw off the tyranny of the concept that the Bible is the Word of God. We must be freed from the tyranny of thought that comes from Martin Luther, John Calvin, [Ulrich] Zwingli, and John Knox."

He discarded the Bible as the authoritative guide for faith and conduct, casting with it such long-accepted truths as the doctrine of man's sinfulness, the doctrine of eternal reward and eternal punishment, the necessity for repentance and justification by faith in Jesus Christ, and the necessity for holy living to please God. Such astounding recommendations can only be grasped when one recalls the words of *Humanist Manifesto I* and *II* (produced in 1933 and 1973), which denied the "existence of a supernatural God who hears and answers prayer."

With all standards and yardsticks removed, society first eased, then rushed toward the extremes of hedonism and nihilism, with increasing numbers finding fulfillment in "doing their own thing."

"If it feels good, do it," comes the advice of everyone from parents to psychologists. This, they say, is freedom. Meanwhile, as we noted earlier, nothing works. Bodies wear out early as sickness and disease soar. Never has there been so much cancer, so much heart disease. Brains, too, wear out. Never have emotional and mental breakdowns run so high; never have suicides reached such levels. Schools fail; businesses fail; governments fail.

Yes, humanism and its society are failing, although seemingly few have perceived the depth of that failure. Most see only symptoms, not the underlying sickness.

Perhaps the bright spot for those of faith is that the collapse of the Soviet Union showed the world the stark and terrible failure of a social and political system founded on humanism. Despite its seemingly unassailable grip on the power centers of Western society, humanism has clearly been exposed as a failed system that cannot withstand the assault of resolute faith. In the 1990s and beyond, the battle is not going to be fought much longer between Christianity and atheistic humanism, but between Christianity and satanic-inspired Eastern religions. In truth the collapse of Communism has opened up for the Soviet Union, the Eastern Bloc countries, and the so-called Third World the greatest religious revival in the history of mankind.

Inevitable Conclusions

The fear has become widespread that our society—and the world's—is beyond repair. There is confusion everywhere. At times the confusion approaches chaos. It seems clear that we will slide further into chaos, the jungle of anarchy: "I've got mine; to heck with you"—"do unto others before they can do unto you"—"every man for himself," or in desperation we will yield to dictatorship. Which will it be?

It matters not that both of the prevailing philosophies of materialism have been proven corrupt and ineffective. Communism said materialism is the goal but the state should control it. Now Communism has fallen. Emerging democracy and capitalism go hand in hand. But unbridled capitalism strives for materialism and the strong control of it. Both systems without a biblical balance will move toward dictatorship, either oligarchical or individual.

Eventually a strong man will be chosen if secular, capitalist materialism fails—unless we turn to the principles of the kingdom of God.

What will we do?

Notes

1. T. S. Eliot, "The Waste Land," 1932.
2. Isa. 59:10–12 NKJV.
3. Isa. 57:21 NKJV.
4. Francis A. Schaeffer, *A Christian Manifesto* (Chicago: Crossway, 1981), 24, 26.

The Devil's Gauntlet

Os Guinness

*D*id you ever visit one of those countries in Eastern Europe when it was under Communist control, where the militiamen went around in threes? The reason for this, it was said, was that the first one knew how to read, the second knew how to write, and the third was there to keep an eye on the other two dangerous intellectuals.

Many churches make us feel like that today. Speak intelligently for more than two minutes and with more than one thought in each, and you are considered dangerously intellectual and unspiritual. But the church today is beset by big problems and big issues, and these must be thought through carefully in light of the Word of God and the situation in our world today. We must forswear simple answers to tough questions and be prepared to pray, think, and sweat intellectually in order to see where we are and what the Lord would have us to do.

One of the most momentous of these questions is this: How should the church today be related to society today? To set the context of this issue I will begin with a story and a question.

The story: Soviet leader Nikita Khrushchev used to tell of a time when there was a wave of petty theft in the Soviet Union. To curtail

Os GUINNESS is a noted lecturer and scholar and author of several books including *The Dust of Death, In Two Minds,* and *The Gravedigger File.* From 1986 to 1989 he was the executive director of the Williamsburg Charter Foundation and one of the drafters of the Williamsburg Charter.

this the authorities put up guards around the factories. At one timber-works in Leningrad, the guard knew the workers in the factory very well. The first evening, out came Pyotr Petrovich with a wheelbarrow and, on the wheelbarrow, a great bulky sack with a suspicious-looking object inside.

"All right, Petrovich," said the guard, "what have you got there?"

"Oh, just sawdust and shavings," Petrovich replied.

"Come on," the guard said, "I wasn't born yesterday. Tip it out." And out came nothing but sawdust and shavings. So he was allowed to put it all back again and go home.

When the same thing happened every night of the week, the guard became frustrated. Finally, his curiosity overcame his frustration.

"Petrovich," he said, "I know you. Tell me what you're smuggling out of here, and I'll let you go."

"Wheelbarrows, my friend," said Petrovich, "wheelbarrows."

Laugh by all means, but when it comes to the issue of church and society the laugh is on us as evangelicals. We have set up patrols to check for secularism all around the country, and the devil has trundled secularization right past our own eyes and on into the church. We have conducted spot checks, looking for any conceivable lapse in biblical authority, and the devil has wheeled anarchy past the front doors of our homes and into our lifestyles.

Back in the early seventies, a professor at Oxford, knowing I was a Christian, asked me, "By the end of the seventies, who will be the worldliest Christians in America?" I must have looked a bit puzzled, so he went on, "I guarantee it will be the fundamentalists."

At the time that seemed startling. Worldliest? Fundamentalists then were world-denying by definition. But after 1987, a lamentable year of Christian scandal and shame, we hardly need to pause to answer that question. What has happened? One of the deepest reasons behind the corruption of evangelicalism and fundamentalism is a profound inadequacy in understanding how the church should engage society.

The quotation: A hundred years ago, the German philosopher Friedrich Nietzsche remarked that when God dies, culture becomes "weightless." When I first read that, I was deeply moved for three reasons.

First, weightlessness is a powerful biblical theme because it is the precise opposite of glory. The glory of God is far more than his renown or radiance. Glory is God's own inexpressible reality, a reality so real that it alone has gravity and weight—the only "really real reality" in the entire universe. Therefore, when things move away from God, they become hollow and weightless, and we can accurately say, "Ichabod" ("The glory has departed"—1 Samuel 4:21). Like Belshazzar (Daniel 5:25–28), we read the handwriting on the wall: *Mene, tekel, parsin* ("You have been weighed on the scales and found wanting"). That's why idols, by contrast with God, are literally "nothings." That's why revival is the refilling of a nation with "the knowledge of the glory of the LORD, as the waters cover the sea" (Habakkuk 2:14).

Second, I was moved because Nietzsche was addressing his remarks to England, my homeland. Nietzsche had looked below the surface and seen the hollowing out that had begun. A generation characterized by "convictions" had been followed by one of "conventions" and was soon to be followed by one of "addictions." England was growing weightless from the inside.

Third, I was moved because many observers say that these are America's weightless years. From families and schools to Wall Street boardrooms and Cabinet dealings, there have been widespread signs of weightlessness, of emptiness of ideals, of the gap between rhetoric and reality—a loss of the real stuff that will keep beliefs strong, ethics decisive, and a nation great. And again, the church shows many of the same signs of weightlessness that you see in the world. One of the basic reasons for this is a lack of engagement in society in ways that are spiritually realistic as well as socially relevant.

In sum, "church and society" is not just one key topic among many. It is the test-bed truth that reveals the character and health of all our truths. If we don't demonstrate Christian truths in the crucible of society, then whatever we profess, they mean nothing. This is far more than a topic for the "socially concerned." When we come to grips with the topic of church and society, we come to grips with all the deep questions of worship and discipleship in the modern world.

The purpose of this essay is to lay out six foundational considerations that need to be burned into our minds and hearts as we engage in society today. Each is a pair of ideas whose two halves are closely linked to each other yet interdependent with the other pairs of ideas. First are two perspectives; second, two principles; third, two great deficiencies; fourth, two reminders of where we are today; fifth, two requirements in relation to society; and last, two requirements in relation to the Lord.

Two Perspectives

The view of society we find in the Scriptures is a bifocal vision. Society is always and everywhere two things at once: God's gift to us and the devil's gauntlet thrown down before us, to challenge us to worship him and not Christ.

On the one hand, society is God's gift to us. To be sure, in comparison with what it might have been if there had been no Fall and what it will be when Christ comes again, what we see today is marred by evil, filled with pain, and ruined with brokenness. Yet even when we have looked evil full in the face, we still know that society is God's gift. God is as decisive in sustaining society as society is decisive in shaping us. Only when we remember the former do we prevent the latter from becoming a fatalism that unnerves us.

Many Christians have forgotten both these truths, and modern individualism is a big reason why. Sin has always pivoted on the claim to the right to oneself, along with the accompanying claim to the right to see things from one's own point of view. Modern individualism therefore bolsters the pretense that we don't need others in any profound way.

But as biblical people, we should know that individualism is a dangerous illusion. We are who we are because we have grown up face to face. We live, work, and play side by side. It is therefore important to us that God decisively sustains the world that decisively shapes us. Despite its fallenness, society is still God's gift to us and we should be thankful.

On the other hand, society is also the devil's gauntlet. However much we experience wonder, love, and joy in it, society is under alien rule. Society is part of the first of the big trio—the world, the flesh, and the devil. Thus, however much it is God's gift, society also contains a spirit, a system, and a structure that stands over against the kingdom of God and his Christ.

Yes, the devil failed once. Out there in the desert, he promised everything, but God's great advocate overcame God's great adversary, and the devil left the field licked.

But the devil knows that where he failed with the Master, he may succeed with the servants. So he comes to us, and he invites us to enter and enjoy society at every level, from our work to our play, from the humblest levels up to the boardrooms of the country. "All this is yours," he says, "if only . . ." Buried in his invitation are the questions, Who is Lord? Have we faced up to the nature of the system? "Pick it up," says the Evil One. "All is yours . . . if you worship me."

Society, in other words, is the devil's gauntlet thrown down before us to induce us toward his lordship rather than Christ's. But that is not because we are the innocents and the world is tempting. Rather, we are the temptable ones. The world is simply our hearts writ large. Our hearts are simply the world writ small. So our view of society needs to be deeply realistic. If society is God's gift to us, it is also the devil's gauntlet and that bifocal vision should shape our perspective.

Two Principles

After the question, How do we see the world? comes a second one, How do we *act* in the world? Two great master principles have characterized the church at its most penetrating. The first is the Protagonist Principle which flows from the theme, "Christ *over* all" and has as its key word *total*.

The story of the exodus provides an Old Testament example. The whole issue with Pharaoh was lordship. He who can liberate is lord. As the contest and bargaining goes on, Pharaoh relents enough to let the Israelite men go, at least for worship. No, says Moses. "Let my people go" means not just the men and not just for worship. Men, women, and children must go, and for good. And then a remarkable little phrase is added: "Not a hoof is to be left behind" (Exodus 10:26).

A New Testament example can be found in Luke 5. Peter, as fisherman, was glad to allow Jesus to preach from his boat. But then Jesus says to Peter, "Put out into deep water, and let down the nets for a catch."

You can almost hear Peter reply: "Look, Lord, I'll listen to you as teacher all day long, but when it comes to fishing, that's my job."

We know the result. Peter found that Jesus was Lord of nature too, and he could only say, "Go away from me, LORD; I am a sinful man!" Christ is Lord of nature as well as truth. He is the Alpha and the Omega. He is the source, guide, and goal of all there is. That is why every eye will one day see him, every tongue will be stopped, and every knee will bow. After all, as Abraham Kuyper said, expressing the Protagonist Principle perfectly, "There is not an inch of any sphere of life of which Jesus Christ the Lord does not say, 'Mine.'"

The second principle is the Antagonist Principle. It flows from the theme, "Christ *over against* all that does not bow to him." Here the key word is *tension*. The Lord himself puts the point unmistakably in the Ten Commandments: "I am the LORD your God. . . . You shall have no other gods before me" (Exodus 20:2–3). Over forty times in Leviticus 18 and the following chapters there is a recurring assertion, "I am the LORD." Each time it introduces a strict instruction not to do as the Egyptians or the Canaanites did, neither following their idols nor copying their ideas and institutions.

The reason? The Lord is the jealous one, the one who brooks no rivals. Since he is our "decisive other," he demands of us a decisive contrast with everything that is over against him and his ways. And most wonderful of all, the deepest reason is not puritanical, but personal. It is "that you may belong to me."

In short, God and the world stand crosswise. We are in the world, but not of it. To be faithful to him, we have to be foreign to the world. We are not to be conformed, but transformed by the renewing of our minds.

Of course, the Protagonist Principle and the Antagonist Principle must never be separated. They go hand in hand. Without the Protagonist Principle the Antagonist Principle would create a we/they division. But the Protagonist Principle means there is no hatred of the world or false asceticism here. Yes, the world is passing away, and we are passing through the world. But, in the memorable phrase of Peter Berger, we are only "*against* the world *for* the world."

Two Deficiencies

The third foundational consideration grows from the question, Where has our engagement with the world gone wrong? Here we have to face the fact that under the conditions of the modern world, or what is called "modernity," a key breakdown between faith and obedience has occurred, one which is proving lethal to Christian integrity and effectiveness.

The full explanation of this breakdown is complicated. (I have discussed this in more detail in my book *The Gravedigger File.*) Let me simply say that its roots are not only theological, but philosophical, sociological, and spiritual. As a result of a whole combination of things, two glaring deficiencies in our discipleship have grown common.

First, as modern followers of Christ, we constantly face a peculiar temptation to break the link between belief and behavior. Anyone who wants to observe religion in the modern world and find the sort of belief that behaves would be advised to look at the cults rather than at Christians. What cult members believe may be bizarre, and the way they behave even worse, but to their credit there is a consistency between their belief and their behavior, which is rare in the modern world.

Some years ago the Queen of the Belgians visited Poland. She went to Mass one day, accompanied by a government official. Noticing that he seemed to know a lot about the Catholic liturgy, she turned to him and asked, "Are you a Catholic?"

The official, looking embarrassed, replied, "Believing, Madam. Not practicing, I'm afraid."

"Oh, of course," she said, "you must be a Communist."

"Not exactly," he said, "practicing, not believing, I'm afraid."

In other words, the breakdown between belief and behavior is not only an evangelical or even a Christian problem. It has affected almost all beliefs, though it hits us harder as Christians because of our specially strong claims as to what faith requires.

There has been considerable discussion recently about "cafeteria Catholicism"—mix your own morals, choose your own church, pick your own preference, and so on. ("Yes, we love the Pope, but we don't follow his teaching.") But if there is a "cafeteria Catholicism," there is equally an "easy-care evangelicalism," and both are a result of the breakdown between believing and behaving.

A simple example is popular evangelical theology, some of the sloppiest and most superficial sentiment that has ever passed for theology. I cited an incident in *The Gravedigger File* that many people thought I had made up. In fact, it was true.

It came from watching a few minutes of a program on the electronic church. A singer sang an old spiritual in a way which threatened to inject reality into the proceedings. But the show's hostess clapped her hands, rolled her eyes heavenward, and cooed, "Fantastic, brother! Fantastic! Christianity is so fantastic—who cares whether or not it's true?"

That incident was a few years ago, and many readers took it as purely funny. But after the scandalous revelations of 1987, the consequences of such corrupt theology in the lives of Jim and Tammy Faye Bakker have proved to be no joke.

Milder everyday examples are common. American evangelicalism is awash in a sloppy, sentimental, superficial, Hallmark-card theology that wouldn't empower a clockwork mouse, let alone a disciple of Christ in the tough, modern world.

The second deficiency in discipleship concerns the broken link between the private world and the public world, through which faith becomes "privately engaging, but socially irrelevant."

The clearest example I know came during a *New York Times* interview with a celebrated business leader who was also a Christian. Asked what he believed in, he replied, "I believe in God, the family, and McDonald's hamburgers. And when I get to the office, I reverse the order."

Let's trust he was being facetious in a manner not picked up in the printed interview. But even if he was, he was only saying what millions of Christians do every single day without realizing it. Their faith flourishes at home, at church, in the prayer breakfasts before work, or in the Bible study group during the lunch hour. But work itself is a different world, with a different way of doing things. Without realizing it, millions of Christians hang their faith along with their hats and coats at the door. The link between the private world of faith and the public world of work is severed.

It is true that there are magnificent exceptions to this problem. It is also true that both these deficiencies are offset by reactions that head in the opposite direction. For example, if one general problem in the church is *permissiveness* ("anything goes"), other Christians have veered to the opposite extreme—a new kind of *particularism.* They see only one particular way as *the* Christian way of doing things—with the added insult that if you don't do it that way, you must not be a Christian.

Or again, if one general problem is the *privatization* of faith, some Christians have recently swung to the other extreme *politicization*. They act as if politics in general and Washington in particular were the be-all and end-all of Christian obedience.

Both those errors, particularism and politicization, are a dangerous trap for disciples. But permissiveness and privatization are the greater problems for evangelicalism as a whole. Dostoevsky's celebrated saying, "When God is dead, everything is permitted," could well be equally translated in America, "When God is dead, nothing is owed." For a characteristic of modern America is the absence of obligation. We owe nothing to anyone except to ourselves. Words mean little, and bind no one. Therefore a deep danger of evangelicalism is that, even as we trumpet our concern for biblical authority, we reveal the disappearance of the Bible's "binding address." The Scriptures still address us in general, but no longer bind us to anything in particular.

Two Reminders

The fourth pair of foundational considerations grows from the question, What is the setting in which we are discussing these questions? Clearly we are not raising these questions in a vacuum or in a purely academic environment. Nor are we living in a great age of faith, such as the Reformation or the first Great Awakening.

Our cultural situation adds an urgent reminder to our discussion at two points. On the one hand, the United States is at a turning point, principally because of the decreasing influence of faith on society. On the other hand, the church is at a turning point, principally because of an increasing influence of society on faith.

I believe that the 1980s will turn out to be an ironic parallel for conservatives of what the 1960s were for liberals. In 1968, liberals hailed victory. For the first time, there was a solid majority against the Vietnam war. In fact, they were right: the majority was against the war. But it was also against liberals. It was Nixon's "emerging new majority." Thus 1968 was both the high point and a turning point, after which the tide flowed relentlessly against them.

In like manner the year 1986 may well prove to be the same for the conservatives. The Statue of Liberty celebrations in July of that year saw the high tide of the claims for the conservative revolution. Now, just a few years later, most of those claims are in tatters. The conservative counter-revolution, like the liberal revolution before it, has been betrayed by its own illusions and inner contradictions.

This means that the period we are entering is one of decisive reckoning because the United States is approaching the close of a generation-long crisis of cultural authority. After the great 1960s lurch in directions liberal, radical, and secular came the great 1980s counter-lurch in directions conservative, traditional, and religious. Now, with the failure of both revolutions on their own terms, we enter the showdown years that will reveal which faiths, which world-views, and which moral principles are going to prove decisive in shaping the nation over the next generations. The nation is at a turning point because of a decreasing influence of faith.

But we can see equally plainly that the church is at a turning point because of an increasing influence of culture. Americans used to speak much of their "exceptionalism." Today there is only one place left where America is still exceptional—the strength of religion. In a world in which modernity and secularity seem to go hand in hand, the United States is simultaneously the most modern and the most religious of modern countries. Yet with the striking discrepancy between religious indicators (church attendance, giving, praying) and the social influence of religion—the former up and the latter down—the exception cannot continue for long. There is too little religion and too much religiosity in the church. The church's showdown period is beginning too, when its true integrity and effectiveness will be revealed.

Two Requirements before the World

The fifth pair of foundational considerations is an answer to the question, What do we most need as we engage with our society? Let me suggest two things that relate to our public witness—the need for a Christian mind and a public philosophy.

In 1976 (*Newsweek*'s "Year of the Evangelical") many observers asked whether the evangelical community would make the impact which its history, numbers, and opportunity might lead one to expect. The answer was generally no, and the main reason given was that evangelicals were unlikely to think in any distinctively Christian way.

Such predictions have proved lamentably correct. Failure to "think Christianly" is the Achilles' heel of English-speaking evangelicalism. While the Puritans were magnificently different, evangelicals since the Great Awakening have by and large displayed only a "ghost mind," hollowed out by various forces which for all their spiritual passion led toward a general anti-intellectualism. Since then, with exceptions only proving the rule, there has been no powerful evangelical mind. Thus at most of the decisive moments in American thinking—Emerson's "intellectual Declaration of Independence" at Harvard in 1837, the rise of higher education and of liberalism, and so on—evangelicals were not so much out-thought as out of it. And they still are today.

When will we face the fact that our deep-rooted anti-intellectualism is worse than ineffective? It is sub-Christian, disobedient, anti-spiritual, and unloving. Only when we root out the last traces of it can we hope to exercise the public influence that faithfulness to Christ demands. For in the end, thinking Christianly is a matter of faithfulness and loving God.

Let me be specific. Since living here in Washington, D.C., the past few years, the single spiritual lesson that I have benefited from most is the reminder of our grand priority: that above all else we are to love the Lord with all our heart, soul, strength, and mind. Christ himself and not "Christianity" is our first love, our primary call, our fundamental loyalty.

There are all too many who love the Lord with all their hearts, soul, and strength, but leave out their "minds" from the list. Under the ostensible guise of spirituality, they rationalize the plain disobedience of anti-intellectualism. Unless this generation of American evangelicals confronts its centuries-old habit of anti-intellectualism, we don't have the slightest chance of penetrating modern society for Christ.

The second external requirement is a contribution to America's public philosophy that has both Christian integrity and public credibility. The United States has always been characterized by its astonishing blend of liberty, diversity and harmony. Consensus-building has become one of America's greatest achievements. Despite change, consensus maintains continuity. It is this common vision of the common good that Walter Lippman called the "public philosophy."

Obviously, a key part of this public philosophy has been an agreed understanding of the place of religion in public life and of the guiding principles by which citizens with religious differences can contend with each other in the public square. But equally obviously, if the public philosophy is in poor shape today, the religious part of that philosophy is in chronic disrepair.

Look at the controversies over religion and politics in the last ten years. The two religious liberty clauses of the First Amendment to the Constitution have been pitted against each other, and there has been an evident breakdown of any shared understanding of how religiously grounded differences should be negotiated in the public square. Worst of all, evangelicals and fundamentalists have often made the problems worse. With their better voices unheard, and those heard relying solely on a confrontational style and being concerned solely with "me/my/our" interests, they too have caused great damage to the public philosophy.

There are deeper issues here than we have space to explore. But let me simply state that we need to be heard to say, "Christian justice is not just justice for Christians; it is justice for everybody." Rights are universal and responsibilities mutual; so a right for one is a right for another and a responsibility for both. A right for a Protestant is a right for a Catholic, is a right for a Jew, is a right for a humanist, is a right for a Mormon, and a right for the believer of any faith under God's wide heaven.

The First Amendment in this sense is the epitome of public justice and serves as the Golden Rule for civic life: rights are best protected and responsibilities best exercised if we guard for others those rights we would wish guarded for ourselves.

Beyond the principled reasons for a public philosophy are pragmatic ones. The recent contentious debates, at least in their high-octane form, are not likely to continue forever. War weariness is already setting in. The public is tired of the trench warfare over religion and public life. But if we are not careful, the danger is of a great change in public attitudes. Instead of faith and freedom being viewed as blood brothers, as they have been for two hundred years, they will come to be viewed as in opposing corners—with titanic implications for the gospel and for the nation.

Two Requirements before the Lord

The last pair of foundational considerations concerns two requirements. If we ask, What is it we most need?, the answer in two words is: God himself—the proclamation of his Word and the visitation of his Spirit.

President Lyndon Johnson used to tell a story of a preacher who prepared a stirring but rather complicated sermon that required notes. Unfortunately on his way to church he dropped the notes, and they were eaten by a dog. Unabashed, he climbed into the pulpit and said, "Brothers and sisters, I'm afraid a dog ate my sermon notes on the way to church. I'm just going to have to rely on what the Holy Spirit tells me, but I promise I'll do better next week."

That may be closer to the situation in many American pulpits than many Americans realize. Having visited almost all the countries in the English-speaking world, I would say that I know none where the churches are more full and the sermons more empty than in America. There are magnificent exceptions, of course. But by and large, I am never hungrier and rarely angrier than when I come out of an American evangelical church after what passes for the preaching of the Word of God. The problem is not just the heresy, though doubtless there is some of that. Nor is it just the degree of entertainment, and there is lots of that. Nor is it even the appalling gaps in theology, for there is far too much of that. The real problem is that in what is said there is almost no sense of announcement from God; and in what is shown there is almost no sense of anointing by God.

Jeremiah attacked the false prophets of his day with the damning question, "Which of them has stood in the council of the LORD to see or to hear his word?" (Jeremiah 23:18). Is such a standard too demanding? I admit that my own expectations have been shaped decisively by the standards common when I came to Christ. As a student I had the privilege of sitting under the ministry of Martyn Lloyd-Jones at his greatest. Before he preached every Sunday, he was alone for an hour with the Lord. Nobody disturbed him. If the prime minister had arrived, someone else could greet him. If a person in crisis had come, somebody else could counsel them. The pastor was with the King of kings. I don't remember Dr. Lloyd-Jones ever saying, "Thus saith the Lord." He didn't have to. His very bearing, quite apart from his words, bespoke that what he said was an announcement from God given with the anointing of God.

As part of our overall secularization we have shifted from a proclamation style to a discussion style, and the result is an endless proliferation of consultations, forums, seminars, symposiums, congresses, and workshops. In most cases, old-fashioned proclamation would seem about as appropriate in those affairs as a full-throated obscenity, and no more likely.

The second requirement is a visitation of the Spirit. I use the old Puritan word *visitation* deliberately, because so many of the words describing revival have been devalued. We have no need of religious *resurgence,* because that word is used of trends that are explicable in purely social terms. Nor can we be content to use the word *revival* merely as a synonym for evangelism. And *visitation* is far beyond what is usually called *renewal.* I am personally in favor of the renewal movement at its best, particularly where it touches personal worship and musical forms. But even at its best, the renewal movement is a million miles short of true revival. Where is its note of profound conviction? Where is the wholesale changing of communities? Where is the developed passion for social holiness, as opposed to personal devotion?

Sadly, revival raises a question to many evangelicals: Do they believe in it still? In 1987 Paul Weyrich, a leading conservative strategist, gave a speech called "Taking Stock." In it he argued in effect, "Even if we conservatives win our entire agenda, we've lost." He shocked his audience further. "Yes," he said, "abortion, school prayer . . . win them all, and we will still have failed." Why? Because social change has changed too much, political change can change too little. Culture is flowing away faster than any piecemeal action can remedy. Nothing short of a total cultural transformation of America will do.

Curiously, evangelicals a generation ago would have taken that as a truism. But in a day when political activism is in vogue, many who used to pray confidently, realistically, and practically for revival no longer have that hunger for a visitation from God.

Show Me Your Glory

Let me draw the threads together. Review these six foundational themes in the setting of your own life and that of your local church. Are those two perspectives burnt into your mind, those two principles mastering your life, those two deficiencies highlighted so that you can avoid them, those two reminders spurring you on, and those two requirements before the world and the Lord being met?

I imagine you feel like many of us. Who is equal to the challenge? Can we really expect to see our culture turned around in our day?

Questions like those make me think of two men under pressure. One was the great German thinker Max Weber. He never shut his eyes to the modern world. He wrestled with it, but the more he wrestled, the more pessimistic he became. One day a friend saw him pacing up and down, nearing the verge of a second breakdown.

"Max," he said, "why do you go on thinking like this when your conclusions leave you so depressed?"

Weber's reply has become a classic of intellectual commitment and courage: "I want to see how much I can stand."

Admirable in many respects, that is not the way for followers of Christ. We are not called to be tragic heroes, or stoics, or spiritual masochists.

A very different response under pressure was that of Moses. Faced by enemies behind, around and ahead, and finding discontent not only among his own people but within his own family, he suddenly met the ultimate threat to his people and his task as leader: God himself. The Lord declared that he would destroy the Israelites himself because of their sin.

His very life and trust in God called into question, Moses stood firm and countered the challenge by putting God on the line (arguing the covenant), the people on the line (calling for a consecration to the Lord even against families and friends) and finally himself on the line (asking that he himself rather than the people be blotted out).

Then, when the Lord had listened to his prayers, agreeing first to forgive the people and then to come with them in person, rather than by an angel, Moses made his supreme request, surely the most audacious prayer in all the Scriptures: "Show me your glory" (Exodus 33:18). He wanted to know all of God that a fallen sinner could be allowed to know, for nothing less would be enough to see him through.

In that prayer we have our answer to Nietzsche. When God "dies" for a nation, a church, or an individual, a weightlessness results for which there is only one remedy—the glory of God refilling them as the waters fill the sea. Wasn't that Jeremiah's message to his generation? To a people who had exchanged their glory for a god altogether nothing, he warned, "Give glory to the LORD your God before he brings the darkness" (Jeremiah 13:16).

G. K. Chesterton, the great Christian apologist, brought the same message to the United States after his visit in 1921. The glory of the American republic, he argued, had not been derived from itself and could not be sustained by itself. Cut off from the source from which it sprang, it would not long endure. He then concluded his book with the magnificent line: "Freedom is the eagle whose glory is gazing at the sun."

If we today stress the spiritual aspects of the gospel without the social, we lose all relevance in modern society. But if we stress the social without the spiritual, we lose our reality altogether. The ultimate factor in the church's engagement with society is the church's engagement with God.

Are we still tempted today to believe that we or anyone else can turn things around? We must forget it. On the other hand, are we overwhelmed by the task, overburdened by the state of the nation and the world? For God's sake, let us forget the eagle and ourselves and turn with Moses to the sun: "Lord, show me your glory."

3

The Destruction of the Foundations of Faith and Freedom

Francis A. Schaeffer

*T*he Founding Fathers of the United States (in varying degrees) understood very well the relationship between one's worldview and government. John Witherspoon (1723–94), a Presbyterian minister and college president, was the only pastor to sign the Declaration of Independence.[1] He was a very important man during the founding of the country. He linked the Christian thinking represented by the College of New Jersey (now Princeton University) with the work he did both on the Declaration of Independence and on countless very important committees in the founding of the country. This linkage of Christian thinking and the concepts of government was not incidental but fundamental. John Witherspoon knew and stood consciously in the stream of Samuel Rutherford, a Scotsman who lived from 1600–1661 and who wrote *Lex Rex* in 1644. *Lex rex* means law is king—a phrase that was absolutely earthshaking. Prior to that it had been *rex lex*, the king is law. In *Lex Rex* Rutherford declared that the law, and no one else, is king. Therefore, the heads of government are under the law, not a law unto themselves.

FRANCIS A. SCHAEFFER was a noted evangelical thinker who founded L'Abri, an international community in the Swiss Alps. He wrote twenty-three books including *Whatever Happened to the Human Race?* and *The Rise and Decline of Western Thought and Culture.* He was also the producer of the acclaimed video series *How Should We Then Live?*

Jefferson, who was a deist, and others knew they stood in the stream of John Locke (1632–1704). While Locke had secularized *Lex Rex,* he had drawn heavily from it. These men really knew what they were doing. We are not reading back into history what was not there. We cannot say too strongly that they really understood the basis of the government which they were creating. Think of this great flaming phrase: "certain inalienable rights." Who gives the rights? The state? Then they are not inalienable because the state can change them and take them away. Where do the rights come from? They understood that they were founding the country upon the Judeo-Christian concept that there is Someone there who gave the inalienable rights. Another phrase also stood there: "In God we trust." There is no confusion here about what they were talking about. They publicly recognized that law could be king because there was a Law Giver, a Person to give the inalienable rights.

Most people do not realize that there was a paid chaplain in Congress even before the Revolutionary War ended. Also we find that prior to the founding of the national Congress the early provincial congresses in all thirteen colonies always opened with prayer. And from the very beginning, prayer opened the national Congress. These men truly understood what they were doing. They knew they were building on the Supreme Being who was the Creator, the final reality. And they knew that without that foundation everything in the Declaration of Independence and all that followed would be sheer unadulterated nonsense. These were brilliant men who understood exactly what was involved.

Do you realize that the first Thanksgiving Day to thank God in this country was called immediately by the Congress at the end of the Revolutionary War? Witherspoon's sermon on that day shows their perspective: "A republic once equally poised must either preserve its virtue or lose its liberty." Don't you wish that everybody in America would recite that, and truly understand it, every morning? Earlier in a speech Witherspoon had stressed: "He is the best friend of American liberty who is most sincere and active in promoting pure and undefiled religion." For Witherspoon, and the cultural consensus of that day, that meant Christianity as it had come to them through the Reformation. This was the consensus which gave religious freedom to all—including the "free thinkers" of that day and the humanists of our day.

This concept was the same as William Penn (1644–1718) had expressed earlier: "If we are not governed by God, then we will be ruled by tyrants." This consensus was as natural as breathing in the United States at that time. We must not forget that many of those who came to America from Europe came for religious purposes. As they arrived, most of them established their own individual civil governments based upon the Bible. It is, therefore, totally foreign to the basic nature of America at the time of the writing of the Constitution to argue a separation doctrine that implies a secular state.

When the First Amendment was passed, it only had two purposes. The first was that there would be no established, national church for the united thirteen states. To say it another way: There would be no "Church of the United States." James Madison (1751–1836) clearly articulated this concept of separation when explaining the First Amendment's protection of religious liberty. He said that the First Amendment to the Constitution was prompted because "the people feared one sect might obtain a preeminence, or two combine together and establish a religion to which they would compel others to conform."[2]

Nevertheless, a number of individual states had state churches, and even that was not considered in conflict with the First Amendment. "At the outbreak of the American Revolution, nine of the thirteen colonies had conferred special benefits upon one church to the exclusion of others. . . . In all but one of the thirteen states, the states taxed the people to support the preaching of the gospel and to build churches. . . . It was not until 1798 that the Virginia legislature repealed all its laws supporting churches. . . . In Massachusetts the Massachusetts Constitution was not amended until 1853 to eliminate the tax-supported church provisions."[3]

The second purpose of the First Amendment was the very opposite from what is being made of it today. It states expressly that government should not impede or interfere with the free practice of religion.

Those were the two purposes of the First Amendment as it was written. As Justice Douglas wrote for the majority of the Supreme Court in the *United States v. Ballard* case in 1944:

The First Amendment has a dual aspect. It not only "forestalls compulsion by law of the acceptance of any creed or the practice of any form of worship" but also "safeguards the free exercise of the chosen form of religion."

Today the separation of church and state in America is used to silence the church. When Christians speak out on issues, the hue and cry from the humanist state and media is that Christians, and all religions, are prohibited from speaking since there is a separation of church and state. The way the concept is used today is totally reversed from the original intent. It is not rooted in history. The modern concept of separation is an argument for a total separation of religion from the state. The consequence of the acceptance of this doctrine leads to the removal of religion as an influence in civil government. It is used today as a false political dictum in order to restrict the influence of Christian ideas. As Franky Schaeffer V says in the *Plan For Action:*

> It has been convenient and expedient for the secular humanist, the materialist, the so-called liberal, the feminist, the genetic engineer, the bureaucrat, the Supreme Court Justice, to use this arbitrary division between church and state as a ready excuse. It is used, as an easily identifiable rallying point, to subdue the opinions of that vast body of citizens who represent those with religious convictions.[4]

The suggestion that the state should be separated from religion and religious influence would have amazed the Founding Fathers. The French Revolution that took place shortly afterwards, with its continuing excesses and final failure leading quickly to Napoleon and an authoritative rule, only emphasized the difference between the base upon which the United States was founded and the base upon which the French Revolution was founded. History is clear and the men of that day understood it. Terry Eastland said in *Commentary* magazine:

> As a matter of historical fact, the Founding Fathers believed that the public interest was served by the promotion of religion. The Northwest Ordinance of 1787, which set aside federal property in the territory for schools and which was passed again by Congress in 1789, is instructive. "Religion, morality, and knowledge

being necessary to good government and the happiness of man-kind," read the act, "schools and the means of learning shall for-ever be encouraged."

In 1811 the New York state court upheld an indictment for blas-phemous utterances against Christ, and in its ruling, given by Chief Justice Kent, the court said, "We are Christian people, and the moral-ity of the country is deeply engrafted upon Christianity." Fifty years later this same court said that "Christianity may be conceded to be the established religion."

The Pennsylvania state court also affirmed the conviction of a man on charges of blasphemy, here against the Holy Scriptures. The Court said: "Christianity, general Christianity is, and always has been, a part of the common law of Pennsylvania . . . not Christianity founded on any particular religious tenets; nor Christianity with an established church and tithes and spiritual courts but Christianity with liberty of conscience to all men."

The establishment of Protestant Christianity was one not only of law but also, and far more importantly, of culture. Protestant Chris-tianity supplied the nation with its "system of values"—to use the modern phrase—and would do so until the 1920s when the cake of Protestant custom seemed most noticeably to begin crumbling.[5]

As we continue to examine the question of law in relation to the founding of the country, we next encounter Sir William Blackstone (1723–80). Blackstone was an English jurist who in the 1760s wrote a very famous work called *Commentaries on the Law of England.* By the time the Declaration of Independence was signed, there were probably more copies of his *Commentaries* in America than in Brit-ain. Blackstone's *Commentaries* shaped the perspective of American law at that time; and when you read them, it is very clear exactly upon what that law was based.

To William Blackstone there were only two foundations for law: nature and revelation. Concerning revelation, he stated clearly that he was speaking of the "holy Scripture." Up to the recent past not to have been a master of William Blackstone's *Commentaries* would have meant that you would not have graduated from law school.

There were other well-known lawyers who spelled these things out with total clarity. Joseph Story in his 1829 inaugural address as

Dane Professor of Law at Harvard University said, "There never has been a period in which Common Law did not recognize Christianity as laying at its foundation."[6]

Concerning John Adams (1735–1826) Terry Eastland says:

> . . . most people agreed that our law was rooted, as John Adams had said, in a common moral and religious tradition, one that stretched back to the time Moses went up on Mount Sinai. Similarly almost everyone agreed that our liberties were God-given and should be exercised responsibly. There was a distinction between liberty and license.[7]

What we find then as we look back is that the men who founded the United States of America really understood that upon which they were building their concepts of law and the concepts of government. And until the takeover of our government and law by this other entity, the materialistic, humanistic, chance worldview, these things remained the base of government and law.

But now it is all gone.

In most law schools today almost no one studies William Blackstone unless he or she is taking a course in the history of law. We live in a secularized society under secularized, sociological law. By sociological law we mean law that has no fixed base. Under sociological law a group of people decides what is sociologically good for society at the given moment, and what they arbitrarily decide becomes law. Oliver Wendell Holmes (1841–1935) made totally clear that this was his position.[8] Frederick Moore Vinson (1890–1953), former Chief Justice of the United States Supreme Court, said, "Nothing is more certain in modern society than the principle that there are no absolutes."[9] Those who hold this position themselves call it sociological law.

As the new sociological law has moved away from the original base of the Creator giving the "inalienable rights," etc., it has been natural that this sociological law has then also moved away from the Constitution. William Bentley Ball,[10] in his paper entitled "Religious Liberty: The Constitutional Frontier," says:

> I propose that secularism militates against religious liberty, and indeed against personal freedoms generally, for two reasons:

first, the familiar fact that secularism does not recognize the existence of the "higher law"; second, because, that being so, secularism tends toward decisions based on the pragmatic public policy of the moment and inevitably tends to resist the submitting of those policies to the "higher" criteria of a constitution.

This moving away from the Constitution is not only by court rulings, for example the First Amendment rulings which are the very reversal of the original purpose of the First Amendment, but in other ways as well. Quoting again from the same paper by William Bentley Ball:

> Our problem consists also, as perhaps this paper has well enough indicated, of *more general* constitutional concepts. Let me refer to but two: the unconstitutional delegation of legislative power and *ultra vires*. The first is where the legislature hands over its powers to agents through the conferral of regulatory power unaccompanied by strict standards. The second is where the agents make up powers on their own—assume powers not given them by the legislature. Under the first, the government of laws largely disappears and the government of men largely replaces it. Under the second, agents' personal "homemade" law replaces the law of the elected representatives of the people.

Naturally, this shift from the Judeo-Christian basis for law and the shift away from the restraints of the Constitution automatically militates against religious liberty. Mr. Ball closes his paper:

> Fundamentally, in relation to personal liberty, the Constitution was aimed at restraint of the State. Today, in case after case relating to religious liberty, we encounter the bizarre presumption that it is the other way around; that the State is justified in whatever action, and that religion bears a great burden of proof to overcome that presumption. It is our job, as Christian lawyers, to destroy that presumption at every turn.

When lawyers discuss the changes in law in the United States, they often speak of the influence of the laws passed in relationship to the Mormons and to the laws involved in the reentrance of the southern states into the national government after the Civil War. These indeed must be considered. But they were not the reason for the drastic change in law in our country. The reason was the takeover by the totally other worldview which would never have given the form and freedom in government we have had in Northern Europe (including the United States). That is the central factor in the change.

It is parallel to the difference between modern science beginning with Copernicus and Galileo and the materialistic science which took over in the last century. Materialistic thought would never have produced modern science. Modern science was produced on the Christian base. That is, because an intelligent Creator had created the universe we can in some measure understand the universe and there is, therefore, a reason for observation and experimentation to be optimistically pursued.

The shift into materialistic science was based on no addition to the facts known. It was a choice, in faith, to see things that way.[11] No clearer expression of this could be given than Carl Sagan's arrogant statement on public television—made without any scientific proof for the statement—to 140 million viewers: "The cosmos is all that is or ever was or ever will be." He opened the series *Cosmos* with this essentially creedal declaration that only matter, energy, and chance exist, and went on to build every subsequent conclusion upon it.

There is exactly the same parallel in law. The materialistic-energy, chance concept of final reality never would have produced the form and freedom in government we have in this country and in other Reformation countries. But now it has arbitrarily and arrogantly supplanted the historic Judeo-Christian consensus that provided the base for form and freedom in government. The Judeo-Christian consensus gave greater freedoms than the world has ever known, but it also contained checks and balances so that these freedoms did not pound society to pieces. The materialistic concept of reality would not have produced the form-freedom balance, and now that it has taken over it cannot maintain the balance. It has destroyed it.

Will Durant and his wife Ariel together wrote *The Story of Civilization*. The Durants received the 1976 Humanist Pioneer Award. In *The Humanist* magazine of February 1977, Will Durant summed up the humanist problem with regard to personal ethics and social order: "Moreover, we shall find it no easy task to mold a natural ethic strong enough to maintain moral restraint and social order without the support of supernatural consolations, hopes, and fears."

Poor Will Durant! It is not just difficult, it is impossible. He should have remembered the quotation he and Ariel Durant gave from the agnostic Renan in their book *The Lessons of History*. According to the Durants, Renan said in 1866: "If Rationalism wishes to govern the world without regard to the religious needs of the soul, the experience of the French Revolution is there to teach us the consequences of such a blunder."[12]

Along with the decline of the Judeo-Christian consensus we have come to a new definition and connotation of "pluralism." Until recently it meant that the Christianity flowing from the Reformation is not now as dominant in the country and in society as it was in the early days of the nation. After about 1848 the great influx of immigrants to the United States meant a sharp increase in viewpoints not shaped by Reformation Christianity. This, of course, is the situation which exists today. Thus as we stand for religious freedom today, we need to realize that this must include a general religious freedom from the control of the state for all religions. It will not mean just freedom for those who are Christians. It is then up to Christians to show that Christianity is the Truth of total reality in the open marketplace of freedom.

This greater mixture in the United States, however, is now used as an excuse for the new meaning and connotation of pluralism. It now is used to mean that all types of situations are spread out before us, and that it really is up to each individual to grab one or the other on the way past, according to the whim of personal preference. What you take is only a matter of personal choice, with one choice as valid as another. Pluralism has come to mean that everything is acceptable. This new concept of pluralism suddenly is everywhere. There is no right or wrong; it is just a matter of your personal preference. On television, for example, the question of the euthanasia of the old has been presented this way. One choice is as valid as another. It is just a matter of personal preference. This new definition and connotation of pluralism is presented in many forms, not only in personal ethics, but in society's ethics and in the choices concerning law.

Now I have a question. In these shifts that have come in law, where were the Christian lawyers during the crucial shift from forty years ago to just a few years ago? These shifts have all come, or have mostly come, in the last eighty years and the great, titanic shifts have come in the last forty years. Within our lifetime the great shifts in law have taken place. Now that this has happened we can say, surely the Christian lawyers should have seen the change taking place and stood on the wall and blown the trumpets loud and clear. A nonlawyer like myself has a right to feel somewhat let down because the Christian lawyers did not blow the trumpets clearly between, let us say, 1940 and 1970.

When I wrote *How Should We Then Live?* from 1974 to 1976, I worked out of a knowledge of secular philosophy. I moved from the results in secular philosophy, to the results in liberal theology, to the results in the arts, and then I turned to the courts, and especially the Supreme Court. I read Oliver Wendell Holmes and others, and I must say, I was totally appalled by what I read. It was an exact parallel to what I had already known so well from my years of study in philosophy, theology, and the other disciplines.

In the book and film series *How Should We Then Live?* I used the Supreme Court abortion case as the clearest illustration of arbitrary sociological law. But it was only the clearest illustration. The law is shot through with this kind of ruling. It is similar to choosing Fletcher's situational ethics and pointing to it as the clearest illustration of how our society now functions with no fixed ethics. This is only the clearest illustration, because in many ways our society functions on unfixed, situational ethics.

The abortion case in law is exactly the same. It is only the clearest case. Law in this country has become situational law using the term Fletcher used for his ethics. That is, a small group of people decide arbitrarily what, from their viewpoint, is for the good of society at that precise moment and they make it law, binding the whole society by their personal arbitrary decisions.

But of course! What would we expect? These things are the natural, inevitable results of the material-energy, humanistic concept of the final basic reality. From the material-energy, chance concept of final reality, final reality is, and must be by its nature, silent as to values, principles, or any basis for law. There is no way to ascertain "the ought" from "the is."[13] Not only should we have known what this would have produced, but on the basis of this viewpoint of reality, we should have recognized that *there are no other conclusions that this view could produce.* It is a natural result of really believing that the basic reality of all things is merely material-energy, shaped into its present form by impersonal chance.

No, we must say that the Christians in the legal profession did not ring the bell, and we are indeed very, very far down the road toward a totally humanistic culture. At this moment we are in a humanistic culture, but we are happily not in a totally humanistic culture. But what we must realize is that the drift has been all in this direction. If it is not turned around, we will move very rapidly into a *totally* humanistic culture.

The law, and especially the courts, is *the vehicle to force* this total humanistic way of thinking upon the entire population. This is what has happened. The abortion law is a perfect example. The Supreme Court abortion ruling invalidated abortion laws in all fifty states, even though it seems clear that in 1973 the majority of Americans were against abortion. It did not matter. The Supreme Court arbitrarily ruled that abortion was legal, and overnight they overthrew the state laws and forced onto American thinking not only that abortion was legal, but that it was ethical. They, as an elite, thus forced their will on the majority, even though their ruling was arbitrary both legally and medically. Thus law and the courts became the vehicle for forcing a totally secular concept on the population.

But I would say for the comfort of the Christian lawyers, it was not only the lawyers that did not blow the trumpet. Certainly the Bible-believing theologians were not very good at blowing trumpets either. Until the twenties and the thirties, few, if any, among the Bible-believing theologians blew a loud horn. By that time it was too late as most of the old-line denominations had come under the dominance of liberal theology at the two power centers of the bureaucracies and the seminaries. By then voices were raised. But with rare exceptions, by that time it was too late. From then on, the liberal theologians would increasingly side with the secular humanists in matters of lifestyle and the rulings of sociological law.

And those Bible-believing theologians who did see the theological danger seemed totally blind to what was happening in law and in the total culture. Thus the theologians did no better in seeing the shift from one worldview to a totally different worldview.

Nor did Christian educators do any better either. The failed responsibility covers a wide swath. Christian educators, Christian theologians, Christian lawyers—none of them blew loud trumpets until we were a long, long way down the road toward a humanistically based culture.

But, while this may spread the problem of responsibility around, that does not help us today except to realize that if we are going to do better we must stop being experts in only seeing these things in bits and pieces. We have to understand that it is one total entity opposed to the other total entity. It concerns truth in regard to final and total reality—not just religious reality, but total reality. And our view of final reality—whether it is material-energy, shaped by impersonal chance, or the living God and Creator—will determine our position on every crucial issue we face today. It will determine our views on the value and dignity of people, the base for the kind of life the individual and society lives, the direction law will take, and whether there will be freedom or some form of authoritarian dominance.

Notes

1. David Walker Woods, *John Witherspoon* (Old Tappan, N.J.: Revell, 1906).

2. Edward Corwin, "The Supreme Court as National School Board," *Law and Contemporary Problems,* 14 (1949): 3, 11–12.

3. Herbert W. Titus (Professor of Law, O. W. Coburn School of Law), *Education, Caesar's or God's: A Constitutional Question of Jurisdiction.*

4. Franky Schaeffer V, "The Myth of Neutrality," *Plan for Action* (Old Tappan, N.J.: Revell, 1980), 37.

5. Terry Eastland, "In Defense of Religious America," *Commentary* (June 1981): 39.

6. Quoted by Perry Miller, ed., *The Legal Mind in America* (New York: Doubleday, 1962), 178.

7. Eastland, "In Defense of Religious America," 41.

8. Francis Schaeffer, *How Should We Then Live?* (Old Tappan, N.J.: Revell, 1976), 217.

9. Ibid.

10. William Bentley Ball has been lead council in litigation in twenty states and has appeared before the Supreme Court in parental rights cases. He was chairman of the Federal Bar Association Committee on Constitutional Law 1970–74.

11. See *How Should We Then Live?* chapters "The Rise of Modern Science" and "The Breakdown of Philosophy and Science," 130–66.

12. Will Durant and Ariel Durant, *The Lessons of History* (New York: Simon and Schuster, 1968), 50–51.

13. See Jacques Monod, *Chance and Necessity* (New York: Knopf, 1971).

4

Meet Secular Humanism

J. I. Packer and Thomas Howard

What Is Humanism?

The secular humanism that we meet today is not the same thing as the Renaissance humanism which one sees in such men as Erasmus and Leonardo da Vinci. Renaissance humanism, despite some murky streaks, was in essence a plea for a rich and robust Christian culture. Nor should we equate secular humanism with the humanism professed by those who teach the humanities professionally; nor should we confuse it with the spirit of sympathetic concern for others' welfare which is often called humanism in these days. Secular humanism is neither a professional field nor a character quality, but an aggressive cultural ideology—that is, a set of ideas expressed in programs designed to change people's lives.

It is a recent growth. Like Kleenex and aerobics, it is a product of the consciously civilized modern West. It appears in various forms, but a single conviction animates them all—namely, the belief that

J. I. PACKER is the Sangwood Youtong Chee professor of theology at Regent College, Vancouver, British Columbia. He is the author of numerous books including *Knowing God* and the coeditor of the *New Dictionary of Theology*.
THOMAS HOWARD is chairman of the Department of English at Gordon College, Wenham, Massachusetts. Among the books he has written are *The Achievements of C. S. Lewis* and *Dialogue with a Skeptic*.

current cultural developments, especially those which claim the name of science, show religion to be irrational and hostile to human happiness. The thought is that only those who know they are on their own in the universe, with no God to worship and no concern about the church, will ever take the bold steps that are needed to set their lives straight. From this it is inferred that the way to help people realize their potential is to disillusion them about religion and so free them from inhibiting superstitions and restrictions. Then, by rational reflection on experience, a wiser code can be devised and a happier generation will be bred.

The heart of secular humanism thus appears as reaction—reaction born, as it seems, of hurt and resentment, outrage and disgust at the tenets and track record of organized religion. It broke surface in the West in the first century B.C. with Lucretius' long poem *De Rerum Natura* (On the Nature of Things). Lucretius wrote to free people from what seemed to him the crippling fear that the gods take notice of men, and to preach to them the Epicurean gospel of a quiet, pleasure-seeking life, devoid of religious concerns. Here is the spirit of modern secular humanism exactly.

Nowhere is humanist reaction currently more visible than in the United States. This is not surprising. In the United States a conversionist folk religion (legalistic, biblicist, revivalist, conservative, credulous, anticultural, authoritarian) has in the past been strong. Such religion naturally prompts reaction among educated and sensitive people. This problem is not, however, unique to the United States, nor to Protestant countries as such. Wherever Christianity has produced what historians call a "popular piety" claiming to be part of the national heritage, anti-Christian reaction among the intelligentsia has followed.

In Roman Catholic and Eastern Orthodox countries, where the church has become an entrenched power structure, revolts that started with anticlericalism, deism, and atheism have ended in Marxism—the embrace of a secular collective juggernaut as a refuge from sacred authority. In England, where the folk religion was a dignified Anglican formalism, cooler, less intrusive, and more laissez-faire than either Orthodoxy or Roman Catholicism, the humanist revolt, though not negligible, has been less strong, probably because fewer there have been hurt by dehumanizing versions of

Christianity. But in the United States the enforcing of substandard Christianity in homes, churches, schools, and communities has inflicted so much emotional hurt, that anti-Christian reaction is marked by a strong head of emotional steam. There is more to secular humanism than the fixated reactionary thinking of the traumatized, but not less; and we shall not understand the movement well unless we give full weight to this factor.

It would no doubt be easy at this point to launch into a diatribe against reaction, pointing out that the reaction of man rarely works the righteousness of God and highlighting the folly of throwing out the baby with the bath water. We could emphasize that really wise people do not let the abuse of things (such as religion) blind them to their proper use. To expand on these thoughts would be very easy— and, as we see it, very wrong. For cheap sarcasm rules out deep understanding, and understanding is what we are after at present.

We are asking what makes humanists tick, and we are saying that one factor is the psychology of the scarred mind. Our thinking about what has traumatized us is regularly negative, adversative, and hostile to the point of obsession. The burnt child, says the proverb, dreads the fire: having been hurt by it, he fears it all his life. This same kind of fear seems to be the reason many humanists are obsessively anti-Christian, just as it is the reason why some Christians, who see humanism as a conspiracy, are obsessively anti-humanist. It is clear that many humanists in the West are stirred by a sense of outrage at what professed Christians, past and present, have done; and this makes them see their humanism as a kind of crusade, with the killing of Christianity as its prime goal. We cannot endorse their attitude, but we can understand it and respect it, and we would like at this point to say so.

What's that? says someone. You can **respect** an attitude that seeks the death of Christianity? Yes, we can, on two accounts.

First, we can justify the disillusionment with Christians out of which the humanist murder plan springs. We know what it is like to be hurt, disillusioned, embarrassed, and disgusted at the words and deeds of professing Christians. We, too, have experienced the damage done by bad Christianity—Christianity that lacks honesty, or intelligence, or regard for truth, or biblical depth, or courtesy, or all of these together. No doubt we have sometimes inflicted this kind of damage, as well as suffered it. Loss of faith caused by bad experiences with Christians is thus often more a case of being sinned against than of sinning and merits compassion more than it does censure.

Second, we honor the humanists' serious purpose of finding the path to human fulfillment and clearing away all that blocks it. This is our own purpose, too; and though we disagree entirely about what constitutes fulfillment and how it occurs, we see their quest as ours and invite them to see ours as theirs.

Meantime, we set on record our conviction that Western humanism, like Marx's Marxism, is best viewed as a prodigal son of Christianity itself. Though it has left its Christian home in search of freedom and fulfillment elsewhere, and though it is driven by the rebel son's passion to strike the father dead, it has no alternative home of its own, but continues to be nourished by elements of its Christian heritage of goals and values.

The Tenets of Humanism

What does humanism offer in place of Christian faith? *The Humanist Manifestos I* and *II* (1933 and 1973) have told the world, and there was never any in-house disputing about it in the humanist camp. Humanism sets human beings at the center of the universe, maintaining that Nature, of which man is the most highly developed component, is all that exists; that happiness and enrichment of human life now is all that we should aim at; that scientific reason is the only tool needed for the task; and that religion hinders the enterprise rather than helps it. Working hypotheses that humanists embrace include the eternity of the universe; the evolution of man and society as a fact of the past and a hope for the future; the autonomy of man as lord of Nature; the absolute uniformity of Nature's laws; utilitarian relativism in ethics, whereby anything that promises happy states and feelings becomes right for that very reason; and a belief that everyone should have a share in all good things.

The 1933 *Manifesto* presented this high-minded, world-centered, science-oriented ethic as an alternative religion (understanding religion as a "means for realizing the highest values of life") and the U.S. Supreme Court recognized it as such in 1961. The 1973 *Manifesto* restated the same view more stringently, with explicit rejection of "intolerant attitudes, often cultivated by orthodox religions and puritanical cultures" that "unduly repress sexual conduct."

The most striking difference between the two *Manifestos* is that whereas the first was signed by thirty-four Americans of whom only John Dewey is known today, the second counts among its signatories philosophers Bland Blanshard and Sidney Hook (American) and Sir Alfred Ayer and Antony Flew (British); authors Isaac Asimov and John Ciardi; scientists Francis Crick, Andrei Sakharov, and Zhores Medvedev; psychologists H. J. Eysenck and B. F. Skinner with sexologists Albert Ellis, Lester Kirkendall, and Sol Gordon; and feminist Betty Friedan; plus the atypical but well-known Episcopal clergyman Joseph Fletcher, fount of "situation ethics." These are, to use the British phrase, top people. The humanist support base has become more impressive. Over forty years, humanism has gathered strength.

The guiding humanist hypothesis about the human condition is evolutionism (the idea that by inevitable progress mankind gets better and better, provided that no one throw a monkey wrench into the works). Where Marxism subordinates the individual to community interests and existentialism mocks him as a passionate absurdity, Anglo-American humanism treats personal welfare as the ultimate value and leaves each individual as free as possible to define welfare for himself in egoistic terms—comfort, convenience, aesthetic pleasure, affluence, self-improvement, sexual satisfaction according to taste, and so on.

The inborn aptitude of the human individual for devising a lifestyle which the rest of us will recognize as good and wise is taken for granted. Modern "values education," which, instead of teaching standards, seeks to draw out of children whatever values are in their minds already, is a latter-day expression of this philosophy.

No doubt some embrace humanism because it allows them behavior which religion forbids. They never become conscious of the radiantly optimistic view of our nature which humanism assumes. But to Christians and others who scrutinize and reject this optimism, humanist permissiveness does not make sense. It seems to them nightmarishly crazy, a canonizing of irrationality and irresponsibility that invites both personal and cultural disaster. But humanists seem happy to give individuals their head however kinky or kooky the results, because they are quite sure of the innate goodness and wisdom of man.

Or are they? Closer inspection reveals disturbing ambivalence at this point. Humanist leaders prove again and again to be profound pessimists, aristocratically contemptuous of human nature as it is and optimistic only about their plans for changing it. Those who start by echoing the second *Humanist Manifesto*—"the preciousness and dignity of the individual person is a central humanist value"—end up as social engineers devaluing all individuals who do not measure up to their ideal. The notorious willingness of some humanists to justify and recommend abortion, infanticide, euthanasia, and the sterilizing or killing of the physically handicapped and mentally limited, as the Nazis did, is clear evidence of the direction in which their basic attitude takes them. It is not that humanists are arrogant and unfeeling, though it seems clear that some of them are. There is a logical inevitability about their impatience with ordinary human beings. After all, when their philosophy aims at a perfectly happy community here on earth, there is no other way for their thoughts to go.

> Morality based on individual sentiment means anarchy and the disintegration of society. Humanists cannot have this, and their writings are filled with fervid arguments in favor of a powerful central state. Autonomous man, they find, needs leadership, and strong leadership is the hallmark of a humanist society. Whether embodied in a committee or personalized in a leader, the elite dominates. Thus, far from being liberation, the anarchy of humanism brings enslavement. The better educated he is, the more likely the humanist is to believe that people are like machines and need to be programmed, and the more likely he is to believe that he should be one of the programmers.[1]

The Marxism of the East, despite its manipulative social policy, called itself humanism; the humanism of the West, despite its name, pursues a manipulative social policy; the two ideologies at this point join hands, revealing beneath their surface differences an elitist family likeness. And both contrast with Christianity in the same stark way. Christianity brings authentic personal freedom through submitting to God; acknowledging his standards as absolutes; and accepting his revealed pattern of social order, law, mutual care, and communal restraint as the milieu for each person's individual life. Both humanism and Marxism, however, while proclaiming freedom from all religious bonds, end up enslaving the individual to some communal program which manipulates and ultimately discounts him in the interests (alleged) of the group.

Thus Western humanism, no less than Eastern Communism, dehumanizes and diminishes the individual whose integrity it professed itself so anxious to safeguard and enhance. Inside its velvet glove of tolerance is an iron hand of tyranny; its professed compassion becomes a sanction for cruelty, and its professed humanitarianism a kind of inhumanity. The preciousness and dignity of the individual person is precisely not its central value, and to claim that it is, as humanists commonly do, is really muddle-headed.

Enlightenment Humanism vs. Promethean Humanism

We need to distinguish between what may be called Enlightenment humanism and Promethean humanism. The Enlightenment was a movement of secular intellectualism; Prometheus was a mythical hero who stole fire from the gods to give to men in order to enrich their lives; and the two humanisms express, respectively, the spirit of refinement and the spirit of revolution.

Enlightenment humanism comes from men like Voltaire and Kant, children of eighteenth-century rationalism which glorified cool reasoners. It has always prided itself on maintaining without Christian sanctions a moral code equal to if not superior to that of Christianity. That is the humanism of refinement.

Promethean humanism, however, stems from men like Feuerbach ("religion means childlike immaturity"), Marx ("atheism is a necessity, since all religions support unjust social structures"), Freud ("religion is an illusion, a wish-fulfillment fantasy"), and Nietzsche ("now that God is dead, everything is permissible"). All these thinkers were products of the nineteenth-century romantic movement, which glorified the heroic rebel. Theirs is the humanism of revolution. Of their ideas and ideologies James Hitchcock has written:

> The new humanism of the nineteenth century embodied a demonic urge to negate and destroy. As Nietzsche saw clearly, it was not only a matter of not believing in God. Once God had

been denied, man could achieve true freedom only by denying all moral constraints on himself and inventing his own morality. The human will alone become sovereign. This type of Humanism has often descended into Nihilism, the urge to destroy and annihilate every accepted good. The older, more genteel type of Humanism has been steadily losing ground to the newer kind, which is in essence profoundly anti-humanistic.[2]

Whereas the spirit of Enlightenment humanism ran through the first *Humanist Manifesto,* the temper of Promethean humanism marks the second. The aggressiveness so often found in current humanist literature suggests that the Promethean spirit is becoming dominant, which in turn makes one wonder whether the humanist movement has not already slid into an irrecoverable decadence. Some decadence is, in any case, inescapable once the relativization of moral absolutes begins.

Hitchcock's word *demonic* points to a motivation in humanism that is deeper than the merely pragmatic and cultural. The humanist movement, particularly in its Promethean form, expresses a defiance of the Creator's just claims, and an instinct for negating value. Viewed from this standpoint, humanism appears as the latest in a series of revolts against Christianity which go back to the first century. In New Testament times the multiform theosophy called Gnosticism tried to swallow up Christianity. At the same time pagan intellectuals ridiculed Christianity's belief in incarnation and atonement, and Rome steadily killed its adherents for the sake of public order. Later Islam emerged, and Arabs and Turks began to wish Christianity dead. The next revolt against Christianity came with the Renaissance. Unlike Medieval thinkers who sought to integrate all knowledge in a single synthesis shaped by God's revealed truth, the Renaissance attempted to free the arts and, later, the sciences from their Christian moorings. In due course this impulse produced the humanism which we know today.

These were all movements of recoil from the Christian call for unqualified submission to God as finally and definitively revealed in Jesus Christ, whom to know is life and to serve is freedom. In this they echoed Satan and the fallen angels, who according to Scripture were the first to refuse to be their Maker's subjects. When all due allowance has been made for the justice of humanist indignation at the sometimes outrageous failings of the Christian church, it has to be said that humanist self-expression often strikes a note of arrogant self-sufficiency and contempt for the very thought of serving God, which is the essence of what Christians mean by original sin. Thus behind humanism's real intellectual seriousness we detect a genuine spiritual problem.

A Biblical Perspective on Humanism

Humanism, like Marxism, sees itself as pointing the way to an ideal society. It is, in other words, a form of utopianism. That is part of its Promethean character. But Christians know that all utopian dreams are foredoomed to failure. When Adam and Eve had defied God by eating fruit from the tree of knowledge, and so yielded to the temptation to seek wisdom apart from God, God said: "'The man . . . must not be allowed to reach out his hand and take also from the tree of life and eat, and live forever.' So the LORD God banished him from the Garden of Eden. . . . After he drove the man out, he placed on the east side of the Garden of Eden cherubim and a flaming sword flashing back and forth to guard the way to the tree of life" (Genesis 3:22–24).

The road to Paradise, whether viewed as the way back or the way ahead, is barred to rebel mankind. The profoundest way to read history is to recognize that the human race has, in effect, been trying to get back to Eden under its own steam all along; the utopian motive has been there, sometimes veiled but always potent, throughout the whole checkered career of humanity. But humanity has never managed to reenter Paradise in this way, nor will it ever. No godless heaven will ever be found, or built, on earth, no matter how far we search or how hard we try. God has decreed that utopianism will fail. He has other plans.

The key to understanding both the gospel and the inadequacy of humanism is found in Genesis 3, which shows God dealing with fallen mankind. It is to this same fallen condition that the gospel declares God's amazing final response in the life, death, resurrection, and promised return of Jesus Christ, through whom he makes all things new. Leaving aside the probably unanswerable questions as to the date of

Adam and the geographical location of Eden and what we would have seen and heard had we been there to observe, we read Genesis 3 not only as narrating man's fall from God, but as picturing the continuing human condition as it was yesterday, as it is today, and as it will be tomorrow. Man, as he has been since the Fall, is portrayed definitively in the story of the Fall. Read thus, as a mirror of mankind's past and present, this chapter shows us the following truths.

From the beginning, man has forgotten that responsive fellowship with God is his highest privilege and dignity. Like Adam and Eve, we have come to doubt whether depending on and responding to our Maker is really the richest life, and we have let ourselves be betrayed into hankering after the will-o'-the-wisp of independence, as if the more independent of God we can be, the nobler we become. Human beings are made for a relationship with God of which total responsiveness in worship and obedience should be the essence, and it is only as we sustain that relationship that real nobility is found in our lives. The supreme proof of this is Jesus Christ, whose nobility sober persons have never been able to deny even when they have failed to see that fellowship with the Father was its source. The Promethean attempt in Eden to live life independent of God was a recipe not for human nobility but for human degradation. So it proved in Adam and Eve's day, and so it is still. How this works out in humanism we have already begun to see.

From the beginning, man has forgotten that he is finite, limited, and weak. Pride prompts in us, as it did in Adam and Eve, the desire to be like God, to play God, to function as God. Pride also leads us to imagine that we have enough strength and wisdom actually to play the divine role, controlling all around us with perfect mastery and glorying in the thought that there is nothing we cannot do. Our whole race suffers from delusions of grandeur, which modern technology serves merely to confirm. The illusion of perfect mastery, like other illusions, is frequently shattered ("Almighty God himself couldn't sink this ship," said the captain of the Titanic), but it forms itself again quickly in most minds. We do not wish to face our limitations, so we encourage ourselves to forget them. We like to think of ourselves as infinitely wise and resourceful, so we indulge self-exalting daydreams all the time. This spirit is universal, and humanism is in no way exempt.

From the beginning, man has made pleasure his prime aim, rather than truth and uprightness. "When the woman saw that the fruit of the tree was good for food and pleasing to the eye, and also desirable for gaining wisdom, she took some and ate it" (Genesis 3:6). What Freud called the "pleasure principle" became in Eden the typical and dominant human motivation, and such it remains. "It looks good, I want it, I shall enjoy it, I must have it; never mind the consequences, for me or for others"—this mentality and mood are universally familiar, being found not only in society around us but also, as honest people admit, in our own hearts. Though we all sometimes make a point of doing what we know to be the right thing, the overall story of our race indicates that egoistic desire is often in control, and that altruism is the exception rather than the rule. There is nothing new (except, perhaps, the degree of openness) in the pleasure-oriented, often immoral motivation that is so much a mark of our times. In essence, it has been that way everywhere since the Fall.

From the beginning, man has felt that God is against him and has reacted to God in a negative and hostile way. The form of Satan's crafty question, "Did God really say, 'You must not eat from any tree in the garden'?" (Genesis 3:1), insinuated that the God of the garden was keeping Adam and Eve down. The statement that followed, "For God knows that when you eat of it (the forbidden fruit) your eyes will be opened, and you will be like God, knowing good and evil" (v. 5), was meant to convince them that God was a jealous potentate unwilling to have peers, while they themselves were creatures of great potential, able to become the equals of their Creator.

Human thought since Eden has been dyed the color of this conviction. Since the Fall it has never been natural to anyone to love God (or his neighbor) with all his heart. Why not? Because, as Paul states, "the sinful mind is hostile to God. It does not submit to God's law, nor can it do so. Those controlled by the sinful nature cannot please God" (Romans 8:7–8).

To say that by nature we are all inclined against God, feeling him to be against us, may be startling. As long as our thoughts of God are selective and determined by our own fancy, we may be inclined to protest that it is not so with us. But no "natural man" can contemplate the God of the Bible without finding it in him to wish that God's claims were less stringent and his judgments less severe. And out of this wish will grow hatred of God—hatred that may well express itself in outraged insistence that "God can't really be like that" and outraged censure of Christians for holding that he is. Humanism, in particular, displays this state of mind.

From the beginning, man has thought that he could escape from God and so avoid the consequences of having defied and disobeyed him. Adam and Eve, we read in Genesis 3:7–8, felt guilty and ashamed the moment they ate the fatal fruit. Their feelings of shame made them want to hide themselves and not be fully seen. This urge found a physical focus, and they donned fig-leaf loincloths, so fulfilling their desire to hide something of themselves from each other. A concealing instinct was part of them now, by reason of their sin. Then they tried to hide from Godtried, because they thought they could do it. But they could not, any more than we can. God knows who we are, what we are, and where we are; and in due course we shall all be called to account.

Here, however, we are in another area where fallen human thinking is constantly wishful and unrealistic. Like Adam and Eve, people imagine that they can sin with impunity, either because they believe retribution is only a sick fancy and will never really happen, or because they are sure they are not bad enough to be condemned, or because they think they can make up for lapses in one department by spurts of moral effort in another. None of this, however, is true, any more than humanism's venture of thinking God out of existence is true. ". . . man is destined to die once, and after that to face judgment" (Hebrews 9:27), and this is something which no amount of thinking otherwise can alter.

From the beginning, man has been unwilling to accept responsibility for his actions and admit that he deserves retribution. The answers of Adam and Eve when God asked them if they had eaten the forbidden fruit show that evading responsibility had already become second nature to them (Genesis 3:11–13). "The woman you put here with me, she gave me some fruit from the tree, and I ate it," said Adam. In other words, it was her fault, not mine! "The serpent deceived me, and I ate," said Eve. In other words, it was not my fault, but his! Reading this, we understand perfectly what was going on in their minds, for it remains one of our most cherished illusions that whatever we have done, we are not to blame; the influence of others, or something in our history, or our circumstances should be censured, but **not** we.

Perhaps the best thing to do with this idea is to laugh it out of court. So we cite the following verses by an anonymous medical man:

> I went to my psychiatrist to be psychoanalyzed,
>   To find out why I killed the cat and blacked my
>   wifie's eyes.
> He laid me on a comfy couch to see what he could find,
>   And this is what he dredged up out of my
>   unconscious mind.
> When I was one my mommy locked my dolly in the trunk,
>   And so it follows naturally that I am always drunk.
> When I was two I saw my father kiss the maid one day,
>   And that is why I suffer now from klep-to-ma-ni-a.
> At three I was ambivalent towards my younger brothers,
>   And that's the reason why, to date, I've poisoned all
>   my lovers.
> And I'm so glad since I have learned the lesson I've been
>   taught,
>   That everything I do that's wrong is someone else's
>   fault.

This is a hit particularly at Freudian determinism; but we do well to remember that behind Freudianism and similar views of a behaviorist-determinist sort lies a craving to shift the blame that is as old as Adam. It is to be hoped, however, that honest laughter will shame it into silence.

But it is no laughing matter when we observe how radically, at least in some of its expositors, humanism canonizes this self-excusing instinct. It starts, as we have seen, by abolishing God—the transcendent ground and guardian of right and wrong—which leaves only a social-utilitarian, culturally relative basis for morality. That, however, is only the beginning. It then proceeds to class antisocial behavior as a form of mental illness, to be treated by medical and psychiatric means (up to the point of brainwashing, if need be). It does this as an alternative to understanding wrongdoing in moral terms. It abolishes the categories of bearing one's guilt and paying one's debt to society.

But this procedure, which is alleged to be kind and humane, actually diminishes and dehumanizes us. For to accept responsibility for our own actions belongs to our dignity as moral agents, however little we like the idea and however much we try to wriggle out of it. Extenuating circumstances there may be, but ultimately we know, and furthermore we know that we know, that those who have done wrong should be made to answer for it, whether to men or to God.

Answering to God for our moral and spiritual shortcomings is in fact inescapable, as we have seen. Nor must this necessarily spell our ruin. Christians know that God in mercy forgives sins, through the atoning death of Jesus Christ. From the recording of God's promise that the woman's seed should crush the serpent's head (Genesis 3:15) and of his provision of animal skin garments for Adam and Eve (v. 21), a gesture which involved killing the animals as was constantly done later when sacrificing for sins, we are probably meant to gather that there and then Adam and Eve found forgiveness, though God's curses on this present life remained in force.

But forgiveness can only come when sin has been confessed as the guilty thing it is. This, however, assumes an acknowledgment of God which humanism does not make. We do not doubt that humanists, like Adam and Eve and everyone else, do in fact feel guilt, even after trying to tell themselves that they shouldn't; and it seems clear that in the humanist universe there is no way they can get rid of it. The sad conclusion is that it must stay as an ulcer on their soul all their days, draining love, peace, and goodwill out of them and souring their spirit, as unforgiven guilt always does.

Humanism Against Humanism

Our response to secular humanism has not taken the form of a general defense of Christianity. That is not, however, because we doubt if such a defense can be successfully made. We are quite certain that it can. The historic mainstream faith for which we stand—"mere Christianity," as the Puritan Richard Baxter and, following him, C. S. Lewis called it—seems to us to be supremely and compellingly reasonable, whereas anti-Christianity in all the forms in which we know it seems to us patently unreasonable by comparison. Let us explain.

The unreasonableness of an anti-Christian commitment seems to us to come out in three ways.

First, anti-Christianity fails to face facts. It can neither explain nor explain away the facts of Bible history, centering in the fact of Christ and his resurrection. Nor can it explain or explain away the courage of martyrs and missionaries; the compassion of Father Damien or Mother Teresa; the character of men like the apostle Paul, Francis of Assisi, and John Wesley; or the communion enjoyed and attested by millions down the centuries in their life of prayer. It has to proceed as if these realities were never there. But to approve a position that is wedded to this ostrich-like course is surely irrational.

Second, anti-Christianity fails to mesh with life. Its diagnoses and prescriptions do not touch our deepest insights, pains, hopes, and needs. Two millennia of Christian influence, plus a plethora of psychological cross-checking during the past century, has established pretty definitely what these needs are. We have a thirst for God, a desire for happiness, a need for friendship, minds that want truth, and an instinct for immortality. We need to know that we are loved, that our lives have significance, and that we have something to look forward to; or our happiness, such as it is, flies out of the window. We know guilt as a burden and see death as a threat, and we need to get rid of the burden and transcend the threat, or once again our happiness will fail.

Christianity ministers to all these felt needs and relieves all these anxieties. Anti-Christianity cannot do any of this, so the only course it can take is to proceed as if these concerns were not there, or at least were not important. Sometimes it tries to bolster itself up by ridiculing those for whom these concerns retain importance, as if this very fact showed Christians to be poor specimens of humanity. But such posturing cannot stop anti-Christianity itself from seeming forlorn for its inability to rival that which it rejects. Nor can it dispel the irrationality of opting for a view which cannot answer our basic questions.

Third, anti-Christianity in all its forms is arbitrary. We see it to be held together by willpower, energy of assertion, and the turning of a blind eye to awkward facts rather than by force of evidence or cogency of argument. But to embrace a view for which such things have to be said is surely irrational.

Explanatory power is, after all, a mark of credibility. The diagnosis of and the prescription for human needs contained in the gospel of Christ fit our actual condition as a glove fits a hand. Anti-Christianity is discredited by its inability to account for the reasonableness of the Christianity it opposes.

The question at the heart of Christianity's debate with humanism is the question of humanness itself; the question of what being human involves. Our review of secular humanism has given this question a preliminary whirl, but it still needs more precise focusing.

When we moderns—Christian or humanist, theist, atheist, or agnostic—say, "man," what we have in view is a functioning psychophysical organism, a conscious embodied individual, male or female, who belongs to the human race. The life-task for us who *are* human is to *become* human in terms of our personal qualities—our character, emotional maturity, relational empathy, appreciation of value, knowledge of God, inner integration, depth of insight, wisdom, goodness, and love. Becoming human in this sense is our primary duty, and the genuineness of any "humanism"—Christian or secular—can be judged best by how effectively it helps us to accomplish this goal.

Secular humanism, which claims to exalt man, actually impedes his becoming human in terms of these personal qualities. Christianity, which starts by humbling man as a sinner, has a directly humanizing effect on him at all these points. Christianity takes man seriously as an immortal soul whom God is preparing for glory; it gives him a sense of the transcendent; it shows him that eternal issues are involved in temporal choices; it draws him into a love relationship of praise and thanks, worship and work, with the Father and the Son through the Spirit; it leads him to the discovery that self-forgetful love to God and men is the holiest and noblest disposition there is ("He showed me that all my preaching, writing and other ministry was absolutely nothing compared to my love relationship with him," wrote David Watson just before he died).[3]

Furthermore, Christianity sensitizes the sinner to moral realities across the board. It stretches him in sympathy and service manward and in fidelity and aspiration Godward; it gives him a hope beyond this world which sustains and refreshes him in this world; it pitches him into grueling fights with himself and the sin that so easily besets him, fights which toughen his moral fiber and deepen his experience of God's power. In short, Christianity makes a man (male or female) of him, a man that without God's grace he never could have been, a man who bears the moral likeness of the Lord Jesus Christ, his Savior, Master, and Friend. Christianity is the true humanism, by reason of its humanizing effect. Christian life is the good life for man.

Clearly secular humanism, as a point of view, is not in the same league as Christianity when it comes to what used to be called "soul-making." It hides from us our eternal destiny, drops God out of our minds, encourages egoism and self-worship, undercuts morality by its relativism and permissiveness, undermines compassion for the weak and helpless who are not socially useful, encourages social programs to manage people as we manage animals, and in all these ways tends to desensitize and dehumanize. If individual humanists are not brash, brassy, arrogant, and insensitive, it will be despite their doctrine, not because of it. It will in fact be because they still bear the impress of the Christianity that they reject.

There are, we know, many such humanists, who have been led to their present views not by the kind of mad pride that turned Lucifer into Satan and caused Adam's downfall, but by a compassionate desire to save others from bad experiences of religion like they themselves have had. With regard to the official humanist scheme, we have already said our piece. We would like, as we close, however, to say a word to this whole class of humanist fellow-travelers.

We say it softly; we know that otherwise we shall not be heard. We are very conscious that we cannot undo their bad experiences and that no apologies from us can cure those wounds which we or our heavy-handed fellow believers have inflicted. Nor can we expect that those who have been thus hurt will quickly cease to suspect that repression, frustration, philistinism, hypocrisy, and cruelty are the natural products of institutional Christianity. Nonetheless, we beg any humanists who will listen to think again, both about what they have let themselves in for and also about what Christian humanism will yield to any who take it seriously.

Notes

1. Herbert Schlossberg, *Idols for Destruction* (Nashville: Thomas Nelson, 1983), 87.

2. James Hitchcock, *What Is Secular Humanism?* (Ann Arbor: Servant Books, 1982), 48.

3. David Watson, *Fear No Evil* (Wheaton, Ill.: Harold Shaw, 1984), 171.

5

Snapshots of Faith in Action

Herbert W. Schlossberg and Marvin Olasky

American Christianity is at a turning point. We face perhaps the greatest challenge—and the greatest opportunity—since the founding of our country. The challenge we face is the tidal wave of militant anti-Christian belief engulfing society and the chaos it leaves in its wake: the AIDS epidemic, the dissolution of the family, the abortion holocaust, growing economic weakness, the crisis of judge-made law, teen pregnancy, widespread financial fraud. These difficult problems and many others are largely the by-product of the humanist idea that man is the measure of all things and that all ethical standards are relative. Frequently proposed "solutions" (for example, "safe sex" and school-based clinics) and ideological fixes (liberal statism, atheistic libertarianism, radical feminism) are proven failures or disasters waiting to happen.

It is becoming painfully apparent that anti-Christian humanism, the guiding force of our society for the last three decades, does not work. The world is in crisis and people want answers. Christianity—which is not an ideology but the truth about God,

HERBERT W. SCHLOSSBERG is a historian and researcher in public policy, who has authored *Idols for Destruction*, *A Fragrance of Oppression* and *Freedom, Justice, and Hope*.
MARVIN OLASKY is associate professor of journalism at the University of Texas, Austin, and senior fellow at the Capital Research Center, Washington, D.C. He is the general editor of the *Turning Point Christian Worldview Series* and author of a number of books including *The Tragedy of American Compassion* and *Abortion Rites*.

man, and the world—provides the answers people want and need. The opportunity for Christians to proclaim the truth, to provide answers, is great. Will we seize the opportunity? Will we share the only real hope there is? But more than this, will we live out our faith in every area of life by showing that Christ is not only Lord of our lives personally but just as much Lord over all of life and culture?

Because of both current crises and biblical imperatives, we do not have a long time to spend pondering these questions. As the epistle of James notes, "Faith by itself, if it is not accompanied by action, is dead" (2:17). James was not suggesting that we earn our salvation, but he was noting that true faith shows itself in action. The author of Hebrews linked faith and action when he wrote of those who "through faith conquered kingdoms, administered justice, and gained what was promised" (11:33). We have to get moving if we are to emulate heroes such as Abraham, Moses, and David, builders of nations. To get moving, we need instruction.

Instruction, though, does not always have to be in the form of a theoretical sermon. The Bible alternates history and formal doctrine, storytelling and message-explaining. Hebrews 11 mentions briefly some of those who put their faith into action; let's begin here by taking "snapshots" of three American Christians who put *their* faith into action during the nineteenth century.

Snapshot 1: Faith in Action, 1816

In 1816 Nathaniel Willis was a thirty-six-year-old Boston printer and former newspaper editor who wanted to get back into journalism. He had many opportunities to put out public relations material for various church denominations, but he wanted more than that. He wanted to publish, in his own words, "a real newspaper."

Willis's idea of journalistic reality was tied to his idea of Christianity. Willis did not identify Christianity with either church buildings or church socials. He had grown up apart from all that, absorbing instead the atheistic philosophies of the French Revolution and coming to edit a radical newspaper. But Willis's sudden conversion was also radical. He wrote, "The Holy Spirit led me to see that there is an eternity—that the Bible is the Word of God—that Christ is the only Savior, and that it is by grace we are saved, through faith."

The new vision changed all of Willis's life, including his journalistic work. He resigned his old editorship and tried to get backing for a new newspaper. It was hard going because he wanted to publish a newspaper that emphasized both individual devotion and societal transformation. Christians then were accustomed to publications that emphasized one or the other, but Willis, without neglecting personal spiritual exhortation, also wanted to report on national and world events. He wanted to cover not only good news but bad as well, for by war and crime, famine and disaster, "God also is teaching us."

Willis had trouble raising start-up funds for a newspaper that would sometimes be unpleasant. He had to wait half a dozen years, but he turned down compromise and finally raised the backing. Once underway, he did not shrink from running a story about how an earthquake turned one city into "heaps of ruins," with "hundreds of decrepit parents half-buried in the ruins, imploring the succor of their sons," and "distracted mothers frantically lifting heavy stones from heaps that covered the bodies of lifeless infants."

For Willis, the remarkable event was that "men and women clinging to the ruined walls of their houses, holding their children in their trembling arms, with mangled bodies all around . . . were imploring the Almighty's mercy." Soon thousands were "falling on their knees and imploring the mercy of God; and shortly after crowding the places of worship, eager to learn what they must do to be saved." Willis developed these and other stories about God's power to urge sinners that they should "immediately seek reconciliation to Him through the Blood of the Lamb."

Willis's strategy was both spiritually and economically successful. In 1822, the year Willis's *Boston Recorder* published that earthquake story, his newspaper had the second highest circulation in New England. Ministers who had feared that attention to "worldly things" would draw away attention from proclamation of the gospel praised Willis for aiding evangelism. Willis continued as editor and publisher for twenty years. For Willis, personal faith had led directly into an attempt to transform American journalism. Willis's public work, in turn, affected many private lives.

Snapshot 2: Faith in Action, 1845

The original Cassius Clay (not the boxer who changed his name to Muhammed Ali) was an affluent slaveholder in Lexington, Kentucky. He could have lived a comfortable life, at least until the Civil War. But Clay believed that chattel slavery was ungodly, and he also believed that society should be ordered on biblical principles.

Clay freed his own slaves and then tried to reach fellow Kentuckians by publishing an antislavery newspaper. When partisans of slavery threatened to destroy his printing press Clay made a fort out of his three-story, red-brick office. He purchased two small brass cannon, loaded them to the muzzle with bullets, slugs, and nails, and stationed them at the entrance, while his friends stockpiled muskets and Mexican lances.

Those measures forestalled the attack. Then Clay took the fight to the opposition, going before hostile crowds to speak his piece. Once, facing his enemies, Clay held up a Bible and said, "To those who respect God's Word, I appeal to this book." Then he held up a copy of the Constitution of the United States and said, "To those who respect our fundamental law, I appeal to this book." Then he took out two pistols and his Bowie knife. He said, "To those who recognize only force . . ."

Clay's writings show both personal faith and a belief in the uses of reason within revelation. He emphasized God's faithfulness not only to individuals but also to societies, and argued that Christians should use their God-given intellects to structure society along biblical lines. Clay wrote, "Let true Christianity prevail, and earth will become the foreshadowing of Heaven." His motivation was to allow the gospel to transform first individuals and then the society.

Clay survived many fights and assassination attempts. Finally he was seized by pro-slavery men and knifed. Gushing blood from a lung wound, Clay cried out, "I died in the defense of the liberties of the people," and then lost consciousness. But he recovered and helped to form the Republican Party during the 1850s. He had many political successes and personal adventures until he died in 1903 at the age of ninety-three.

Snapshot 3: Faith in Action, 1871

In 1871 Louis Jennings, a faithful Christian, was editor of the *New York Times,* a newspaper begun by Christians twenty years earlier. Jennings could have viewed the faith described in Hebrews as a private religion to be left out of the newspaper office. But he saw abortionists operating openly throughout his city and resolved that "It is useless to talk of such matters with bated breath. It is time to rouse ourselves. The evil that is tolerated is aggressive," and the good "must be aggressive too."

We tend today to think of abortion as a problem that arose about twenty-five years ago, but that is an error. In mid-nineteenth-century America, abortion services were advertised in major newspapers and almost never interrupted by police. The *British Medical Journal* noted that American abortionists have a "large and lucrative business" and are "never in want of engagements." Both pro- and anti-abortion physicians repeatedly estimated that at least 20 percent of all pregnancies were ending in planned abortion.

Who would oppose such a terror? Some ministers tried. Frank Howe of Indiana pledged to "sound the cry of MURDER!" Even then, though, some ministers suggested that abortion was a private matter, or one too controversial to tackle. A Michigan preacher worried that sermons on abortion would "turn the pulpit and church into a place that many people would not like to visit." A New York observer noted that congregations were hearing "rose water balderdash" and "cream-cheese platitudes" from ministers who "remained silent lest the namby-pamby sensibilities of fashionable 'fops' should be hurt."

On the abortion issue, mid-nineteenth-century American Christians were starting to show the hesitations that have hindered faithful action in the twentieth century. But it was still possible then to sound a strong call and receive widespread backing. Jennings suggested that abortion was a disgraceful attack on not only children but the lordship of Christ.

First, he ran stories about "thousands of human beings murdered before they have seen the light of this world." Jennings boldly used specific detail: "Human flesh, supposed to have been the remains of infants, was found in barrels of lime and acids, undergoing decomposition." He described the political connections of abortionists, and quoted one abortionist's description of "the class of people that come to us. We have had Senators, Congressmen and all sorts of politicians, bring some of the first women in the land here."

Then, when the nude body of a young woman was found inside a trunk in a New York railway station baggage room, and when the autopsy showed that her death had been caused by an abortion, Jennings saw a chance to begin closing down the abortion businesses. He ran descriptions of how the woman had been crammed into a trunk two feet six inches long. Seen even in this position and rigid in death, the young girl, for she could not have been more than eighteen, had a face of singular loveliness. But her chief beauty was her great profusion of golden hair, that hung in heavy folds over her shoulders, partly shrouding the face.

The sensational "trunk murder" detective story received full play in the *Times* during the next several days as police tried to identify the perpetrator. The abortionist eventually was found, arrested, and convicted. The *Times* kept up the pressure. When Philadelphia police, on a tip, dug in one cellar and found "the bodies of 21 infants who had been killed before birth," the *Times* gave full details of a trial in which jurors were shown a cigar box containing the bones of the murder victims: "Whenever the box was moved, they rattled like hard withered leaves. There were many bits of skulls among them, some almost complete."

The newspaper accounts awakened the public. Officials under pressure tightened laws and stepped up enforcement. Abortion was driven underground. It was not ended, but the number of abortions sharply declined. Instead of wasting an opportunity, Jennings and other nineteenth-century Christians had worked hard to build a society more attuned to the Bible on at least this issue.

Twentieth-Century Scorn

We've looked at three snapshots of those who followed in the footsteps of the heroes of Hebrews 11. It doesn't take away from the impressive faith of Willis, Clay, and Jennings, though, to say that in one sense they had it easy: They were writing for and speaking to people who may not have had biblical faith, but at least respected it. Clay, even amidst a crowd out for his blood, could hold up a copy of

God's Word and receive a respectful hearing. The situation today, though, is quite different. Let's look now at three snapshots that show the difficulties of putting faith into effective action in a hostile culture.

Snapshot 4: 1925

Early in the twentieth century academic and media leaders adopted Darwinian evolution as established fact rather than speculative theory. A few Christians fought back, trying to avoid the adoption of Darwinism as official state religion. Tennessee legislators made it a misdemeanor for public school teachers to teach as fact the belief "that man has descended from a lower order of animals." Evolutionists hired the most famous lawyer of the era, atheist Clarence Darrow, to bring a test case against the law.

Significantly, the "monkey trial" battle was not primarily one of science vs. religion. Creationists praised the proper use of reason. Governor Peay of Tennessee correctly viewed Darwinian theory as one "that no science has established." One anti-evolutionary organization even called itself the Defenders of True Science versus Speculation. This group contended that evolution "is a theory not yet approved by science," particularly since species-transitional fossils ("missing links") had not been found. The conflict was between two faiths, creationism and evolutionism.

Christians countered the presence of Darrow with a nationally-known figure of their own, former presidential candidate and Secretary of State William Jennings Bryan. At the trial Bryan stressed the inability of evolutionists to explain how life began, how man began, how one species actually changes into another, and so on. He pointed out the irreconcilability of Darwinian doctrines of extra-species evolution with the biblical account of creation, original sin, and the reasons for Christ's coming. His arguments were coherent, but evolutionist reporters called them "grotesque" and "imbecilic."

Throughout the trial Bryan and Tennessee Christians were lambasted in the nation's media. Few journalists even tried to explain the issue. A typical newspaper lead attacked "Tennessee's quarantine against learning." The supposed battle was "rock-ribbed Tennessee" vs. "unfettered investigation by the human mind and the liberty of opinion of which the Constitution makers preached." Bryan's face was said to be "a panorama of curdled egotism." If the creationists were to win, "The dunce cap will be the crown of office, and the slopstick will be the scepter of authority."

Journalists saw Christians as "treewise monkeys" who "see no logic, speak no logic and hear no logic." The biblical position was said to be one of "bigotry, ignorance, hatred, superstition, every sort of blackness that the human mind is capable of." The creationist position was said to represent a "breakdown of the reasoning powers."

Many Christians responded to the media barrage in one of two ways. Some said, "If you can't beat 'em, join 'em." On the issue of evolution they were *rationalistic,* contending that a view contradicting the Bible, when proclaimed by some of the leading thinkers of the period, had more credence than the biblical position. Others said, "If you can't beat 'em, ignore 'em." They practiced *pietism* by turning their backs on what was going on in the wider culture.

Bryan himself died one week after the trial.

Snapshot 5: 1948

While one story was coming to an end in Tennessee, another was beginning in New York: In 1925 a young man, Whittaker Chambers, became a Communist. After working in Washington as a spy for the Soviet Union during the early 1930s, Chambers became a Christian, resigned from the Communist Party, and gave investigators solid evidence of Soviet espionage in the State Department. Chambers charged that former State Department official Alger Hiss had been a spy, and produced microfilm and other evidence to back up his accusations.

Chambers, for his efforts, was at first scorned. "Insane," the headlines read. When it became obvious that Chambers's evidence was irrefutable, he was hated by those who were crying "peace, peace," and did not want anyone to upset their fantasies. Chambers tried to communicate essential Bible-based truths to the American public. He told of the true *evil* of communism's worship of man (not just mistake, or misfortune, or trying too hard to make progressive changes, but satanic evil). He described the grace of God (not just existing in some abstract form, but actively changing men's hearts and creating the opportunity for new lives).

Chambers brought a biblical worldview to twentieth-century problems. He criticized "the great alternative faith of mankind," the Communist vision of "man without God . . . man's mind displacing God as the creative intelligence of the world." Chambers argued that many non-Communists also had the modern "vision of man, once more the central figure of the Creation, not because God made man in His image, but because man's mind makes him the most intelligent of the animals." Chambers testified that he had been consumed by this sinful vision also until God changed his heart through grace. He explained that his reason had been twisted when he embraced twentieth-century rationalism, but now he was free to think worshipfully.

Sin and grace—Chambers's story was impossible to understand unless those concepts were taken seriously. But, with a few exceptions, journalists and intellectuals seemed incapable of even understanding these biblical categories of thought. The major universities and communications outlets were almost entirely lost to Christians. Consequently, Chambers's message of warfare, not between Soviet materialism and American materialism, but between humanism and theism, was lost also.

Snapshot 6: 1962

The year after Chambers died, two events symbolized drastic movement away from a biblical worldview.

In Arizona, a woman openly announced her intention to have an abortion. Sherri Finkbine, faced with a 20 percent possibility that her child could be born with serious birth defects, flew to Sweden to kill the baby. Mrs. Finkbine was praised throughout the United States for an "unselfish" willingness to sacrifice her privacy to promote "more humane" abortion legislation. One Catholic newspaper was caustic—"Brush away the sentimental slush of a thousand sob-sisters and the cold fact remains that this woman wants to kill the child now living within her"—but other reporters, and then public opinion polls, gave broad support to what was euphemistically called "baby surgery." In another decade, no-questions-asked abortion would become the stated law of the land.

Meanwhile, in Washington, the Supreme Court ruled that it was unconstitutional for children to recite a twenty-two-word nonsectarian prayer addressed to "Almighty God." Some senators, including Prescott Bush and Willis Robertson, reacted critically. Some clergymen gave passionate sermons. Coverage of the Sherri Finkbine abortion incident lasted for about a week after the death of her child. Coverage of the prayer controversy petered out after about the same length of time. Thus, a physical death and a spiritual vacuum symbolized the decline of Christian influence in America. Anti-Christians would have had good reason to proclaim that Christianity was going out with not even a bang, but a whimper.

Recent Years

As these snapshots illustrate, Christianity has often had a dramatic impact in the past. Today, however, Christians frequently seem reluctant to get involved with the important issues and actually make a difference. Why is this?

The reason for our hesitation is simple. Although we now commonly assert that the Bible provides the standard for every area of life, we rarely make it *become* the standard. That's partly because we don't always obey the truth that we know, but partly also because we do not know how to use biblical beliefs to make judgments about what we read in the newspaper every morning, hear at work or school during the day, and watch on television at night.

In the ordinary course of life, most of us quietly take in a stream of ideas from the surrounding society. Even though many of those ideas contradict biblical teaching, many Christians believe one and the other at the same time, without realizing the contradictions. Thus Christians are done—and consequently *do*—considerable harm, or at least become ineffective in living out the full message of the gospel.

The harm that is done when that happens has its effect in more than just major issues of public policy. To mention a recent example, one woman of our acquaintance visited a high school counselor about some problems her son was having. Even though it was a public high school, the counselor did not try to hide her Christian beliefs; she had in her office a shelf full of Bibles and related materials. But when she was asked about a situation in which a teenager had committed a sinful act, her advice was for the parents to reflect on their own faults.

Why did she say that? Evidently because her understanding of psychology and counseling was based on the assumption that people act as they do solely as the result of environmental influences. The environment, and not any decision the boy made, was said to account for the way in which he behaved.

The counselor's advice was curious but predictable. She was not being hypocritical. When she thought as a Christian, she regarded her own sins as behavior for which she was responsible and for which she would have to repent. But when she thought as a trained psychologist, she concluded that the boy's behavior was controlled by his environment. She assumed that must be the case because her professors and textbooks had taught her so. She did not realize that the scientists who taught her that behavior is controlled by the environment were advancing a theory that has never been demonstrated scientifically, or that they were teaching her their own assumptions (or, it may as well be said, their own theology). She may have been well-educated, but she remained helpless in her ignorance as far as her callings as a Christian and an educator were concerned.

Why couldn't she do better? She lacked a way of understanding the biblical revelation which could enable her to make judgments about the truth of the science she was being taught at the university. She truly wanted to help, but her advice was based on a perspective that came from an anti-Christian point of view. Her advice, therefore, was full of bad theology. Since that was so, it also was bad advice.

This high school counselor was laboring under the handicap of having a mind divided into two airtight compartments: the wisdom compartment, informed by the Bible, and the knowledge compartment, informed by her university studies. She assumed that she could learn theology when she studied the Bible and then lay it aside when she attended the university classroom, where she would learn science.

This is not only psychologically unhealthy—a fact which better science than she was learning at the university could have taught her—but also incompatible with Christian discipleship. The disciple of Christ is to bring every thought and every action into obedience to Christ. Believing false ideas prevents that from happening. Under those conditions, she could not bring her ideas into conformity with the truth of divine revelation; nor could she practice her calling as a counselor in such a way as to bring glory to God.

We're not saying that we learn everything about biology, psychology, and chemistry from the Bible. We are saying that everyone, including the most adamantly "secular" scientist, is ruled by what can legitimately be called a theology—a view of what the world is like and what is ultimate in it. We're saying that bad theology leads to defective science. The "secular" professor may be able to disguise this, even from himself, by publishing studies that deal only with the narrow, technical side of his discipline. But as he wanders further from the narrow specialty and tries to derive broader meanings from the data, his conclusions increasingly reflect his theology.

Christians who have good theological understanding should arrive at conclusions different from those arising out of ungodly beliefs. Yet millions of Americans who claim to be born again show no signs of having a different moral and intellectual perspective than Americans in general. Unthoughtful attitudes involving such matters as government, education, culture, sexual morality, abortion, and so on suggest that Christians have not learned to make the right connections between piety and reason. We must practice making this connection and working out the implications of God's Word for all of life if we are to truly demonstrate Christ's lordship.

6

Abortion: The Way Forward

F. LaGard Smith

> A politician thinks of the next election; a statesman of the
> next generation.
>
> J. F. Clarke

On January 22, 1973 in the case of *Roe v. Wade,* the U.S. Supreme
Court surprised the nation by striking down the abortion laws of most
states and severely limiting the states' power to regulate abortion.[1]
The Court in *Roe v. Wade* blithely overturned centuries of precedent
in which abortion had been considered both morally and legally un-
acceptable. Never before nor since has there been such sweeping disregard for fundamental morality in the halls of American justice.

Specifically, the Court held that in the *first* trimester of pregnancy a decision to abort must be left to the woman and the medical judgment of her physician. From that point up to the point of
viability—basically the *second* trimester—the state may regulate the
abortion procedure if restrictions are related to the health of the
mother. Subsequent to viability—essentially the *third* trimester—
"the State in promoting its interest in the potentiality of human life
may, if it chooses, regulate, and even proscribe, abortion" except
where it is necessary to preserve the mother's life or health.

By this decision, therefore, individual states were *permitted,*
but not *required,* to regulate abortions in the second trimester and

---

F. LaGard Smith is a professor of law at Pepperdine University School of
Law in Malibu, California. He is the author of *Out on a Broken Limb* and
other books dealing with provocative current issues. He divides his time
between teaching in California and writing in rural England.

to forbid them in the third. If a given state decided neither to regulate nor to forbid abortions under the Court's guidelines, abortions in that state could be legal throughout the entire nine months of a pregnancy—up to the day a baby is born, if so desired by the mother. In a worst-case scenario, if a state were not to act in regulating abortion, nothing in the language of *Roe v. Wade* would prevent the killing of a near-term child even if a woman decides at the last minute that she simply doesn't want to experience the pain of giving birth.

By contrast with that seemingly stark possibility, virtually all states have in fact enacted *some* form of abortion regulation and have generally forbidden abortions in the third trimester, except where the mother's life would be threatened. An example of such state regulation is found in the widely disputed 1989 case of *Webster v. Reproductive Health Services.* In *Webster,* a bitterly divided Court held that a Missouri statute was Constitutional in requiring that, before performing an abortion on a woman 20 or more weeks pregnant, the physician must first determine whether the unborn is viable.

That "fine tuning" of *Roe v. Wade* was hardly the disaster that pro-choice advocates have bewailed ever since, nor the major victory that pro-life advocates have thought it to be. State regulation is still where the ball game is to be won or lost. No new Constitutional ground was covered in *Webster.*

Time to Overturn Roe v. Wade?

So where do we go from here? Should *Roe v. Wade* be overturned? If so, how? The answer to the first question is clearly "Yes!" As it stands, *Roe v. Wade* gives Constitutional protection to abortion in individual states which might wish *not* to regulate or forbid it. Given that latitude, the laws of individual states do not go far enough in the protection of human life in the womb. Indeed, under *Roe v. Wade* they *cannot* protect life in the first trimester, and even under *Webster* they are fairly limited in protecting life in the second trimester.

From almost any perspective, the decision in *Roe v. Wade* is a judicial calamity. In "balancing the interests" (which, sadly, is the only alternative for judicial review once absolute moral values are rejected) the Court demonstrated a dreadful paucity of moral insight.

Employing the language of "right of privacy," the Court elevated a woman's right of choice over the value of developing human life. Such a moral gaffe is all the more remarkable in light of the highly questionable Constitutional basis for the so-called "right of privacy" in the first place.

Certainly *Roe v. Wade* was not the first case to talk about a "right of privacy." This novel concept had been developed in the earlier case of *Griswold v. Connecticut,* which dealt with the use of contraceptives by married couples (a seemingly benign use of "right of privacy," given the high moral ground of marital relations). But even by the time of *Roe v. Wade,* the Court was still unsure where exactly the "right of privacy" was to be found in the Constitution. Note, for example, this implicit admission in the *Roe* decision:

> The right of privacy, whether it be founded in the Fourteenth Amendment's concept of personal liberty and restrictions upon state action, as we feel it is, or, as the District Court determined, in the Ninth Amendment's reservation of rights to the people, is broad enough to encompass a woman's decision whether or not to terminate her pregnancy.[2]

Unable to pinpoint just exactly where in the Constitution the so-called "right of privacy" was to be found, the Court nevertheless was certain that, wherever it might be located, it was "broad enough" to permit abortions! In this unprecedented fishing expedition, the Court was sure it had come back with a very big fish, despite the fact that no one could ever prove there had been such a fish of any size swimming around in the murky waters of Constitutional language.

But even if one were to allow such a judicial *fabrication,* one can hardly overlook the judicial *legislation* which followed on its heels. It would be one thing if the Court judicially legislated in a matter such as racial integration. Whatever opinion a person might have regarding court-ordered busing to achieve racial balance in public schools, there is at least a Constitutional foundation for such judicial action. Without any question, racial discrimination violates the Constitutional guarantee of equal protection.

By contrast, in *Roe v. Wade* the Court judicially legislated such novel concepts as "trimesters" and "viability" on the strength of an already-judicially-fabricated "right of privacy." As the country gentleman reputedly said, "If we had any ham, we could have ham and eggs, if we had any eggs!" Either fabrication without legislation, or legislation without fabrication, might possibly pass muster. But judicial fabrication bolstered by judicial legislation is simply asking too much.

Putting the Cat Back into the Bag

It is in this abuse of judicial power as a "Superlegislature" that *Roe v. Wade* is vulnerable to attack by the current Court. There is already precedent for the Court to turn its back on a prior decision, by acknowledging that it had no right to act as a "Superlegislature" in the first place—in other words, in a given case, that what was called a *judicial* decision was actually a political decision.[3] Significantly, that precedent came in an area of Constitutional law far more settled than the gossamerlike "right of privacy." Therefore one would hope that, at a minimum, the current Court would overturn *Roe v. Wade* on this precedent-laden judicial basis.

In this way the Court could deprive abortion of any supposed Constitutional justification and thereby give its approval to state legislation prohibiting abortion altogether (or perhaps with limited exceptions), as long as such legislation met a "rational basis" test. Without question, the protection of human life in the womb would stand as an eminently rational law, deserving at least the same level of protection as racial equality.

If it wished to do so, of course, the U.S. Supreme Court could take even more affirmative action in protecting human life in the womb, on the basis of the Fourteenth Amendment's equal-protection clause. Many states, such as California, now prohibit the unlawful killing of a fetus (interpreted to mean a "viable" fetus). The intent, of course, is to punish anyone other than the mother who intentionally kills such a viable, unborn fetus. An equal-protection argument could run in either of two directions: (1) protecting a viable fetus from being killed by its own mother, just as it is protected from an unlawful killing by anyone else; or (2) protecting all unborn fetuses—whether viable or not—just as *viable* fetuses are now protected by the laws of homicide.

The equal-protection arguments are straightforward: (1) If human life is worthy of protection from all third parties other than the mother, it is equally worthy of protection from its own mother; and (2) since any distinction between "viable" and "nonviable" fetuses is arbitrary, or at best inventively contrived (not to mention shifting with every advance in medical technology), no valid distinction can be made in the protection given to one type of fetus as opposed to the other. A more overarching equal-protection argument would hold that the protection of *newborn* infants from infanticide—a protection given by all states—must equally extend to *unborn* infants, without whom there would be no newborn infants.

The importance of the equal-protection approach is that unborn human life would be accorded *Constitutional* protection. The shoe would then be on the other foot: No longer could individual state legislatures *permit* abortions any more than they could choose to permit racial discrimination. No longer would lower courts have the liberty to elevate women's rights over the interests to be protected in unborn human life.

Under the current climate of national debate, however, this approach is probably more than one might reasonably expect from the Court. More likely is a return to the pre-*Roe v. Wade* stance in which states are permitted to regulate or prohibit abortion as they best see fit.

In the absence of any recognized Constitutional protection for the unborn, we will always and interminably be locked in an impasse between pro-choice and pro-life advocates from one state to the next. Legislative battles will be endless, and gubernatorial vetoes will be the subject of enterprising oddsmakers. Unborn babies in the womb will be kicked around forever as a political football. There is no escaping the dilemma: Pro-choice advocates *will* not relent, and pro-life advocates *cannot*.

Amending the Constitution

If the abortion controversy is ever to be put to rest, it most likely will have to come in the form of a Constitutional amendment—itself a political process with all the built-in difficulties already mentioned. The advantage of *this* political referendum, however, would be to settle the issue once and for all. Once for all *time,* and once for all *jurisdictions.* No more fads in point of view. No more bitter, unresolved civil war.

A Constitutional amendment would also have the advantage of clarifying the present Constitution. Any argument that the Constitution is too vaguely worded to encompass a right of protection for the unborn, or that "state action" must be shown before the power of the Court is invoked, would no longer pose a problem. The law would be clear, unequivocal, and fairly decided.

Who knows whether a Constitutional amendment to guarantee protection to unborn human life is possible at the present time? Although those who personally oppose abortion outnumber those who support it, today's pro-choice sentiment is at a fever pitch. Certainly no Constitutional amendment appearing to threaten a woman's right to decide would be viable until the issue of personal choice is clearly distinguished from the issue of abortion itself. So far, the pro-choice generation has lacked either the sophistication or the will to make that distinction.

So for the time being we may be left with skirmishes at the state level over the many sub-issues which seem to accompany the controversy: Whether minors seeking abortions should be required to notify one or perhaps both parents; whether there should be "waiting periods" or perhaps pre-abortion counseling; whether public funding ought to be available in support of abortions for those who cannot afford them. Like the first Civil War, our present conflict is set to last far beyond what anyone on either side would wish.

The Focus of Legislation

Looking down the road, when pro-life advocates consider prohibiting abortion through legislation, it is important for them to handle carefully the legal concept of murder for women who have abortions. As previously discussed, not all criminal homicides are automatically classified as murder. Given the anguished decision made by many women who choose to abort, the more appropriate classification for many cases might be manslaughter. Manslaughter denotes the presence of mitigating circumstances, consistent with the moral ambivalence which many women experience.

For women who have abortions coldly and calculatedly, it may be right to refer to abortion as murder. However, it is ultimately only God who can judge the moral severity with which women will be held accountable.

As a practical matter, when some pro-life advocates talk in terms of abortion being "murder," the public often assumes that pro-life legislation would jail women who have abortions (just like any other cold-blooded murderer) for 25 years to life. However, that notion plays into the hands of the pro-choice propaganda which suggests that under pro-life legislation women will be jailed as vicious criminals.

Historically, a woman seeking an abortion has not been the target of abortion statutes. Nor would she be the target under a *Roe v. Wade* reversal. Just as in statutes prior to *Roe v. Wade,* the proper target is the *physician or other person who performs illegal abortions.* Cut off the availability of legal abortions, and for the most part abortions will cease. It is the same principle—already in place in several jurisdictions—in which statutes punish the *supplier* of illegal marijuana but not the *user.* No one is eager to throw women into jail for having illegal abortions. The idea is to *deter* them from having abortions in the first place.

If it should be argued that many women would then seek illegal abortions, the fact is that there is little the state could do in legal terms from that point forward in any case. Women who choose to go outside the law would be doing so at their own risk, both physically and morally. But at the very least the state would have ceased to be in complicity with the killing of unborn children. And that is a statement which *must* be made in whatever way it can be made. (Of course, the greater statement would be to support women in ways which will not make abortion the only apparent option.)

Death in a Pill

Unlike pre-*Roe v. Wade* abortion statutes, future legislation will have to reach beyond illegal abortionists to deal with new technology which promises to revolutionize the manner in which pregnancies are terminated. Perhaps no scientific development in our time has more potential for condemning our collective conscience than the new French-developed RU-486 abortion pill. What it achieves, of course, is nothing different from any other means of abortion: It terminates a pregnancy; it kills a newly conceived life. Yet what it potentially represents in the public mind is an outrageous statement about the legitimacy of "over-the-counter death."

For many feminists, the prospect of RU-486 (or some pill like it) being introduced into the United States signals a welcomed end to male-dominated medical abortions. As popularly perceived, RU-486 may be taken in the privacy of the home, economically and with relative ease. In truth, RU-486 is designed for supervised *clinical* use—not for unsupervised *in-home* use; and its threat to women's health has been criminally understated. Actually, many feminists are adamantly in agreement with that evaluation. The prospect of RU-486 has split feminists right down the middle.

The most damning evidence against RU-486 has finally surfaced—ironically at the very core of attempts to achieve population control and a better quality of life in China. Because of potential adverse side-effects from unsupervised use in rural areas of China, RU-486 has now been withdrawn from the most pro-abortion nation in the world.

Given that evidence, one can only wonder in amazement at how Planned Parenthood and NOW activists can steadfastly persist in their demand that the United States test RU-486 and begin the Food and Drug Administration approval process. How could the interests of women ever be engulfed in more abject confusion?

The real problem is that the debate over RU-486 is in the wrong venue. The principal reason the drug is running under a yellow caution flag in the United States is concern about safety and legal liability, not about the morality of its use. Even if RU-486 were certifiably safe for women, its widespread use would make a social statement almost beyond belief: that human life can be *taken* with the same ease as it can be *prevented*.

Since its introduction as a widely used contraceptive, "the Pill" has made its own statement about sexual freedom. If the Pill brought an enhanced quality of life for married women, it also played a significant role in creating a sexually promiscuous society. And it is not without its own share of blame for health risks to women. But whatever other adverse consequences it may have brought into play, the Pill *prevents* conception of new life rather than *killing* new life once it is conceived. By contrast, RU-486 is specifically designed to kill innocent human life. That we could even seriously consider the eventual possibility of over-the-counter death of unborn children is a mark of how far we have gone in a pro-choice generation.

Pornography used to be on the back shelf, if at all. Condoms used to be behind the counter. Now it's all up front with glossy covers and slick advertising. If some people have their way, we will see the day when abortions come packaged in plastic bottles with brand names like "Oops!" and "Second Chance." Abortion-by-vending-machine will make abortion-on-demand look absolutely antiquated! For many people any future abortion pill will be the ultimate guarantor of the selfish "good life."

Speaking at the 1989 American Medical Association conference for science writers, Dr. Etienne-Emile Baulieu, developer of RU-486, explained the *social* significance of an abortion pill. "In practical terms, choice is synonymous with freedom," said Dr. Baulieu. "Science cannot dictate how we believe," but it can increase people's choices and improve their quality of life.[4]

"Freedom," "choice," and "quality of life." With all that going for it, who could object to an "abortion pill"? However, what few people stop to consider is the natural progression of the pro-choice philosophy outlined by Dr. Baulieu. He stopped short of the full explanation, which is this: *Quality of life* in a pro-choice generation is synonymous with the *right to choose;* which is synonymous with *freedom;* which, in the case of RU-486, is synonymous with *freedom to kill;* which, because of the nature of the victim, is synonymous with *freedom to kill an innocent human being.*

Without question, RU-486 and its inevitable commercially produced successors must be thwarted by appropriate legislation. Pro-choice must not be allowed to accomplish through the back door what is forbidden through the front door. Death in a pill is no different from death at the end of a suction tube, unless by its ease of availability it becomes even more pernicious.

But Can Morality Be Legislated?

If there is any one statement about which everyone seems to be in agreement, it is that "morality can't be legislated." The idea is that one person's morality is as good as another's, so society is not at liberty to adopt moral standards through legislation. But if there is no one statement about which everyone seems to be overlooking the obvious, it is the same statement: that "morality can't be legislated."

As Judge Robert H. Bork has put it, "Indeed . . . we legislate little else."[5]

Bork is also correct in pointing out that "if the statement that one man's moral judgment is as good as another's were taken seriously, it would be impossible to see how law on any subject could be permitted to exist. After all, one man's larceny is another's just distribution of goods."[6]

However, Bork freely admits that even he did not always appreciate that point. In the spirit of academic candor, Bork relates the story of a seminar on constitutional theory which he taught along with Alex Bickel. In the seminar, Bork says he took the position that it was "no business of society what conduct that did not harm another person took place out of sight." Bickel then posed a hypothetical:

> Suppose, he said, that on an offshore island there lived a man who raised puppies entirely for the pleasure of torturing them to death. The rest of us are not required to witness the torture, nor can we hear the screams of the animals. We just know what is taking place and we are appalled. Can it be that we have no right, constitutionally or morally, to enact legislation against such conduct and to enforce it against the sadist?

Bork says he cannot remember what answer he gave, but he now realizes that Bickel was right. "Morality, standing alone, is a sufficient rationale to support legislation."[7]

"There is no objection," Bork reminds us, "to segregation or even to slavery other than moral disapproval."[8] More pointedly, as recently as 1986 the Supreme Court upheld—at least as to homosexual sodomy—a Georgia statute making all sodomy criminal.[9] To that list I would add virtually all criminal laws, from "Thou shalt not kill" on down. Where do we think we got such laws? Simply out of a secular vacuum, or solely as a matter of social contract?

Perhaps no laws better illustrate the point that morality *can* be legislated than the so-called "statutory rape" laws, which criminally punish a man for having sexual relations with an "underaged female." The age limit itself has varied from 18 all the way down to 14, even in modern times. However, the law's thrust has always been the same: the protection of underaged women from male sexual aggression. It's a matter of morality—nothing less.

What's more, it is a matter of strict liability. We don't take any alleged ignorance as an excuse. Even in the last two decades of sexual liberation, only California has dared to give any defense at all to a man who claims to have been mistaken about the young woman's age. Other jurisdictions have specifically refused to follow California's lead.

Even more surprising is the fact that a man may be put in jail if convicted of "statutory rape," when for no other strict liability offense would so severe a punishment be allowed. Sexual liberation or no sexual liberation, Americans have a low tolerance for moral manipulation of the sexually naive.

Because "statutory rape" is rarely the subject of actual prosecution, it may speak to another aspect of legislating morality, to be discussed shortly. But make no doubt about it, morality can *be* legislated, and it *is* legislated. In fact, hardly any phrase is more familiar to lawyers than "the state's police power to regulate conduct adversely affecting the community's peace, health, safety, *morals*, and general welfare."

Should Morality Be Legislated?

However, simply because morality *can be* and *is* legislated does not necessarily mean that morality *should be* legislated. No one seriously proposes that all morality ought to be the subject of oppressive laws. Even if one could prove envy, greed, hatred, or misdirected lust, such immoral motives taken by themselves do not fall within the boundaries of man-made laws. (Nor would even outwardly-manifested immoral *acts* be worthy of the law's scrutiny in every case.)

When it comes to an issue like abortion, pro-choice advocates believe adamantly that there is no place for pro-life morality in legislative halls. Kate Michelman, executive director of the National Abortion Rights Action League (NARAL) has offered a letter presenting just that concept, in the hope that *Woman's Day, Family Circle, Good Housekeeping,* and *Ladies' Home Journal* might publish the letter for their readers. When at the invitation of Helen Gurley Brown the editors of those magazines recently met with the editors of more politically-activist publications, such as *Ms.* and *Cosmopolitan,* the letter was presented as one which readers could send to state and federal legislators.

The letter says in part, "Religious extremists must not be allowed to impose their narrow beliefs on society as a whole; rather, each of us must be permitted to heed our own conscience and faith."[10] If *"religious* extremists" must not be allowed to impose their narrow beliefs, why should *secular* extremists? The belief that a woman should be able to kill her unborn child is just as much a moral belief as is the personal conviction that doing so is wrong. In such a case, one person's *immorality* is another's *morality*. In truth, it is the *pro-abortion* morality that has already been imposed upon a nation which—counting heads—is personally opposed to abortion.

Isn't it interesting how everyone wants to get in on the act? When the political fur was flying over animal rights in the recent Aspen, Colorado, referendum regarding a proposed ban on the sale of items made from animal skins, there was an odd sense of déjà vu. Almost predictably we had Mark Kirkland, president of the pro-fur lobby, saying, "The mayor's trying to legislate his morality." Kirkland argued that "freedom of choice" would be "legislated away" if the measure passed.[11] One can only wonder how this argument goes down with animal-rights activists, most of whom are pro-choice on the issue of abortion!

Once again, that is where pro-life activists have a leg up on animal-rights activists. Nothing could be more sacred—and thus more worthy of protective legislation—than human life. And at least some pro-choice advocates are honest enough to admit the obvious. Columnist Anna Quindlen, for example, is pro-choice all the way ("Today, on the issue of choice, it is time for us to choose it or lose it"), but she is keenly aware of the limitations to the "imposed morality" argument:

> Those people who believe that abortion is murder are morally obligated to oppose it. To say that is imposing religious beliefs on others is absurd. We have long ago agreed as a society that killing innocent people is the worst of our crimes.
> The people who are convinced that abortion is the killing of a human being have no choice but to fight until they win.[12]

As always, it comes back to the question of whether the unborn fetus is human life. If it is not, then pro-lifers are unjustifiably imposing their judgments upon others. However, *if in fact* human life is at risk in an abortion, then society has every right to protect it through appropriate legislation. Indeed, it *must* do so.

Public Versus Private Morality

University of Michigan law professor Carl E. Schneider moves the issue of legislated morality closer to a resolution in observing, "It is hard to say to what extent the law should encourage people in their better impulses. Many of the law's attempts to do so—Prohibition comes to mind—have been moralistic in the narrowest sense and unsuccessful in the broadest sense."[13] Why was Prohibition such a notable failure? Because it attempted to impose a morality which only indirectly affected innocent third parties. If it is true that when you are intoxicated you might possibly kill someone (as in an auto accident), it is also true that you can be intoxicated *without* killing anyone. No one else need *necessarily* be involved.

In abortion, by contrast, there is *always* an innocent party affected. As opposed to intoxication, which is not in each case a direct threat to society, abortion cannot help but be a public offense in the strongest sense of the word. A woman may have a "right of privacy," but the killing of an innocent life is never a private matter. That is why it is fitting and proper to punish someone for the act of abortion, just as we find it altogether proper to punish those who, under the influence of intoxication, end up killing someone else. In the death of innocent human life, the killing always "goes public." At its heart and soul, killing human life is always a matter of morality—*public* morality.

There is another sense in which Professor Schneider's observation about Prohibition moves the argument along. It is altogether true that in the area of *private* morality—when it is *truly private*—the law is rarely the best vehicle for promoting one's personal conduct. Those who wish to drink will tend to do so regardless of any law prohibiting it. The same with those who wish to smoke marijuana or even, to some extent, to ignore the nationally mandated speed limit. In this sense, and in this sense alone, it is correct to say that "you can't legislate morality." If you could, we would all be moral robots. No amount of legislation can force any of us to do the right thing. No degree of harsh punishment can make us "good people."

In a particularly insightful article entitled "Justice Without Conscience Is Dead," James T. Burtchaell argues a case for even those laws which seem to fail, but which make an important statement of national conscience:

> The law will always fail if it is unsustained by the common conscience. But that is no reason for repealing the unsuccessful law, because the law has a further purpose: not to transform people, but to declare and disavow publicly what we commonly believe to be unfair or damaging. Laws are part of our public profession of justice. They are what we, as a people, are willing to promise out loud to one another.[14]

Burtchaell concludes with this thought-provoking observation: "You probably cannot tell the moral character of a people by reading their laws. But you can learn something about a people's character by observing what laws they lack."[15] What does it say about the moral character of the American people that they do not prohibit the killing of their own children?

The Role of Law in Fostering Morality

Morality is a response to various calls for us to act according to the highest good—whether those calls come from family upbringing, social traditions, religious instruction, or from the law itself. In the past, public morality was not a matter of "personal choice," but was woven into an intricate tapestry of our collective conscience, by which everyone was held personally accountable. Now that very tapestry is deteriorating at a rapid pace, and being pulled apart strand by strand by a pro-choice generation.

Look how each strand has been pulled away: Family upbringing has been shredded by broken homes; social traditions have been replaced by a value-neutral, "do-your-own-thing" philosophy; and religious instruction has dwindled into virtual oblivion, along with the shrinking influence of the liberal church. What is left but the law? Only the *law!*

At this point there ought to be red flags, bells, and whistles. In the wake of the demise of traditional sources of both public and private morality, the only moral source for a secular society is the *law.* For a pro-choice generation bereft of any transcendent point of reference, there is but one natural conclusion: If it's *legal,* it must be *moral.*

Who says we can't legislate morality? Legislation itself has *become* our morality! Too often our *only* morality!

How many of us, for instance, simply *assume* abortion is moral, particularly in what has become known as the first trimester, because the Supreme Court just happened to permit it during that time? Likewise, how many of us assume something is *wrong* with abortion in what has become known as the third trimester, because that is where the Supreme Court happened to draw the line? Can we say that our own view of abortion has not been colored by what the Court arbitrarily has deemed to be legal or illegal?

Shed the garment of transcendent morality, which causes us to ask what we *ought* to do, and we find ourselves standing morally naked, asking ourselves only what we can *get away with.* What does the *law* allow? As much as the law is shaped by the moral impulses of those who legislate, interpret, and administer it, the law is also the Great Shaper of society's morals.

Law—particularly judicial law—often runs before public opinion. At certain times it has been for the good. In the case of *Brown v. Board of Education,* for example, it was the Supreme Court that boldly led the way to racial justice. It encouraged us in our *best* impulses at a time when as a nation we did not have the courage of our inner convictions. But sometimes, as in the case of *Roe v. Wade,* the Supreme Court permits our *worst* impulses to have free play. What could be more disastrous than a pro-choice Court leading a pro-choice generation wherever it wants to go?

In Search of Consensus

Something in me wants to agree with John Leo, who insists that "abortion may be a great evil, but it is folly to try jamming through a law. As Aquinas says, where there is no consensus, there is no law. And there is no consensus now either way."[16] But when law has become the very touchstone of morality, I wonder if we any longer have a choice but to attempt "the folly of jamming through a law."

Aquinas had the luxury of living in a time when a moral superstructure was deeply embedded throughout society, even apart from the law. In his day, under the heavy influence of the church, morality was hardly a matter of individual choice. Even where there was no consensus on a given issue, there was a crucial widespread consensus on the basic assumptions underlying those issues. There may have been disagreement in detail and nuance, but the general framework was agreed upon. It was a theological framework into which all moral questions ultimately could be fit.

It is here that philosopher Alasdair MacIntyre contributes this keen observation:

> The most striking feature of contemporary moral utterance is that so much of it is used to express disagreements; and the most striking feature of the debates in which these disagreements are expressed is their interminable character. . . . [T]hey apparently can find no terminus. There seems to be no rational way of securing moral agreement in our culture.[17]

MacIntyre is not saying that there is no such thing as capital "T" Truth in matters of morals, but only that we are not playing on the same field when we try to decide the outcome. We can't make any progress in our negotiations because some of us insist on sitting at round tables while others insist on square tables. It's not our *conclusions* that separate us, but our *premises*. We don't disagree about abortion as much as we disagree about the value of individual rights, and what "quality of life" is all about, and whether human life itself is accidental and therefore dispensable, or sacred and therefore inviolable.

In our generation there is no agreed-upon framework. *All* issues are up for grabs. Morality no longer has any broad-based theology upon which to rest its case. We are no longer a "Christian nation," not even a "Judeo-Christian culture." We are a pro-choice generation: ad hoc, faddish, trendy, and self-directed. Therefore we are left either to political power struggles—to try "jamming through a law"—or to set our aim for the moral high ground, to claim it back from the secularist mind-set, and to call a floundering nation back to its best impulses.

Leading, Not Pushing

Thomas J. Gumbleton is a Roman Catholic bishop in Detroit, Michigan, but carries well-earned liberal credentials as president of

Pax Christi U.S.A., the National Catholic Peace Movement. For my money, when all is said and done, Gumbleton has elegantly shown us the way forward:

> As much as I wish that laws against abortion would solve all our problems, I do not believe they would. We need above all to change the hearts and minds of people. This is really the root of the whole problem. To some extent we have put so much effort into getting laws on the books that we have failed to persuade people of the basis for our moral stance.
>
> Changing hearts and minds is always the most difficult task; it is also the most essential. I would like us to spend a lot more time and effort on it. If we did, we might come to more agreement on the profound moral questions involved. Then the development of the legal structure would follow quite quickly.[18]

Unfortunately, changing hearts and minds is not always as simple as blocking a doorway and causing a teenage girl to decide at the last minute not to have an abortion. What is needed in the long run is a reasoned response to pro-choice that captures America's moral imagination. Some greater view of human life that calls people higher. Some appreciation of life in the womb that excites human compassion. Some challenge of conscience that will deny the urge to do that which is beneath our dignity.

Gumbleton's call for a moral revolution is seconded by Harvard Law School professor Mary Ann Glendon, who has scrutinized the Western world's abortion laws in her 1987 book, *Abortion and Divorce in Western Law*. Like Gumbleton, professor Glendon calls for "legal condemnation of abortion (even if it must be accompanied with exemptions from punishment in limited circumstances)" as an "essential first step toward repairing the damage the Supreme Court has done to our social fabric by lending its prestige to the position that abortion is 'private,' that it involves only a woman and her body, and that morality has no place in public discourse about life."[19]

But also like Gumbleton, Glendon recognizes that the larger battle will not be won at the statehouse. In her survey of other countries, Glendon discovered that there are sometimes major discrepancies between a country's laws and its abortion rate. Nor should we confuse the taking of the high moral ground with any particular religious perspective. Glendon notes, for example, that abortion is much more socially disapproved in both Northern Ireland and in the Republic of Ireland—by Protestants and Catholics alike—than in Catholic France or Protestant England.[20]

Comparisons like these put us on notice that a person doesn't have to buy into a particular religious faith—or a formal faith of any kind, for that matter—to be appealed to on the basis of his or her own sense of morality. Those who believe that human life is sacred because we are made in the image of God must also believe that in every human being there is a moral sense to which an appeal for human justice can be made—if made respectfully calmly, knowledgeably, and with patience.

I find it interesting that both Gumbleton and Glendon isolate on what may be the most important factor of all in winning the hearts and minds of a pro-choice generation: proven concern for the women who are the current targets of America's abortion mania. Glendon, for example, favors systems of rewards and sanctions that "make abortion less attractive and motherhood less risky"—that is, medical care and adequate housing for women who otherwise would feel they have no choice but to have an abortion.[21]

Thomas Gumbleton stretches our horizons even further in lamenting how tragically we have prioritized our social concern:

> One tragic effect of the controversy is the waste of time and effort that ought to be devoted to social programs that would provide alternatives to abortion. We need to change structures that cut health care and food programs, that force women and children to live in poverty. This is our common ground and our common work. Our groups, and all who value life, need to align our efforts with greater determination in these areas.[22]

For all of us, James Burtchaell makes the critical tie between caring social action and the winning of hearts and minds: "It is only when people's hearts and minds are touched and they undergo moral conversion that they can find the motivation to observe law. And the major force for moral conversion is usually the example and the appeal of a religious community."[23]

Rising to the Challenge

The greatest challenge we face is neither secularism nor the pro-choice philosophy. The greatest challenge we face is our own commitment to the cause of transcendent moral values and the welfare of our fellow human beings. Convincing rhetoric is the easier task; truth is on the side of human life and moral absolutes. The more difficult task is to lead a pro-choice generation to choose the good by what they see in *our own* choices.

Public morality is but an extension of private morality. The question that each of us must answer is: What kind of public morality would there be if everyone else's private morality were exactly like my own? Inquiring minds truly *do* want to know whether we practice in social concern what we preach so eloquently in condemnation.

If pro-life advocates are right to demand that the quality of life in the womb be recognized as of equal value with the quality of life outside of the womb, then pro-choice advocates are right to make the same demand in reverse. Pro-life must extend beyond the womb into every aspect of society. If each individual life is sacred, so is all of life. The only thing worse than single-issue politics is single-issue morality.

In the great battle for hearts and minds, a wistful pro-choice generation is watching. Have we given them reason to choose life? Have we given them reason to put the God of Creation before individual choice? Or indeed have we given them every reason to follow along blindly in the footsteps of another generation of whom it was said: "In those days Israel had no king; everyone did as he saw fit" (Judg. 21:25).

There may be a place for banners and bumper stickers. There may be times when doors should be blocked. And surely there must come a time when *Roe v. Wade* is overturned, for abortion is the ultimate miscarriage of justice. But the victory will be achieved only when, as a chorus of one people joined together in pained conscience, America cries out in anguish at our greatest national sin. When that day comes, there will be no more need of laws, and the lion will lie down with the lamb. Not until then will we be at peace. Not until then will the battle over abortion have ended.

Notes

1. *Roe v. Wade,* 410 U.S. 113 (1973).

2. Ibid., 153, 164–65.

3. See *West Coast Hotel Co. v. Parrish* (1937), 300 U.S. 379, and *Day Brite Lighting, Inc. v. Missouri* (1952), 342 U.S. 421.

4. Rita Rubin, "'Abortion Pill' Developer Claims Spotlight," in *Dallas Morning News,* October 4, 1989.

5. Robert H. Bork, *The Tempting of America* (New York: The Free Press, 1990), 246.

6. Ibid., 249.

7. Ibid., 124.

8. Ibid., 122.

9. *Bowers v. Hardwick* (1986), 478 U.S. 186.

10. Cal Thomas, "Journalism Conspiracy?" in *Los Angeles Times Syndicate,* 1989.

11. Ron Harris, "The Fur Is Flying in Trend-Setting Aspen," in *Los Angeles Times,* December 25, 1989.

12. Anna Quindlen, "There's No Middle Ground to Abortion Rights Issue," in *The Register-Guard,* February 4, 1990.

13. Carl E. Schneider, "Rights Discourse and Neonatal Euthanasia," *California Law Review,* vol. 76, January 1988, 151.

14. James T. Burtchaell, "Justice Without Conscience Is Dead," *Christianity Today,* 12 June 1987, 26.

15. Ibid.

16. John Leo, "The Catholic Politics of Abortion," *U.S. News & World Report,* February 19, 1990.

17. Alasdair MacIntyre, *After Virtue,* 2d ed. (Notre Dame, Ind.: University of Notre Dame Press, 1984), 6.

18. Thomas J. Gumbleton, "If All Life Is Sacred, So Is Each Life," *Los Angeles Times,* 9 December 1989.

19. Randy Frame, "Will Our Planet Be Prolife?" *Christianity Today,* 19 February 1990, 32.

20. Ibid.

21. Ibid.

22. Gumbleton, "Life."

23. Burtchaell, "Justice," 26.

7

Euthanasia and the Right to Die

C. Everett Koop

*T*he term *euthanasia* comes from the Greek and means painless, happy death (*eu*—well, plus *thanatos*—death). Webster's dictionary goes on to define euthanasia as "an easy and painless death, or, an act or method of causing death painlessly so as to end suffering: advocated by some as a way to deal with victims of incurable disease." The Euthanasia Society of America, founded in 1938, defines euthanasia as the "termination of human life by painless means for the purpose of ending severe physical suffering." Gradually the meaning of one word changed from the connotation of easy death to the actual medical deed necessary to make death easy. Finally it reached the connotation of "mercy killing." The idea that abortion is not killing is a brand new idea. However, the fact that euthanasia is not killing has really never existed. The common synonym for euthanasia in both lay and professional vocabularies has been mercy killing. In any discussion of euthanasia an understanding of terminology is essential. The deliberate killing of one human being by another, no matter what the motivation might be, is murder. Some distinction is usually made between a positive, decisive, death-producing act and the act of permitting death to occur by with-

C. EVERETT KOOP is the former Surgeon General of the United States. As the co-chairman of the National Ready-to-Learn Council, he continues to campaign for the health and wellness of Americans. Dr. Koop is the author of *To Live or Die: Facing Decisions at the End of Life* and coauthor of *Whatever Happened to the Human Race* with Francis A. Schaeffer.

holding life-support mechanism or life-extending procedures which in common parlance might be called heroic and in medical terminology might be called "extraordinary means."

The current discussions of the right to die are, in essence, a broad reflection on the moral and ethical problems created by an understanding of the term *euthanasia.* A consideration of the right to die carries with it the implication of the right of how to die. Does a patient have the right to expect a painless, comfortable death? Does he have the right to expect that his physician should see that it is so? Does he have the right to expect that the physician might take an active role in his dying process to shorten it for the sake of the patient's comfort or peace of mind? Does the patient have the right to expect the physician to terminate his life if the physician deems it advisable? Could this ever be an active role on the part of the physician or may he assume only a passive role? Is there a difference between an active and a passive role in this regard; is a deed of omission less reprehensible than a deed of commission legally, ethically, or morally? Does the patient have the right to participate in the decision, or better yet, to influence it?

The way one answers any of these questions will depend a good deal upon his view of life. If he is God-oriented in the sense of being either a conservative follower of Judaism or if he is a Christian, and if he indeed believes that the Scriptures are the Word of God and teach that life is precious to God, he will view life as a holy thing, its end not to be decided upon by man. Yet, many physicians who truly believe that the Scriptures are the Word of God and that they give specific admonitions concerning the sanctity of life, will, in the role of physician, act passively in certain circumstances rather than carry out what the laity might call heroic measures to prolong life.

If, on the other hand, the individual's view of life is atheistic, agnostic, or utilitarian, his decisions about participating in the dying process actively or passively are not so much matters of conscience. In between these two views will probably lie the great majority of people who are faced with this kind of decision making, either as a privilege or an obligation. Although they might not wish to carry the label of a situational ethicist, they would in general be making decisions on the basis of the situation. The situation would encompass for them the patient's state of health, his alertness, his understanding of what was happening to him, and his spoken desires on the matter. But all these would be in the light of the physician's understanding of that patient's disease and that patient's ability to withstand it at all, to withstand it comfortably, or to succumb to it quickly or slowly. One can already see that several physicians might have completely different points of view in a given situation depending upon their previous knowledge of the disease entity in question, but also tempered by their previous experience in similar situations where they had been proven right or wrong or where their ethical decisions were affected by the morality which grows out of experience and contact with repetitive problems.

Another facet that the situational ethicist must deal with is the situation in respect to the patient's family. In many situations, for example, there comes a time when the patient's consideration is essentially out of the picture. The patient may be unconscious, truly comatose, definitely out of pain, and waiting for an inevitable death which may be days, weeks, months, or in rare situations even years away. There are emotional factors to be considered in reference to the family and there are definitely economic factors. There may be times when these economic factors may have far-reaching implications. The financial undergirding for the education of a child, for example, might disappear while her unconscious grandmother has the financial substance eaten up by medical bills. The motivation on the part of a family to see a rapid demise in a dying grandmother would understandably be varied, but one can see the obvious temptation for a change in motivation as the aforementioned hypothetical example drags on and on.

Can the physician who is in the business of prolonging life and relieving the suffering of the sick and injured be asked to reverse his role and shorten life even while ministering to the needs of the suffering? How much credence should he give to the pressures of the family to terminate life? How can he sort out the motivation that leads to the request? How can he balance his obligation to his patient against his compassion and his understanding for the family? If the right to live and the whole question of killing an unborn baby in the womb raises multiple dilemmas, they are as nothing compared to the dilemmas that are inherent in the question of the right to die.

Extension of Human Life

Probably nowhere in the development of medical technological advances has our ability been greater than in the specific area of the prolongation or extension of human life almost at the will of the physician. The life-support systems which are available in almost any intensive care unit attest to this fact. It has always been far easier to exterminate life quite painlessly than to prolong it. The medical profession now has a two-edged sword: the extension of human life by artificial means and the painless termination of life by drugs. The ability of man to wield this sword has moral and ethical as well as practical considerations that are mind boggling.

Whenever a discussion centers around dying and the shortening of life, the antithesis of this, namely, the prolongation of life, must be considered. Technologically, medicine has advanced so quickly that older, unwritten understandings of "ordinary" and "extraordinary" care no longer seem applicable. What might have been considered "extraordinary" care a few years ago is now so commonplace as to be called "ordinary" (respirators, pacemakers, kidney dialysis machines, etc.). Furthermore, what starts off in a given case to be "ordinary" care such as the application of a respirator to a patient who is unable to breathe, turns out, when it becomes evident that the patient never can assume normal respirations on his own, to have been "extraordinary care," if one is permitted the liberty of changing the adjective after the fact. Perhaps an example would help to clarify this. If one were struck down by a car and had a serious head injury which rendered him unable to breathe and made him unable to respond, and if his bladder sphincter were in spasm so that he could not urinate, he could be placed on a respirator, he could be artificially fed intravenously or by a stomach tube, and his urinary obstruction could be taken care of by the proper placement of a catheter. If it were assumed that he would recover in a matter of a few days, all of these things would be "ordinary" care. If on the basis of superior knowledge of the neurosurgeon attending him at this time it were known that there was essentially no way he could be expected to recover, all of these things might be considered "extraordinary" care, since without them his injuries would produce death.

If one had acute appendicitis and postoperatively developed a situation where his kidneys did not function, to put him on a dialysis machine (an artificial kidney) which could handle his urinary function temporarily would be an extraordinary act and might at times be considered to be "extraordinary" care. However, in a vigorous, alert, productive individual with a normal life expectancy of several decades ahead of him, it should not be considered "extraordinary" care. On the other hand, if in a ninety-year-old individual the same kidney shutdown took place and was the result of a disease process that inevitably would take this patient's lie, the institution of dialysis would be an "extraordinary procedure" and would definitely be thought of, by any medically competent individual, as providing "extraordinary" care. Here the difference perhaps is less difficult to ascertain than in the previously mentioned case of head injury.

To show how difficult predictions might be, *Medical World News* on May 5, 1974, reported a case of a woman with myasthenia gravis who lived "artificially" for 652 days in intensive care and then made a remarkable recovery. Said a hospital representative at the Harbor General Hospital in Torrance, California, "She made us recognize that there was no such thing as inordinate effort. She had such a tenacity for life we felt that everything we did, no matter how extraordinary, was appropriate to the situation."[1]

It is most difficult to judge medical action from the standpoint of what is legal justice alone. If one gets into the pure aspects of ethics, there could be concern that the use of a pain killer in a dying individual could so cloud his conscious response that he might not in his dying moments be in a position to make decisions which in theological terms might bear upon his eternal destiny. It is essentially impossible to control pain in most instances, particularly in a debilitated or dying individual, without at the same time temporarily impairing his ability to think. From a purely ethical point of view, because clouding of judgment accompanies relief from pain produced by drugs, the situation seems to be insurmountable and therefore has become acceptable.

With the technological advances in medicine, the opportunities for physician participation in momentous decisions concerning life and death increase dramatically. But so do the temptations to misuse this newfound expertise. The physician of a generation or two ago was practically powerless to extend life but on the other hand he faced fewer dilemmas.

Dilemmas for Doctors and Laymen Alike

The dilemmas presented by euthanasia are not dilemmas for the medical profession alone. They are dilemmas for laymen as well. The situation is somewhat akin to the remarks that are made about the malpractice crisis in American medicine today. Many people say: "The doctors certainly have a difficult problem." The fact of the matter is that it is the patient who has a difficult problem. Who do you suppose will pay for the doctor's malpractice insurance premium which has increased in cost fivefold? You, the patient, will pay that. What other dangers exist for the patient in an era where the specter of malpractice suits hangs over the head of the responsible physician at all times? First of all, the physician will treat you not on the basis of what his experience and learned intuition dictates, but rather he will do those things which he feels would absolve him from eventual guilt were he ever sued, and he will neglect to do those things which you might need but which involve a high risk concerning a malpractice. In short, the patient's physician must practice defensive medicine and the loss is not only the physician's, it also is the patient's.

So it is in the dilemmas surrounding euthanasia. Sooner or later you, the reader, will have to face some of these questions in reference to a member of your family and eventually your family will have to face these questions in reference to you. Indeed, you may be party to the latter dilemma as you approach the end of your life.

Once any category of human life is considered fair game in the arena of the right to life, where does it stop? If the mongoloid [Down's syndrome] is chosen as the first category whose life is not worthy to be lived, what about the blind and the deaf? If the hopeless cripple confined to a wheelchair and considered to be a burden on society is the first category to be chosen, what about the frail, the retarded, and the senile? It does not take much fanciful imagination to extend these categories to include certain categories of disease such as cystic fibrosis, diabetes, and a variety of neurologic disorders. The population-control people who are concerned about food supply have been very effective in influencing society's thinking on abortion; it seems very logical that eventually one of their targets could be the obese individual who not only has eaten too much already but has to eat a lot to sustain his large body.

It is very easy to slip into moral deception in a discussion of euthanasia. One starts from the point of view of abortion and says, "I can see why you are against abortion because after all someone, preferably the law, must protect the fetus because the fetus is not in a position to protect itself. But when one is talking of euthanasia, if the person is willing to undergo a 'mercy killing,' why should other people object?" The answer is really the same as it is for abortion. Abortion-on-demand opens up other abuses of which euthanasia is number one. Euthanasia opens up the opportunity at this early stage of the game for almost inconceivable fraud, deception, and deceit. Think of the burdensome elderly people, economically burdensome, whose rapid demise could be looked upon as an economic blessing for their family. Think of the temptation to hasten a legacy. Think of how easy, when there are ulterior motives, to emphasize the surcease from suffering and anxiety that comes with painless death.

Practical Considerations

I don't think a medical student is ever told what his or her mission in life is. Certainly no one told me when I was a medical student what was expected of me as a lifetime goal in assuming the role of a physician. Yet it is very clearly and indelibly imprinted upon the mind of the physician that the first obligation toward the patient is to heal him and cure him and to postpone death for as long a time as possible. The second goal is more difficult to enunciate and ever so much more difficult to practice: When cure is not possible the physician is to care for and comfort his dying patient. There is in here a gray area where the physician is not certain about the possibility of cure and yet is not ready to treat the patient as one who needs comfort in dying. The other side of that coin has to do with the behavior of the physician who, realizing that the opportunity for cure is passed, has two options: first, that of maintaining the life of a "dying" patient through the extremely difficult times of transition from active life to inactive life and from inactive life to death, or, secondly, to withhold certain supportive measures which would enable nature to take her course more quickly.

Let me illustrate. There is a unique tumor of childhood called the neuroblastoma in which I have been interested for more than thirty years. Because of this, I have developed a broad clinical experience with the behavior of this tumor as it affects the lives of my patients. I have perhaps had more neuroblastoma patients referred to me than would normally be the case, because of my special interest in this tumor. I present this background in order to establish the fact that with this particular tumor I have considerable expertise in understanding the clinical course and have been able to predict with relative accuracy what will happen in a given patient when certain signs and symptoms occur or when certain responses to treatment are known. In a given situation I might have as a patient a five-year-old child whose tumor was diagnosed a year ago and who, in spite of all known treatment, has progressed to a place where although her primary tumor has been removed she now has recurrence of the tumor (metastases) in her bones. On the basis of everything I know by seeing scores of patients like her I know that her days of life are limited and that the longer she lives the more likely she is to have considerable pain. She might also become both deaf and blind, because those are sequelae that might be expected when this tumor spreads in the bones of the skull.

If this five-year-old youngster is quite anemic, her ability to understand what is happening her might be clouded. If her normal hemoglobin level should be 12 and is now 6, I have two choices. I can let her exist with a deficient hemoglobin level knowing that it may shorten her life but also knowing that it will be beneficial in the sense that she will not be alert enough to understand all that is happening around her. On the other hand I could be a medical purist and give her blood transfusions until her hemoglobin level was up to acceptable standards. In the process of so doing she would become more alert, she would be more conscious of the things happening around her, she would feel her pain more deeply, and she might live longer to increase the problems presented by all of these things.

In the second place there are anticancer drugs which I know beyond any shadow of a doubt will not cure this child, but which may shrink the recurring tumor in several parts of her body, postponing the inevitable death by a matter of a few days or weeks. However, it is possible that the effect of these drugs will not be very dramatic on the tumors in the skull. They may relentlessly expand, producing blindness and deafness. Would it be better to let this little girl slip into death quietly, with relatively little pain, and with her parents knowing that she can both see and hear—or should we prolong her life by two or three weeks, increase the intensity and duration of the pain she would have, and possibly run the risk of the added terrible complications for the family to witness: blindness and/or deafness? In such a circumstance I opt to withhold supportive measures that would prolong miserable life for the patient to bear and the family to see.

I well remember the occasion on which I decided that this would always be my course of action in this particular tumor unless I was forced to do otherwise or there were some very extenuating circumstances. One of my patients was approaching the aforementioned condition and had been sent home because of the approach of the Christmas holidays and the desire of his family to have the child with them. In the days before his discharge I had promised him a chemistry set as a Christmas gift and on the day before Christmas I delivered the gift in the afternoon. His family took me into their living room, and there before the Christmas tree was a big mound on the floor which looked like a heaped-up beige blanket. Under it was my patient on his hands and knees slumped down as though hands and knees could no longer support his weight. The story was most pitiful. Earlier he had asked to come down from his bedroom to see the electric trains under the Christmas tree and found a measure of comfort on his hands and knees before the trains. He asked not to be moved because he had found a position in which he seemed more comfortable than when lying in bed. He died the next day in that same position.

In a situation such as I have just described one gets to the very nonlegalistic moral core of the relationship of a physician with his patient. Whether the patient is a child and the relationship has to be with his parents, or whether the patient is an adult and the physician's relationship must be with the patient himself and his relatives, there has to be a sense of trust and confidence that the physician will do the "right" thing whether the disease process is curable or is one which will cause death. There have been many occasions in my life when I have clearly described the thoughts that went through my mind as I outlined to parents why I planned what

I did plan to do with their child. But much more often than that there has been between parent and physician an understanding which exceeds the bounds of pure trust and confidence, where the family seems to know, and I encourage them to think, that their child is in understanding hands as well as in competent hands, that their child will be kindly treated in this terrible process of dying to which death brings a sense of relief and release. Here the family senses that I will treat their child the way I would like someone in my position to treat my child were he in the same circumstance. Yet through all this there is the understanding that this life, waning though it may be, is precious to the patient, is precious to the family, is precious to me, and—in my particular belief—the understanding that this life is also precious to God.

Therefore, it should be very clear that the decisions that are made in any circumstance are tailored to the problems at hand, the background and experience if the physician, the depth of understanding of the family, and the relationship which exists between patient and physician and family and physician. There is no way that there can be a set of rules to govern this circumstance. Guidelines may be possible, but not rules. I can think of no more tragic circumstance to come upon the practice of medicine and no more tragic circumstance for a future patient to face than to have a legal decision made by someone in the field of jurisprudence who has not lived through these circumstances, and who could not in a lifetime of testimony understand what the problems are and how they should be handled. His training, his experience, and his emotions have not been intimately involved with similar circumstances in the past where his decision and his decision alone is the one that must answer all the questions, no matter how inadequately.

The arrival of the era of organ transplantation adds another series of dilemmas to the practice of medicine in reference to the ethics and the morality of the prolongation of life on the one hand or its extermination on the other. Add to all of the other questions that have been raised previously, the new one of terminating one life to make possible an organ transplant to another individual in order that the second individual's life may be meaningfully prolonged. Some of these decisions are relatively open and shut, as for example in brain death of an individual, perhaps young, who is kept alive by a respirator in the presence of a functioning heart. But one can also easily imagine the pressures that develop from the family of a patient consigned to death because of the lack of a vital organ, when the patient could have his life significantly prolonged by the removal of that organ from another individual whose life may not be considered by the patient and other interested parties to be worthy of extraordinary care. These pressures are felt especially by those engaged in kidney transplant programs.

Theology, Morality, and Ethics

Although the termination of unborn life precludes the living of the life for threescore and ten years, whereas euthanasia only shortens a life that has already been lived, this is no reason to regard the taking of a life by euthanasia as any less serious a moral decision than that by abortion.

Obviously, the great majority of people realize that a decision concerning abortion will never be theirs to make personally. It naturally follows that many people will be indifferent to the implications of liberalized abortion laws, not recognizing how the change in our understanding of abortion affects so many other aspects of our lives today and in the future. But when it comes to death, there is no one who can say that a decision concerning the way his death is managed will be of no concern to him. The death rate is still one per capita.

It has always been of considerable interest to me that any discussion of human life rapidly and inevitably becomes associated with theological discussions. The fact that as distinguished a journal as the *Human Life Review* would contain technical articles on population, learned discourses on jurisprudence, and publish them side by side with the theological implications of man's regard for human life suggests to me incontrovertibly that life and death are God's business.

As with abortion, any discussion of euthanasia by the individual leans heavily upon that individual's understanding of the sanctity or lack of sanctity of human life, upon an understanding of man's understanding of God, and upon whether or not in the synthesis of these things the individual believes that there is life not worthy to be lived.

My own perspective of the dilemmas presented by euthanasia represent an understanding produced by the synthesis of where my belief in biblical revelation crosses my experience in medicine.

Each reader must face the fact that his own beliefs on these matters may be based on theological arguments of which he is not aware, as well as on Christian spinoffs that regulate society.

To one raised in Judeo-Christian moral philosophy, life might be considered on a much higher plane than the right considered inalienable by Thomas Jefferson. If one considers life as a sacred privilege, that understanding can be extended to include the view that this sacred privilege was indeed designed by God in order that a creature might relate to the Creator in a personal way—in a relationship in which God is sovereign.

If man was indeed created in the image of God and he was created for a life of fellowship with God, then death is alien to anything that God in his creation of man intended before man's fall. From a theological point of view the sanctity of life represents, or rather understands, man as a trinity: he is a soul, he does inhabit a body, and he has a spirit. In the trinitarian Christian view there is a sanctity of life for each of these.

The term "death with dignity" has caught on because of its alliterative catchiness rather than because it represents anything based upon Judeo-Christian moral principles.[2] The Judeo-Christian understanding of the fall of man is essential to an appreciation of this point of view. Man was created in the image of God and would have lived in fellowship with Him, had it not been for the disobedience of the progenitor of our race, Adam. Anything that exists within man's nature to enable him to have fellowship with God must be regarded as a gift from God and, in a sense, the worthiness of this life has meaning only insofar as it has this relationship to God.

In a sense the whole problem of the right to live and the right to die, centering around one's understanding of abortion and euthanasia, has a significant analogy to the behavior of Lucifer. We do not know whence his temptation came, but we do know that he sought to be "like the most high."[3] Our society, having lost its understanding of the sanctity of human life, is pushing the medical profession into assuming one of God's prerogatives, namely, deciding what life shall be born and when life should end.

A great deal of our Western civilization with its concomitant culture is based upon Christian principles, Christian ethics, Christian morality. Even though many refer to this era as the post-Christian era, there are a remarkable number of spinoffs that we accept as everyday rights and privileges which would never have been part of Western society except for Christian influence.

If one were to superimpose a map of the Western world showing those places where the Christian gospel has been preached, where Christian morality and influence has had its greatest impact, upon another map showing those parts of the Western world where what used to be called social reforms were most prevalent—literacy, education, hospitals, orphanages, homes for the aged, institutions for the retarded and the insane available to all regardless of creed—these maps would be almost identical.

Without theological insights that help to form the basis of one's understanding of matters relating to the life and death of patients, I would find it impossible to make judgments in these matters. I suspect that theological principles, some of which may be vague implantations from early religious training are probably at work in the minds of the great majority of physicians as they face some of these decisions.

If there is not to be a Judeo-Christian ethic in the preservation of life in matters relating to euthanasia, what does the future hold? To assume the role of prophet, I can almost hear the arguments that will be given by the proponents of euthanasia outlining the safeguards that the state can build into euthanasia laws to prevent euthanasia from becoming perverted as it once was in the days of the Nazis in Germany. It comes down to the question as it does in reference to any matter of life: "Is there life not worthy to be lived?" The day may come when a death selection committee may objectively consider my life not to be worth much. On the other hand the subjective worth of my life in my eyes and those in my family who love me might be quite different. Many cases will be open and shut, but the number of cases in the gray area will exceed those where physicians have clarity of thought and relative unanimity of opinion. Certainly the rights of individuals will disappear; depersonalization and dehumanization will reign. If our human-value concepts are to be preserved, no one should take the life of another human being even passively without the deepest concern and consideration of all the attendant implications. Once the human-value ethic becomes weakened or tarnished, it doesn't take long for inhuman experimentation on human bodies to take place. Auschwitz could be in the offing.

Where Do We Go from Here?

The decision of the Supreme Court in favor of abortion on demand literally hands over the decision on the survival of one person's life to another person. All of the economic, social, emotional, and compassionate arguments that are used in favor of abortion very suddenly become the same arguments for euthanasia.

It does not take long to move rapidly to a new set of standards once we have learned to live for a short time with an abrogation of a former principle. Take the medical profession, for example. For four centuries longer than the Christian era, doctors have taken the Hippocratic oath. To be sure, there are many things that are outdated because of the difference in culture between the time of Hippocrates and this modern era. To be sure, there are changes in our understanding of modern medicine which alter or render obsolete certain areas of the Hippocratic oath. But the one thing that the public could rely on was that the medical profession, functioning on the traditional oath of Hippocrates, was in the business of being on the side of life. Life was to be preserved just as suffering was to be alleviated. But nowhere were the skills of the physician to be used as intervention to lower the health standards of the patient or to shorten his life.

If the medical profession abandons the life principle embodied in the Hippocratic oath and sees its privilege to extend to the interruption of unborn life in the womb and to exterminate painlessly a waning life much as the veterinarian would put an ailing dog to sleep, it will have changed its raison d'etre. The patient can no longer look at his physician as his advocate for the extension of life—because when in the mind of that physician that patient's life is waning, the sick person has no guarantee that the physician will approach him in the role of life preserver. He may be coming as executioner. The medical profession has been disappointingly silent as they have heard the intellectual arguments, Supreme Court rulings, and population-concern pressures that have begun to alter the fundamental basis which has for so long set them apart as the proponents of the healing art.

Before the century is out, it is quite possible that the elderly will exceed in numbers those who bear the burden of their support, whether as family or under some legal technicality such as the Social Security Act. If the question of euthanasia presents a dilemma now on moral and ethical grounds, think of what it will present in days to come when, in addition to moral and ethical considerations, there is the overpowering question of economics. Unless we get our ethics and our morals straightened out now, the death selection committee that decides for you may be motivated more by money than by ecological concerns.

Most of the dilemmas that present themselves in reference to the dying patient have been described. If the reader feels at this juncture that he or she does not have a good grasp of how the author would act in every imaginable circumstance, then the reader has grasped the situation rather well. It is almost impossible to present in capsule form how one feels on this subject, so extenuating are the circumstances in different situations.

Perhaps no more difficult question is ever asked of me by an intern or a resident than to summarize in a few sentences my feelings on this subject. When asked to do so, I put it somewhat like this: "As a basic principle, keep as many men at as many guns for as long a time as possible; that's how you win the war. I am in the life-saving business and that comes first, but I recognize also that I am in the business of alleviating suffering. I never take a deliberate action with the motive of terminating a patient's life. It is possible that a patient's life might be shortened by some therapeutic measure I employ with the intent of relieving suffering. In some circumstances where I believe that I have sufficient experience and expertise with the life history of a disease process and my patient's response to that disease as well as to his therapy, I might withhold treatment that could be considered extraordinary or heroic in the given circumstance in reference to the quality of life that might be salvaged for a short period of time." Even as I write these words I recognize full well the chance for errors in judgment. Because of that I try to err only on the side of life.

Notes

1. *Medical World News,* 5 May 1974.

2. Editorial, *The Philadelphia Inquirer,* 12 November 1975. William A. Reusher, Op-Ed page, *The Philadelphia Inquirer,* 23 November 1975.

3. Isaiah 14:14.

8

Word and Deed

Peter Waldron with George Grant

Servanthood

*T*here is a direct connection between service and authority. It is only as Christian men and women become the benefactors of the people through servanthood that they are able to become the leaders of the people.

Jesus was a servant. He came to serve, not to be served (Matthew 20:20). And he called his disciples to a similar life of selflessness. He called them to be servants (Matthew 19:30).

Unfortunately, servanthood is a much neglected, largely forgotten Christian vocation today. Most Christians are obsessed with leading. They want headship. They want prominence. They want dominion, not servitude. Their obsession with power has been, and continues to be, self-defeating.

Jesus made it plain that if Christians want authority, they must not grasp at the reigns of power and prominence. They must serve. It

PETER WALDRON is host of "Peter Waldron Live," a talk radio broadcast, and has served as a political consultant. He is the author of several books including *For the Love of Justice* and *The Making of a Wise Man.*
GEORGE GRANT is the executive director of Legacy Communications and the author of numerous books on public policy including *Grand Illusions, Bringing in the Sheaves,* and *The Dispossessed.* He is the instructor for the *Living By The Book* course, "Current Issues By The Book."

is only by service that they become fit for leadership. Jesus said, "Whoever wants to be first must be your slave" (Matthew 20:27). The attitude of all aspiring leaders "should be the same as that of Christ Jesus: Who, being in very nature God, did not consider equality with God something to be grasped, but made himself nothing, taking the very nature of a servant, being made in human likeness. And being found in appearance as a man, he humbled himself and became obedient to death—even death on a cross! Therefore God exalted him to the highest place and gave him the name that is above every name" (Philippians 2:5–9).

This principle is reiterated throughout the biblical narrative. The theme of the suffering servant who later triumphs, who serves faithfully and then succeeds, is, in fact, the commonest of scriptural themes.

Jacob served his ruthless uncle Laban under difficult and demeaning circumstances for more than fourteen years. But then, God exalted him to high honor and position (Genesis 1:1, 36–42).

Joseph served faithfully in Potiphar's house only to be falsely charged and imprisoned. But then God raised him up to become Pharaoh's second-in-command (Genesis 39:1, 7–20; 41:38–43).

David served in the court of King Saul as a musician and a warrior. And though the king ultimately turned on him, David remained steadfast. In the end, that faithful service won him the crown (1 Samuel 16–19; 23; 24:20).

Daniel served as an exile in the courts of Nebuchadnezzar and Darius. His faithfulness stirred the envy of the power-seekers and the power-brokers. Their vicious plotting landed him in the lions' den, but he prevailed nonetheless. His service earned him victory (Daniel 6:3–28).

In the same way, Paul and Silas won Philippi from a dark, dank dungeon cell. Jeremiah won Judah cloaked in sackcloth and ashes. And Hosea won Israel from under the rubble of a broken home. They won because service leads to authority.

If Christians are going to rebuild the walls of this culture, if they are going to help to restore America's greatness, they are going to have to learn the lost art of servanthood. They are going to have to comprehend the connection between service and authority.

As James said, "What good is it, my brothers, if a man claims to have faith but has no deeds? Can such faith save him? Suppose a brother or sister is without clothes and daily food. If one of you says to him, 'Go, I wish you well; keep warm and well fed,' but does nothing about his physical needs, what good is it? In the same way, faith by itself, if it is not accompanied by action, is dead" (2:14–17).

Modern men are looking for *proof.* They want *evidence.* When the great heroes of the faith wedded Word and deed, the people of the day got their proof. They needed no further evidence. They could *see* that the biblical solutions to societal woes were not simply pie-in-the-sky. They were, instead, cause for hope—real hope.

True service verifies the claims of Scripture. It tells men that there is indeed a sovereign and gracious God who raises up a faithful people. It tells men that God then blesses those people, and gives them workable solutions to difficult dilemmas.

It is not enough for Christians today merely to *believe* the Bible. It is not enough simply to *assert* an innate trust in scriptural problem-solving. Christians must validate and authenticate their claims. They must *serve,* backing up Word with deed.

Whenever and wherever Christians have effected righteous change in their society, that change has come on the heels of an explosion of good works. From the time of Paul's missionary journeys to America's Great Awakening, Christian cultural influence has always been accompanied by selfless service. Hospitals were established. Orphanages were founded. Rescue missions were started. Alms-houses were built. Soup kitchens were begun. Charitable societies were incorporated. The hungry were fed, the naked clothed, and the homeless sheltered. Word was wedded to deed.

This is as it should be. Even today. Christians are to stand before the world as "an example by doing what is good" (Titus 2:7). They are "to be ready to do whatever is good" (Titus 3:1).

Sadly, the welfare state humanists have absconded with that legacy and taken it for themselves. They have stolen the moral high ground from the Christian community. Despite the fact that their civil rights measures have been more rhetoric than reality and their war on poverty has been more a "war on the poor," they have taken a servanthood pose while Christians have been idle and apathetic.

Their pose has won for the humanists cultural authority. They have served as the people's benefactors while the church has become increasingly obsolescent. So, guess who has won the right to rule and judge?

If Christians are going to help turn this nation around in any measure, then they will have to recapture their place of authority. But in order to do that, they will have to wrestle from the humanists the mantle of servanthood. They will have to become the people's benefactors.

A Time of Open Opportunity

The unchanging standard of Scripture must be matched with the unwavering commitment of servanthood. Only then can Christians hope to overcome the humanist assaults against life and liberty in this land. Listen to how the prophet Isaiah addressed his generation:

> Is not this the kind of fasting I have chosen: to loose the chains of injustice and untie the cords of the yoke, to set the oppressed free and break every yoke? Is it not to share your food with the hungry and to provide the poor wanderer with shelter—when you see the naked, to clothe him, and not to turn away from your own flesh and blood? Then your light will break forth like the dawn, and your healing will quickly appear; then your righteousness will go before you, and the glory of the LORD will be your rear guard. Then you will call, and the LORD will answer; you will cry for help, and he will say: Here am I. If you do away with the yoke of oppression, with the pointing finger and malicious talk, and if you spend yourselves in behalf of the hungry and satisfy the needs of the oppressed, then your light will rise in the darkness, and your night will become like the noonday. The LORD will guide you always; he will satisfy your needs in a sun-scorched land and will strengthen your frame. You will be like a well-watered garden, like a spring whose waters never fail. Your people will rebuild the ancient ruins and will raise up the age-old foundations; you will be called Repairer of Broken Walls, Restorer of Streets with Dwellings (58:6–12).

The needs of contemporary society are indeed great. Today Christians have numerous open opportunities to regain the moral high ground by demonstrating true, Christlike servanthood.

The plight of the poor provides believers with an open opportunity. In 1950, one-in-twelve Americans (about 21 million) lived below the poverty line. In 1979, that figure had risen to one-in-nine (about 26 million). In 1992 one-in-seven (nearly 34 million) fell below the line.

More than one-fourth of all American children live in poverty (up from 9.3 percent in 1950 and 14.9 percent in 1970). And for black children under the age of six, the figures are even more dismal: a record 51.2 percent.

Today, about two-thirds of single elderly women live in poverty, all too often in abject poverty, up from 37 percent in 1954.

Between 500,000 and 2 million Americans are homeless, living out of the backs of their cars, under bridges, in abandoned warehouses, atop street-side heating grates, or in lice-infested public shelters. Even at the height of the Great Depression, when dustbowl refugees met with the "grapes of wrath" on America's highways and byways, there have never been so many dispossessed wanderers.

The fact is, the Reagan Recovery of the eighties never reached into the cavernous depths of the bottom third of the economy. Shelters are bulging at the seams. And social service agencies are buried under an avalanche of need.

If only Christians would undertake the God-ordained task of charity—serving the needy, helping the helpless, and caring for the hopeless—not only would they be able to transform poverty into productivity, but they would regain the moral high ground as well (Proverbs 11:25, 14:21, 28:27). By serving the despised and rejected, they would obtain the cultural authority they need to help restore America's greatness.

The frightening dilemmas posed by the AIDS plague provide believers with an open opportunity. In 1980, AIDS was virtually unknown outside Central Africa. Only about one hundred cases had been reported in the United States. By 1982, there had been about a thousand diagnosed cases in the United States, but panic had yet to set in.

By 1984, there were nearly a million confirmed cases and the media had begun to hype the story. By 1987 the number of cases was doubling every ten months. The disease had broken out of homosexual enclaves and into the general populace. Medical experts began admitting that a cure was, at best, many years away, and the trauma on the entire fabric of American society was everywhere apparent.

By 1992, 12 million people carried the HIV virus worldwide. And in America, there were 250,000 confirmed cases of AIDS, with about 1 million people unknowingly carrying the HIV virus. Tossed to and fro on waves of doubt, fear, ignorance, intolerance, and hopelessness, an entire generation of Americans has been shaken from their sure and secure cultural moorings.

If only Christians would undertake the God-ordained tasks of reconciliation and healing—tending the sick, rebuking the wicked, and forgiving the repentant—not only would they be able to offer the suffering the medicine of hope, but they would regain the moral high ground as well (Matthew 10:8; Luke 10:29–37). By serving the afflicted, they would obtain the cultural authority they need to help restore America's greatness.

The difficulties faced by working mothers provide believers with an open opportunity. Over the last decade, per capita family income has increased 7.1 percent. At the same time, however, the consumer price index has inflated a whopping 11.2 percent. Add to that the fact that only 20 percent of all United States jobs pay enough to lift a family of four above the poverty line, and working mothers become a foregone conclusion.

In 1970, only 39 percent of America's mothers had entered the work force. By 1980, 54 percent were working. And by 1985, 61 percent were. Today, nearly 47 percent of all American families have both parents working.

According to the Bureau of Labor Statistics, 43 percent of those working mothers have children under the age of six. This poses an additional burden in and of itself: day care cost. Nearly 20 percent of those working mothers are so overextended financially that they cannot afford day care at all and are forced into latch key arrangements for their youngsters.

The emotional pressure, the physical fatigue, and the spiritual entropy that working mothers face day in and day out can be utterly debilitating, and with no relief in sight.

If only Christians would undertake the God ordained task of biblical compassion—encouraging the distraught, upholding the distressed, and refreshing the discouraged—not only would they be able to help working mothers, but they would regain the moral high ground as well (Isaiah 1:17; James 1:27). By serving the immediate emotional, physical, and spiritual needs of women and their children, believers would obtain the cultural authority they need to help restore America's greatness.

The isolation and frustration faced by the handicapped provide believers with an open opportunity. They are the forgotten and the neglected. And there are millions of them. According to the best statistics available, as many as 16.3 percent of all Americans (or about 37 million) suffer from some sort of crippling disability—congenital or accidental. There are 6.6 million mentally retarded Americans, with an additional 15.4 million suffering from severe learning disorders. There are at least 1.2 million men, women, and children with total hearing loss, and 6.4 million with total visual impairment. Still another 6.6 million are restricted by paralysis, atrophy, deformity, amputation, degeneration, or immobility.

Abandoned by families, shunned by peers, frustrated by dependency, and incapacitated by loneliness and doubt, the handicapped are all too often society's pariahs.

If only Christians would undertake the God-ordained tasks of nurturing and sheltering—cherishing the uncherished, respecting the unrespected, and loving the unloved—not only would the handicapped be grafted into the productive mainstream, but believers would regain the moral high ground as well (Psalm 82:4; Luke 14:12–14; Acts 20:35). By serving the disabled, believers would obtain the cultural authority they need to help restore America's greatness.

The awful calamity facing displaced homemakers provides believers with an open opportunity. The liberalization of divorce laws, the breakdown of family solidarity, and runaway immorality have combined to create a whole new underclass in American society: the abandoned housewife.

The number of displaced homemakers rose 28 percent between 1975 and 1983 to 3.2 million women. Another 20 percent increase from 1983 to 1987 brought that number to nearly 4 million. An astonishing 61 percent of those women suddenly left alone had children under the age of ten at home.

Often without job skills and stranded without alimony or child support, as many as 70 percent of these women make less than $10,000 a year, and 50 percent are employed at minimum wage or less. It is thus readily apparent why a full 75 percent of all Americans living below the poverty line in the United States are women and their children.

Caught between traditionalism and feminism, these women have no advocate. No matter where they turn, they don't fit in. They know no context.

If only Christians would undertake the God-ordained task of ministering to orphans and widows—upholding the weak, upbraiding the lax, and uplifting the vulnerable—not only would women be given their proper due, but believers would regain the moral high ground as well (Exodus 22:22; Psalm 146:8–9). By serving displaced homemakers, believers would obtain the cultural authority they need to help restore America's greatness.

The severe crisis in education provides believers with an open opportunity. According to the United States Department of Education, 23 million Americans are functionally illiterate. Just fifty years ago, only 1.5 percent of white, native-born Americans struggled with this liability. Today that figure has peaked at more than 10 percent. Urban blacks fifty years ago faced an illiteracy rate of about 9 percent. Today the figure is an astonishing 40 percent. And this, despite a multi-billion dollar splurge by the government on schools all across the United States.

Even in the area of physical fitness the public schools are a dismal failure. The President's Council on Physical Fitness found that 40 percent of boys and 70 percent of girls aged 6–12 could not do more than one pull-up. Nearly 55 percent of the girls could not do any. Half of the girls aged 6–17 and 30 percent of the boys aged 6–12 could not run a mile in less than ten minutes. Almost 45 percent of the boys and 55 percent of the girls could not hold their chin over a raised bar for more than ten seconds. And 40 percent of the boys could not even reach beyond their toes while seated on a floor with legs outstretched.

Apparently, Johnny can't read and Susie can't spell. Willie can't write and Alice can't add. And all four of them are terribly out of shape. According to another presidential study, the demise of America's schools has made this once great land "a nation at risk."

If only Christians would undertake the God-ordained tasks of teaching and training—establishing schools, equipping communities, and preparing for the future—not only would the blight of ignorance be banished, but believers would regain the moral high ground as well (Deuteronomy 6:4–9; Ephesians 6:4). By saving the young, believers would obtain the cultural authority they need to help restore America's greatness.

Opportunity after opportunity presents itself through service: to the elderly, to the victims of child abuse, to women in crisis pregnancies, to recovering alcoholics, to the terminally ill, to single parents, to repentant homosexuals, to the mentally ill, and to drug addicts on the rebound: "Be wise in the way you act toward outsiders; make the most of every opportunity" (Colossians 4:5).

Christians must learn to recognize and seize these opportunities. They must begin to comprehend the pivotal and powerful influence that service plays in the flow of human history. They must wed Word and deed.

Where the Rubber Meets the Road

Any businessman can tell you that the best kind of advertising is word of mouth. People can only be hyped so much and so far. Commercials, campaigns, programs, and strategies are innately limited. People are influenced most by people. That is why when Jesus sent his disciples out to win the world and to transform society, he told them to get personally involved with people (Matthew 28:19–20). They were to start with the folks they knew (Acts 1:8). They were to nurture relationships (2 Timothy 2:2). They were to be personable, loving, kind, gentle, and a joy to be around (Galatians 5:22). The way the Christian wins his battles involves winsomeness as well as confrontation (1 Peter 3:1–2). After all, love covers a multitude of sins (1 Peter 4:8).

Christianity has answers. It offers solutions to the nagging, plaguing problems of our day.

Some of the solutions Christianity offers are overtly political. But only some. Christianity is a fully rounded worldview, and so it includes politics in its broad purview. But it also includes much, much more. Christianity is by no means a political cult.

In the plan to redeem society that God implanted in the Bible and entrusted to Christianity are innumerable other institutions, strategies, and agendas. If any one of them is slighted, then the efforts of Christians in the political arena are doomed to failure. Every area of life must be yielded to the lordship of Jesus Christ: politics and personal relationships; families and churches; institutions and communities—that's where the rubber really meets the road.

Rebuilding Relationships

The scandal-racked Christian community is held in anything but high esteem by the citizenry at large. And it is not simply because a few highly placed TV evangelists have been exposed as frauds. Graft, greed, corruption, and materialism are common among Christians. Christian divorce rates are skyrocketing. The lives of believers are all-too-often indistinguishable from the lives of unbelievers. Is it any wonder that the world holds Christians in low regard? If this nation is to be turned around, Christians will have to regain and retain high and honorable reputations among their neighbors, friends, and peers.

Christians must also work hard at constructing deep and abiding friendships. Very few people have real friendships past the days of adolescence. The trust, confidence, loyalty, honesty, integrity, transparency, dependency, and accountability that comes with true friendship has been lost. As a result, we do not have the reserves of strength, boldness, certainty, and commonality necessary for protracted spiritual and cultural warfare. Christians are picked off by burnout, fanaticism, loneliness, or temptation simply because they have attempted to live and work as "Lone Rangers." And that simply does not, cannot, and will not work. Christians need to relearn the art of creating and maintaining godly, intimate friendships.

Fellowship is also necessary for discipleship. Disciples are made one person at a time. It takes time, effort, and personalized attention. In this instant-everything world, Christians tend to neglect the one-on-one dynamic of discipleship. They tend to abandon the time-consuming model of apprenticeship, of accountability, of oversight, and of responsibility that is inherent in the scriptural program of discipleship. The fact is, most Christians are left to grow—

or stagnate as is so often the case—all on their own. They are expected to figure out inductively what to do, how to act, what to change, and whom to associate with. Evangelism is all too typically a "love 'em and leave 'em" affair. But the fact is that there is no such thing as impersonal discipleship.

Restoring Families

If the family is weak, unstable, insecure, debilitated, demoralized—as it is in our land today—the entire structure of civilization is gravely at risk. Leadership is a function of happy, wholesome, righteous, active, loving, vibrant, and challenging homes, not of conservative political parties. Vision, character, stalwartness, courage, efficiency, incorruptibility, excellence, confidence, dynamism, and integrity—these are all the fruit of Christian homes, not of civil orientation programs.

Christians need to work hard at integrating spiritual nurture into their families. Parents are charged by God with the awesome and fearsome responsibility of raising their children up "in the training and instruction of the Lord" (Ephesians 6:4). That's not primarily the job of the preacher, the Sunday School teacher, the youth director, the summer camp counselor, the TV evangelist, or the Christian school educator.

It is the job of parents to inculcate prayer habits in their children by actually praying with them. It is their job to establish Bible study disciplines in their children by actually studying with them. It is their job to nurture a commitment to the church by actually fellowshipping with them. It is their job to confirm a respect for the throne of God by actually worshiping with them. It is *their* job. It cannot be delegated, relegated, or dispatched. Christians need to reorder their priorities and place spiritual nurture at the forefront of their families' agendas.

Christians also need to work hard at integrating financial responsibility into their families. Again, God has charged parents with an enormous series of responsibilities. They are to guard their children from the ravages of greed, materialism, graft, and corruption on the one hand and poverty, deprivation, and debt on the other. They are to model in their own lives godly stewardship through budgeting (Luke 14, 16), saving (Proverbs 6), setting goals (Proverbs 1), investment

(Matthew 21), the eradication of debt (Romans 13:8), and, of course, the tithe (Malachi 3:8–12).

All too often Christians rant and rave about the fiscal irresponsibility of Washington, while their own houses are in utter disarray. We need to get our own houses in order by untangling the complex snarl of financial irresponsibilities in our families and establishing patterns of holy and consistent stewardship.

Finally, Christians need to work hard at spending quality time with their families. Tragically, the modern careerist myth that you can spend quality time with your family without having to spend quantity time with them has been accepted in a wholesale fashion by Christians. Quality time isn't something that can be conjured at will out of a void. It is the natural product of nurture, constancy, consistency, and familiarity. Quality time takes time! It is only as intimate personal relationships slowly develop that parents and children, brothers and sisters, and husbands and wives can become what God really intended: a real family.

Revitalizing Education

"If you want to lead," quipped Napoleon to his generals, "you'll have to read." And he was right. Those men and women God raises up to influence and reform society must be well-informed, well-educated, and well-read. Solomon accumulated a massive library and was an encyclopedic chronicler of human knowledge (1 Kings 4:32–34), and the apostle Paul cherished his books and parchments, yearning for them even during his imprisonment (2 Timothy 4:13). The early church fathers were brilliant and literate men who hungered for learning like mustangs hunger for cool, sweet bluegrass: Clement of Rome, Ignatius, Gregory of Nyssa, Chrysostom, and John of Damascus.

Contrast that with the awful state of affairs in the community of believers today. Due to a heritage of anti-intellectualism and pietistic isolationism, illiteracy and alliteracy run rampant in the church. Only about 11 percent of the community of faith ever visits a bookstore or library. And only about half of those actually buy books. The others purchase cards, or music, or trinkets, or gifts. The hardback book trade is supported by a mere 5 percent of the Christians in this country.

How are Christians supposed to turn this nation around if they don't know what's going on in the first place? How are they going to restore the foundations of grace, mercy, and truth to this culture if they have yet to study, analyze, critique, research, read through, compare, contrast, synthesize, and summarize the vast storehouse of wisdom at their disposal in books? How seriously should the humanists take the gospel agenda if the majority of its adherents are basically illiterate?

To remedy this problem, Christians need first of all to restore spiritual vitality to the curriculums of their children. Education is not simply a transfer of naked neutral facts to the ready receptacles of young minds. It is the communication of an entire worldview. Facts are meaningless until they are fitted into a grid of interpretation, until they are located on a map of reality. That is why the Bible describes education as a parent-directed process of discovery and discipleship, as opposed to a professionally-directed program of dictation (Deuteronomy 6:4–9). It is not simply designed to enable children to draw from a repertoire of historical or mathematical trivia on command. Instead, it is the sovereignly appointed means of passing on the legacy of the covenant from one generation to the next. Readin', writin', and 'rithmetic are, thus, just as clearly opportunities to communicate the grace of Jesus Christ as "Bible class" is.

There is no generally accepted term in our educational vocabulary for this kind of learning—the Germans call it *erziehung,* the Russians call it *raspitanie,* and the French call it *educatione.* The best English equivalents would be something like "upbringing," "character training," or "admonitive nurture," expressions that sound oddly irrelevant to the schooling process to us. They speak of values, morals, motives, ethics, and patterns of social response. In our society we've actually tried to separate those things from the educational system. Of course, in so doing, the educational system has been crippled. If we are to see America return to greatness as a nation, Christians will have to insure that the educational programs of their children are infused with moral and spiritual content.

Equally important, Christians need to restore academic excellence to the curriculums of their children. At the time our nation was founded, a basic liberal arts education included a study of Greek, Hebrew, Latin, and the literary classics of Plato, Aristotle, Thucydides, Aristophanes, Josephus, Augustine, Aquinas, Luther,

Calvin, Knox, Milton, Rutherford, Rousseau, Voltaire, and Locke. It included physics, astronomy, geography, history, civics, logic, philosophy, theology, biology, composition, grammar, oratory, architecture, music, literature, and navigation. And that was just a basic education. Even in the rough-and-tumble pioneer schools—where kids could only attend between harvests, where every age group crowded into one room, and where time, money, and resources were extremely limited—the curriculum put to shame our modern and sophisticated schools.

It's not that under the threat of a hickory switch those schools could command a higher level of academic discipline. They actually created a hunger for learning. They stimulated in their students a desire to grow and learn. They were rooted in the idea that nothing less than the best is good enough for servants in the kingdom of the Lord Jesus.

Sadly, that holistic approach to glorifying God with all our minds has been lost in our day. When was the last time you heard a believer talk nonchalantly and inconspicuously about genuinely intellectual pursuits? Such things are scorned in the church today. They are perceived as superfluous and prideful. But, if this nation is to be turned around, Christians will have to begin to give the educational programs of their children a stout transfusion of academic excellence.

Finally, Christians need to restore functional practicality to the curriculums of their children. Life is rough in the big city. The cold, cruel world comes as quite a shock to most kids fresh out of high school or college. More than 76 percent of all high school graduates and an astonishing 6 percent of all college graduates have no readily transferable job skills. And we wonder why it seems like we have to start from scratch economically with each new generation!

The fact is that, since we have abandoned the age-old systems of apprenticeship, our kids are forced to enter the marketplace without the skills necessary to succeed. Education has become a combination of therapy and babysitting. Instead of laying the foundations for a life of industry, productivity, service, and stewardship, our kids are just "doing time." They idle their days and weeks and years away. And when they walk out into the work-a-day world they have no trade, no vocation, and no future.

Reviving Churches

The church has become the spurned and neglected stepchild of the modern evangelical movement. But the fact is, what the church does and doesn't do directly affects the course of civilization. It determines the flow of historical events (Revelation 5–6). It is a hub around which the gusting, swirling winds of time turn.

It is the church that has the keys to the kingdom (Matthew 16:19). It is the church that has the power to bind and to loose (Matthew 18:18). It is the church that shall prevail over the gates of hell (Matthew 16:18). It is the church—not parachurch groups, not evangelistic associations, not political action committees, not special interest groups, not ecumenical rallies—that can catalyze the kind of social transformation necessary to turn this nation around.

Often Christians get so involved in the political struggle for life and liberty that they forget about the pivotal role that revived churches can play in rebuilding the walls of this land. But we can remedy this critical omission.

First, Christians need to restore a fully functional body life to the church. Mutual ministry is the way the church is supposed to operate. That is why the New Testament so heavily emphasizes the "one another" commands as the primary relational qualifiers in the body. Because they are members of one another (Ephesians 4:5), Christians are to love one another (Romans 13:8), build up one another (1 Thessalonians 5:11), serve one another (Galatians 5:13), defer to one another (Philippians 2:3), admonish one another (Colossians 3:16), comfort one another (1 Corinthians 12:25), and encourage one another (1 Thessalonians 5:11). They are to spur one another on toward love and good deeds (Hebrews 10:24), always bearing with one another (Colossians 3:13), accepting one another (Romans 15:7), waiting on one another (1 Corinthians 11:33), and fellowshipping with one another (1 John 1: 7). They are never to speak against (James 4:11), complain against (James 5:9), or judge one another (Romans 14:13).

Instead, they are to be of the same mind (Romans 12:16), being subject to (Ephesians 5:21), and having forbearance for one another (Ephesians 4:2). They are to bear one another's burdens

(Galatians 6:2), living in peace with one another (1 Thessalonians 5:13), and confessing sins to one another (James 5:16). In short, Christians are commanded by God to give preference in their lives to one another (Romans 12:10). When they actually do that, not only is the entire church fit for the work of the ministry, but the entire culture falls under the sway of wave after wave of confident, zealous, and thoroughly equipped believers (Ephesians 4:12–13).

Sadly, this kind of interrelatedness has all too often been relegated by the modern evangelical church to the realm of theory. Mutual ministry has been replaced by professional ministry. Spiritual gifts lie dormant and unused.

Second, Christians need to restore effectual discipline in the church. Blatant, flagrant, perpetual sin simply must not be harbored and sheltered by God's chosen people. If sin is casually tolerated, the church is defiled (1 Corinthians 5:6–13), evangelism is stifled (1 Corinthians 5:1–5), and victory is denied (Joshua 7:1–15).

Every member of the church fails and falls from time to time (Romans 3:10–23), but patterns of heinous sin cannot and must not enter their lives (1 Corinthians 6:9–11). If those patterns do crop up, the church is obligated to take disciplinary action (Matthew 18:15–20). The purpose of church discipline is not punitive but restorative. It builds into the body accountability, responsibility, and respectability. It erects a hedge of protection and a boundary of fear around the people of the covenant.

This dimension of God's plan for the church has been ignored by the modern evangelical church in America. It seems that what the Bible has to say about internal integrity is simply too harsh, too controversial, too difficult, and too combative for churches whose concern is primarily larger congregations and cash flow. Clearly, Christians need to rekindle the fires of holiness and integrity by restoring accountability and discipline to the church.

Third, Christians need to restore genuine spiritual refreshment to the church. Yes, church membership involves duty, responsibility, commitment, service, obedience, deference, and sacrifice. Yes, Christians should go to church to learn, to share, to serve, to give, and to work. But, first and foremost, they are to relax in the joy of the Lord as they collectively recall the divine order of redemption.

The modern church has lost sight of this important reality and, as a result, the people of God come away from worship no more refreshed, no more ready for the battles ahead, than when they went in. Ignoring sanctity, sanctuary, and sacrament, most evangelical churches practice: "lecture hall" worship, "entertainment hall" worship, or "existential encounter" worship. They ignore the rich legacy of the past and rush headlong into modern diversions and distractions. The modern tendency to turn the church into an "ecclesiastical Disneyland" is a far cry from the biblical ideal of a vibrant, dynamic, and vivifying wellspring of strength, hope, and gladness. There can be no question that if this nation is to be spiritually revived, Christians will have to return to the sure and secure foundations of true worship, restoring genuine spiritual refreshment to the church in our day.

That's where the rubber really meets the road.

9

Recent Trends in the Arts

Leland Ryken

Art as a Substitute Religion

*T*he secularization of Western culture was accompanied by the elevation of art to the position of a substitute religion to replace Christianity. We may think this is a movement limited to artists and does not extend to the masses, but we should not quickly conclude this. The case has been made that in our own secular culture, movies and popular music have replaced the pulpit as the leading influence on people's thinking and values.

There is a right and wrong Christian response to such idolatry. The most common response has been for Christians to say, in effect, "See—this is what contact with the arts leads to. A person had better stay away from art." But this is to adopt an unbiblical scorn for art and to turn the whole artistic enterprise over to the unbelieving segment in our culture.

Let us remember that the non-Christian mind elevates much besides art to the status of a substitute religion. We do not avoid cars or ball games or clothes or science or good works because some people have made idols of them. The Bible teaches us to value art. We can love it without worshiping it. The Christian doctrine of creation should spare us from both the worship and the rejection of art.

LELAND RYKEN is professor of English at Wheaton College, Wheaton, Illinois. His writings include *Worldly Saints, Words of Delight,* and *Windows to the World.*

The Artist as Superior Genius

Before the nineteenth century, there was an underlying agreement that what set writers, painters, and musicians apart from ordinary people was their skill with their chosen artistic medium. What distinguishes the artist, in this view, is an ability, just as cooks have the ability to prepare food and doctors to diagnose and treat illnesses.

But the romantic movement of the nineteenth century introduced an important shift by defining artists, not by their ability to manipulate the techniques of a given craft, but by their personal and moral qualities. In this theory, art is not a voluntary creative activity but an inherent superiority of person. Artists thus became viewed as a separate race of great souls.

Once this attitude became entrenched, it produced some notable and unfortunate results in the lives of writers, painters, and musicians. Arrogance was only the beginning of woes. Much more troubling was a prevailing belief among artists that their genius put them above ordinary morality. The personal lives of artists, especially in the twentieth century, have frequently been sordid. Some of the best known of such artists have committed suicide. Reading their biographies reveals not only the moral aberrations of the artists themselves, but also the assumption of some biographers that their subject's genius makes him or her exempt from ordinary morality.[1]

Naturally, the belief of artists that they could do as they pleased affected the works of art they produced. Art increasingly became an assault on traditional morality and a shock to conventional standards of good taste.

The Christian View of Art as God's Gift

A Christian worldview finds no place for such a theory of the artist as superhuman. The Bible describes how God endowed the artists who beautified the tabernacle. Here we find the Christian view of the artist in kernel form, and the important idea is that God is the ultimate source of artistic talent. He endows artists with the specific abilities that their art requires. Artists, like everyone else, are the recipients of grace. They are stewards of what has been given to them. God gave them the gift of artistic ability, not for unrestrained self-indulgence, but to glorify God and serve their fellow humans.

It goes without saying that the very idea that anyone is above morality is repugnant to everything we find in the Bible. No one, whether king, priest, or servant, is exempt from moral criticism in the Bible.

The Isolation of the Artist

Beginning late in the last century, writers, artists, and musicians self-consciously cultivated their alienation from their society. They flaunted their scorn for the middle-class masses. They lived in communities of artists (especially in Paris) in splendid exile from their native culture. "By example and reason," says one scholar, "they announced the independence of art, its freedom not only from society and moral convention but from nature itself."[2]

Such exile naturally affected the art, literature, and music that artists produced. Above all, it produced a new obscurity in the arts. Writing and painting for self-expression rather than communication, artists produced works that few can understand. These works exhibit structural disjointedness and esoteric allusions instead of relying on the inherited cultural framework of myths and symbols. The resulting obscurity has made most modern art and literature inaccessible to all but a handful of people who study it in college courses.

The Christian Ideals of Community and Servanthood

What does the Christian faith say about a movement that removes art from the population at large? Before we denounce obscurity in modern art, we should acknowledge that not all modern art is equally inaccessible. Some of it is on a par with the poetry of Shakespeare and Milton or the symphonies of Beethoven or the paintings of Rembrandt. Great art is never transparent. It requires and then repays serious effort from a reader, listener, or viewer. Once a person has gone to the initial intellectual effort to master a piece of modern art, he or she can "walk into" the work and possess it at will.

Having said that, it is also true that most modern art, music, and literature does not aim to be accessible to society at large. I see no reason why a person should feel guilty about leaving such art untouched. Communication is a two-way street. There is enough great art from the past to go around. If modern artists are uninterested in communicating, they should be granted their wish. We can legitimately regard intelligibility in art as a qualifying exam: if it cannot even pass that criterion, we are relieved from inquiring further into its qualities.

But what about Christian artists who must choose a contemporary style in which to compose their works? They should begin with the premise that they are not exempt from the Christian ideals of community and servanthood. The Christian poet John Donne captured the essence of Christian belief about community when he wrote that "no man is an island, entire of itself."[3] The Bible never considers the possibility of an individual achieving full meaning apart from community. The obligation to serve one's fellow humans is written large in both Testaments.

For Christian artists to regard these as their foundational premises will naturally set them apart from prevailing trends. It is the glory of their Christian vocation to see themselves as serving a genuine social function (see 1 Peter 4:10–11). In a Christian scheme of things, no artist has a right to isolate himself or herself from the human race. The reverse is also true: Christians at large cannot exile the artist from their midst.

Subjectivism in Art

The decline of Christianity as the intellectual system that most Americans and Europeans accepted as truth is the biggest cultural movement of the last two centuries. The roots of that decline can be traced back at least as far as the eighteenth century, which is commonly known as "the Enlightenment" or "the Age of Reason." In the two centuries since then, a thoroughgoing secularism has replaced Christianity as the dominant intellectual and moral force in society. In the twentieth century, most artists are either oblivious to Christianity or treat it as an anachronism—a museum piece from the dead past.

When Christianity became just one intellectual force among others, artists could no longer base their vision of the world on a publicly-shared system of values. This was a great watershed in the cultural and intellectual history of the West. Private experience replaced public (shared) experience as the standard of reality. This revolution of thinking about what constitutes reality is well illustrated in William

Wordsworth's definition of poetry: "All good poetry is the spontaneous overflow of powerful feelings."[4] Prior to this time, artists believed that the subject of art was the external world of people and things. Wordsworth's definition is really revolutionary. It locates both the source and substance of literature within the mind of the poet.

The same theory has dominated art and music for the past two centuries. Artist Oskar Kokoschka writes, "Consciousness is the source of all things and of all perceptions."[5] Similarly, two cubist artists theorize that "there is nothing real outside ourselves."[6] This is obviously an artistic manifestation of philosophic relativism. Its working assumption is that truth is whatever is true for a given individual.

What were the implications for art? At its most innocuous, subjectivist theories simply produced a new interest in human psychology as a subject for art. In its more extreme forms, it became another impetus for obscurity in art. Painters, for example, filled their canvases with images that expressed their inner feelings and perceptions but that often represented nothing recognizable to the viewer. Poets developed their private mythologies in apparent indifference to whether the resulting poetry was intelligible to the world at large.

The Christian Conception of Truth

Subjectivist theories, of course, contradict the Christian conception of truth and reality. In a Christian scheme of things, God and everything he created are real and important. Truth moreover, is supernaturally grounded. Artists do not create truth; God is its source and revealer. Truth is not relative to every individual; it exists objectively as God creates and reveals it. Nor should artists deny their ties with the human race in their quest for a purely private reality.

Having criticized the more extreme theories of subjectivity in art, I should add that there is no reason to be as negative about the movement as some Christian critics are. There is always an element of subjectivity in art. Artists necessarily portray reality as they perceive it. Inner feelings and perceptions have been one of the richest subjects of art, from the Old Testament psalms to the latest song. The crucial question is whether an audience can find anything recognizable and universal in what an artist produces.

Nihilism in Art

Twentieth-century art has been dominated by a denial that the universe has meaning. In fact, modern artists have expended some of their best energy and ingenuity in devising forms that will express the meaninglessness they find in the universe. The arts have been the vehicle by which philosophic nihilism and despair have become the prevailing spirit of our age.

The literary tradition of nihilism appears in concentrated form in the so-called absurd movement. It began as "the theater of the absurd" in the middle of this century. What did playwrights mean by "the absurd"? Eugene Ionesco defined his understanding of it thus: "Absurd is that which is devoid of purpose. . . . Cut off from his religious, metaphysical and transcendental roots, man is lost; all his actions become senseless, absurd, useless."[7]

Rooted in a philosophic belief that human life in this world has no ultimate meaning, writers in the absurd tradition applied their ingenuity to inventing plots and characters and literary structures that would strike an audience as absurd. Farfetched situations, bizarre characters, and disjointed jumps from one event to the next became the stock-in-trade of dramatists and novelists. Disorientation of the audience became a chief aim.

There are parallels to the literary tradition of the absurd in the visual arts and music. A familiar type of modern painting is the one in which disjointed fragments are brought together to suggest the subject announced in the title. Surrealistic painters have chosen grotesque scenes and caricatures of people to suggest the absurdity of the world. Painters in many modern movements give their paintings titles that have so little correspondence to the content of the painting that they strike a viewer as absurd.

Modern forms of abstract art also have a foot in this camp. By painting shapes that represent nothing in the real world, abstract artists give us paintings devoid of rational meaning. It is possible to find delight and beauty in the designs and colors themselves, but this is not what most modern abstractionists have in mind. The failure of their paintings and sculptures to suggest anything in the world around us is an implied comment that the world contains no meaning. Faced with the failure of the painting to communicate a recognizable and definite meaning, the viewer has little choice but to conclude that in the painter's view, life does not make sense. Abstract art need not fail to communicate meaning, but in the modern era it usually has done so.

The Denial of Hope

With the loss of belief that the universe makes sense came a denial of hope. Modern art is characterized by a metaphysical and temperamental pessimism. There are several ways in which this pessimism shows itself.

Until the modern era, the Christian and classical traditions generally agreed on certain assumptions about people. They agreed that people, despite all their faults, have a capacity to be good as well as bad. They have within their psyche a reasoning faculty that can control their appetites, emotions, and physical impulses. In this view, people are morally responsible beings with the power of choice. Most of the art, music, and literature produced within this framework of belief portrayed people as significant beings, capable of courage, love, heroism, and other virtues.

Modern art changed all that. Its prevailing spirit is called *naturalism*. Naturalism is a view of people and the universe that is pessimistic and deterministic. It believes that people are the victims of four types of determinism—cosmic, societal, hereditary and psychological. Given these types of determinism, people do not have a significant power of choice. They are the victims of their environment and their glands. Modern literature repeatedly portrays characters carried away by self-destructive and irrational impulses.

Naturalism is also a theory of the universe. It pictures the universe as hostile, cruel, and impersonal. There is no God in this universe that victimizes people. The people who inhabit it are essentially isolated figures, powerless to control their destiny. Naturalism posits a fourfold alienation: people are cut off from other people, from God, from their natural environment, and from their true selves.

Even the subjects that modern artists choose to portray reveal a denial of hope. Modern artists have singlemindedly agreed that ugliness, violence, and human misery are what art today should portray. Everywhere we turn in modern literature, music, and art, we are bombarded with this type of subject matter. In the contemporary section of a typical art gallery, we have no choice but to stare at contorted human forms, despairing faces, ugly city landscapes, and tawdry objects from modern life. Much contemporary music concentrates on dissonance instead of harmony, disorganization rather than pattern, anguish instead of peace. Modern literature seeks by every means available to convince us that the rose bush in front of the house is much less real than the garbage can behind the house.

A Christian Assessment

Enough has been said to suggest how widespread the denial of meaning and hope is in modern art, literature, and music. Christians cannot avoid some contact with such an outlook because it is everywhere in our culture. How, then, should they view the phenomenon?

They can begin with an awareness that these works of art embody attitudes really held by large numbers of people in the twentieth century. It is not an insignificant phenomenon but one that Christians need to understand. If the value of the arts in our day is that they state the problems to which the Christian faith has the answers, then we can accept modern art as "primary data" for defining the problem.

The Element of Truth in Nihilistic Art

Another reason why Christians should not make a simplistic rejection of nihilistic art is that it contains an element of truth. Christianity postulates a threefold view of people and the world: perfect as created by God, fallen and therefore partly evil, and capable of restoration through Christ. The tradition of nihilism expresses part of this truth, though not the whole truth.

According to the Bible, life lived apart from God and biblical values is meaningless. This is the theme of the book of Ecclesiastes, for example. So Christians can begin their assessment of nihilistic art on a note of agreement. Ephesians 2:12 speaks of unbelievers as "without hope and without God in the world." What does that condition look and feel like? For an answer, all we need to do is read some modern fiction and poetry, visit an art gallery, or listen to some modern music.

The Untruth of Nihilistic Art

The agreement between nihilism and Christianity soon ends, of course. This tradition of modern art is guilty of falsifying reality in several ways. It is false first of all by its concentration on the ugly and violent aspects of life. If sentimental, wish-fulfillment art is a false view of reality, so is nihilistic art. There is a realism of grace as well as realism of carnality. The rose bush in front of the house is as real as the garbage can behind the house. The art of nihilism and despair presents an incomplete vision of what is real.

The nihilistic viewpoint also contradicts basic doctrines of the Christian faith. An important aspect of the biblical view of people, for example, is that they are capable of moral and spiritual choice. The deterministic premise of naturalism directly contradicts this view.

Christianity is ultimately a vision of hope. It is based on the Good News, not the bad news. This point has been well stated by Hilda Graef, who begins her book *Modern Gloom and Christian Hope* with the premise, "Our point of view is solely that of the Christian, for whom hope is one of the theological virtues and despair a sin."[8] Christianity is based on a minor theme and a major theme. The minor theme is the fact of evil and despair in the world and in the lives of Christians. The major theme is the redemptive awareness of God's forgiveness and the hope of eternal life. Judged by such a doctrinal framework, we can reach a somewhat paradoxical assessment of nihilistic art as being partly truthful without telling the Truth.

We know from the creation itself that God values beauty and form. The world that God created and declared to be "very good" stands as a model for the type of things that artists should create. Order, design, and beauty are norms for art, rooted in the very nature of God's creation and human creativity.

These norms apply to the audience of art as well as to artists. Jesus told us to "consider the lilies of the field" (Matthew 6:28). It is possible to see a whole theory of art in that great aphorism. What, after all, do we see when we consider the lilies of the field? We see a natural beauty so captivating that "even Solomon in all his glory was not arrayed like one of these" (v. 29). Artistic form and beauty have value because God gave them to the human race. The modern disparagement of artistic form is at odds with a Christian attitude.

The Assault on Morality

Along with the assault on traditional notions about the meaningfulness of human life in this world, the attack on traditional morality has been the most troublesome aspect of modern art. The relation between art and morality is complex and much misunderstood, and it will require patience to untangle the threads. Let me say at the outset that in discussing immorality in modern art and literature I am not talking about censorship. Censorship is what a society decides to do about immoral art. My concern is to discuss theoretically how to determine whether art is immoral.

The morality of art should not be confused with its intellectual truth or falseness. Morality has to do with human behavior, especially between one person and another. Applied to works of art, this involves the behavior portrayed in works of art and the effect of works of art on the behavior of its audience.

Morality enters the artistic enterprise in three ways. In an ascending order of importance, they are (1) the subject matter portrayed in works of art; (2) the perspective toward that subject matter embodied in works of art; and (3) the response of an individual to works of art, literature, and music.

It is easy to define what constitutes moral and immoral art. The difficult issue is determining what works of art fit the definitions. Moral art is art that recommends moral behavior for approval and that stimulates an audience to behave morally. Immoral art offers immoral behavior for approval and influences an audience to behave immorally.

Realism in the Bible

Thinking Christianly about realism begins with an awareness that the Bible affirms the necessity and legitimacy of realism as an artistic technique. The Bible depicts the full range of human depravity and as such adopts the basic strategy of realism. Stories of sexual immorality in the Bible include the stories of homosexuality in Sodom (Genesis 19); the rape of Dinah (Genesis 34); Onan's interrupted intercourse with Tamar (Genesis 38:1–10); Samson and the harlot of Gaza (Judges 16); the "concubine at Gibeah" incident (Judges 19);

the adultery of David and Bathsheba (2 Samuel 11); and the incest of Amnon and Tamar (2 Samuel 13).

Realism also includes the portrayal of violence. Stories of violence are everywhere in the Bible, especially in the Old Testament. Ehud's assassination of Eglon in Judges 3 is a good example.

The presence of realism in the Bible lays down a basic premise for art and its audience: Realism itself is not immoral. If we did not need it, the Bible would not give it to us. As a religious book, the Bible does not escape from life. It uses the technique of realism to tell us something that we need to know, namely, the sinfulness of the human condition and the misery of a fallen world.

The presence of realism in the Bible refutes a common misconception that works of art automatically encourage approval of everything they portray. This is a totally untenable position. Art has two main themes: life as it should be and life as it fails to match that ideal. As with the Bible, much art portrays things that the artist wishes to reject and denounce. The only way to offer a negative perspective on something is to portray it in a negative light. But notice in the meantime that artists have to portray evil before they can show their indictment of it.

In some Christian circles it has become fashionable to reject all forms of artistic realism. I recently saw an interview on national television with a high school student who had won his battle to be exempt from reading Aldous Huxley's *Brave New World* in a literature course. He expressed the belief that this was a victory for God. I doubt that this is so. *Brave New World* is not an immoral book, and its realism is essentially no different from what we find in the Bible.

Legitimate Realism in Modern Art

We can infer from the example of the Bible that one function of art is to present human experience as it really is. If modern life is ugly and depraved and perverted and violent, we can expect modern art to be the same in the subject matter that it portrays. By itself, such realism is not immoral, even though it may be distasteful. Whether or not it passes the boundary of morality depends on how the artist treats the subject. The modern painter Georges Roualt painted prostitutes in such a way as to reveal the devastation and emptiness of sin.

In appropriating what is legitimate in modern realism, Christians may have to put up with some objectionable subject matter in order to gain whatever positive benefits a work has to offer in terms of insight and the enlargement of our sense of compassion. This will surely require a willingness to assess artistic works as wholes. We cannot judge the morality of a book, for example, only by a few isolated passages of realistic description. The question that a Christian must therefore answer is: Does the moral or intellectual significance of a work exceed in value the possible offensiveness of any of its parts? The answer will vary for individual Christians with individual works, and it will even vary for the same person from one occasion to another.

The Immorality of Modern Realism

Although realism is not immoral in principle, much modern realism raises moral problems for Christians. I have said that the Bible affirms realism in principle, but to say only this obscures an important point: The realism of the Bible is realism within definite bounds. Modern realism frequently differs from biblical realism in the following ways:

- The Bible does not contain a preponderance of depravity in its account of human experience. It does not leave the reader with the impression that degradation is all there is to life, or that there is no alternative to ugliness and depravity.

- The Bible does not dwell on the sordid details of sexual immorality. It avoids dramatizing profanity by using narrative summary instead. It does not share the clinical or descriptive approach of so much modern literature and art in the portrayal of sex.

- The Bible never condones the evil that it depicts. A majority of modern art and literature, however, portrays immorality as a normal and inevitable part of human behavior.

The Bible probably does not fix the limits for the kinds of art and literature that we can consider moral. But biblical realism establishes a pattern that Christians can trust. As a model, the Bible strikes a balance. It gives us realism within certain bounds. Biblical realism serves as a reliable model to guide Christian artists and consumers of art.

When we look at modern realism through the lens of the biblical model, we find much that fails to measure up to that moral standard. Four types of realism are particularly troublesome: (1) art or literature that delights in the immorality that it depicts, or that encourages the audience to approve and emulate that immorality; (2) pornography, or art that elicits lustful thoughts and actions; (3) art or literature that is filled with profanity, blasphemy, obscenity, and sacrilege (ridicule of the sacred things of the Christian religion, including God or Christ); and (4) the explicit and unrestrained portrayal of violence. All of these are prominent features of the modern artistic landscape, as they are of modern life. By Christian standards of morality, they are examples of artistic immorality.

The Realistic Portrayal of Sex

Several things are objectionable about the detailed portrayal of sex. We can object on artistic grounds, first of all. Edmund Fuller argues that the criteria for including descriptions of sexuality in fiction should be: What does this illumine? What does it reveal that was not known before or that cannot be left as tacitly understood? Does this add anything to our understanding of character that was not already clear?[9] We can also object to the realistic portrayal of sex on broadly humanistic grounds, as Roland Frye does when he argues that "the primary objection to glandular fiction . . . is simply that it belittles man."[10]

There is a great difference between art that uses sex as part of a thorough analysis of human experience and art that lingers over the details of the human body or sexual activity. The Bible portrays sex in the former but not the latter way. Immersion in art and literature that portray sex in the clinical manner usually does what such art was designed to do, namely, inflame the audience's sexual appetite. At the very least it fills the mind and imagination with sexual images, making voyeurs out of an audience. Jesus extended lust and adultery to include a person's thought life when he condemned the mental act of lust in one's heart (Matthew 5:28). Modern psychology claims that there is an element of possessing in the act of looking at something intently and habitually.

The encouragement that the arts today give us to "let go" is not limited to the sexual appetite. Almost as common are songs and stories that give vent to our impulses to express aggression, anger, violence, and greed. Here, too, we become the sum of our indulgences. The effect of the hedonistic bias that we find in modern art has long been an immoral influence in our society. Christians and moral people in general have reason to be alarmed.

Christians also have standards of purity and morality in regard to the related phenomena of blasphemy, profanity, sacrilege, and obscenity. Obscenity may be one of the things proscribed by the statement in Colossians 3:8 to avoid "foul talk," and it is certainly what is in view in Ephesians 5:4, which prohibits "filthiness and silly talk, or coarse jesting" (NASB). There are, incidentally, vulgarities that may violate a standard of good taste but which fall short of what I am here calling obscenity and profanity.

Christians are responsible for the furniture of their minds and imaginations. What they take into themselves is not morally neutral. It is like food that they digest and that becomes part of them. Some food is poisonous to the system. So are some forms of art, literature, and music.

"Sincerity" Does Not Make Art Moral

It is fashionable in the secular world to condone pornography and blasphemy in art because the artist is serious or sincere in the portrayal of depravity. In fact, to portray immorality seriously may make it more, not less, blameworthy. A scene of illicit love may be portrayed "sensitively," but its sensitivity does not mitigate its immorality and may actually increase it.

Many artists have defended the unrestrained portrayal of human depravity on the criterion of "lifelikeness." If it happens in life, runs this argument, the artist has a right to portray it. But the fact that something happens does not make it morally good either in life or art. Madeleine L'Engle observes that the root meaning of obscene is "offstage; that which should not be seen on stage."[11] Traditional artistic and literary standards have agreed that some forms of human behavior should remain "off-stage."

Perspective as Moral Determiner

The arts take all of life as their domain. Sex, violence, and evil are not themselves immoral topics for artistic portrayal. It all depends on how the artist treats them—in other words, on the artist's perspective. Moral art is not art that avoids evil as a subject, but that finds ways to discredit evil and encourage good. Calvin Seerveld has written that "art is Biblically Christian when the Devil cannot stand it. . . . The Devil cannot stand exposure of sin as sin, dirty, devastating misery for men; it unmasks him."[12]

How does art embody an immoral perspective toward its subject matter? Essentially it does so by offering an immoral attitude for the audience's approval. The means by which it does so include these: making immoral acts attractive; leaving goodness "bereft of its proper beauty";[13] generating sympathy for immoral characters and actions; belittling characters whose actions and attitudes are moral; omitting models of morally good behavior that would serve as a foil to immoral models and thereby offer the audience an alternative; treating immoral acts in a comic tone, thereby prompting a reader to refrain from moral judgment; portraying immoral acts as something people have no choice in rejecting.

By contrast, a work of art possesses a moral perspective whenever an artist constructs it in such a way as to recommend moral behavior. Here, too, there is a wide range of techniques: making the good appear attractive or ultimately satisfying (even when there is a price tag attached); displaying models of morally good behavior in such a way as to make an audience wish to imitate them; generating final sympathy for morally good characters and actions; exposing the self-destructive nature of evil; including foils to immoral behavior as a way of showing that people have a power of choice to resist evil.

The example of the Bible shows that subject matter by itself does not determine the morality of a work of literature. The Bible portrays experiences that are realistic, sordid, and evil. Yet the overall effect of reading the Bible inclines a person to be moral in behavior. It is not hard to see why. The perspective from which evil is portrayed in the Bible is a strongly moral one.

The Final Determiner of Morality in Art

Thus far I have explored the role of subject matter and perspective in determining the morality of a work of art. Both of these are tendencies in the work. But more important in determining the morality of art is something that lies outside of the work, namely, the individual viewer, reader, or listener. No artistic response is automatic. The same work of art produces far different moral responses in different people. Even reading the Bible does not automatically produce moral behavior in readers.

The ultimate responsibility rests with the individual reader, viewer, or listener to be moral in his or her response. When we read a novel or look at a painting or listen to the lyrics of a song, we do not need to be victimized by the perspective embodied in the work. What, after all, happens when a moral reader encounters literature that recommends immoral behavior? The most common response is to be repelled by the immorality that is commended and to have one's own moral resolve strengthened.

If a moral person can assimilate a work of art in a positive way contrary to an artist's intention, the reverse is also possible. Immoral readers can twist a work's inherent moral tendencies, or seize upon isolated scenes that portray immoral behavior, in a perverse way. People who want to do so can treat the Bible as a pornographic book, or can use it to rationalize immoral behavior.

Christians should scrutinize their own moral responses to works of art. Just as all education is ultimately self-education, the only effective type of censorship is self-censorship. Christian consumers of the arts need to be aware of how they are being affected morally by what they read and listen to and view. Works of art are moral and immoral persuaders, but we are not persuaded against our will. If the effect of a work of art is one that pushes us toward immoral attitudes, feelings, or actions, the antidote is simple: we can either cease contact with the work, or exercise a stronger moral control over the influence that the material is exerting. The moral controls on art rest ultimately with the individual.

The Christian and Modern Art

The problems posed for the Christian by modern art are so complex that the general tendency has been to adopt simple responses. These fall into three categories. One is wholesale endorsement of modern art, combined with the attitude that anyone who finds modern art offensive is an ignoramus. Another is wholesale condemnation of modern art. And then there is the desire to resolve the issue with lists of approved and disapproved works. My belief is that the issues must be handled on a much more individualistic basis. The general principles that we establish must be applied by each person in connection with every particular work of art.

I believe simultaneously in the necessity and danger of a Christian's contact with modern art, music, and literature. Christians need modern art because it expresses the mind and soul of their own culture. That mind and soul are not predominantly Christian. I am not asking Christians to approve of the contemporary arts. But the most profound and articulate expression of the modern spirit can be found in the arts.

The media claim to tell us what is happening in our culture, but they are terribly superficial. They bombard us with facts but ignore the meaning of those facts. By contrast, the arts lay bare the inner movements of our own time. We should have contact with modern art, not necessarily because we enjoy it, but because we recognize it as a necessary way of keeping abreast of our own culture.

Furthermore, one function of the arts (though not their only function) is to present human experience and reality as they actually exist. Truthfulness to reality is one of the reasons for art. We have no right to avoid the truth telling impulse of modern art. By presenting human depravity and misery for our contemplation, modern art, at its best and most responsible, aims to increase our understanding of the human predicament in the modern world. One function that such art can fill is to open the eyes of Christians to the needs of people whose physical and moral plight they might otherwise comfortably avoid.

We must also remember that modern art embodies the attitudes really held by large numbers of people in the twentieth century. Modern art records contemporary people's quest for meaning, even when it portrays persons who search for it in such vulgar ways as sexual license and violence. Christians cannot sweep aside the views espoused in modern art as being unimportant, for the fact is that they are important in the culture in which we live.

Moreover, contact with modern art is a way of achieving a sympathetic understanding of non-Christians. Someone has written that "if we truly want to communicate with our contemporaries we must understand them; and there is no more readily available way of understanding them than by reading what they have written for us and for each other."[14] In a similar vein, Roland Frye comments that if "we are to see clearly the ultimate problems of man's life for which Christian truth must have relevance if it has value, we can scarcely do better than to study man as his lot is clarified through enduring literature."[15] One of the lessons that modern art can teach the Christian is that persons who deserve our moral condemnation should at the same time elicit our pity and compassion. We can also be reminded that people who live without hope in the world do not usually enjoy their despair.

Finding a Balance

Our final stance should be a middle-of-the-road attitude that both affirms and rejects modern art. We must affirm its importance as a force in contemporary culture and therefore our need for it as a means of understanding our culture. We can affirm the necessity for some contact with art that portrays evil in a realistic manner since the presence of realism in the Bible leaves us no option on this score. And we can agree that art is intended to be not only a source of artistic pleasure but also a truthful reflection of reality.

Whenever we find ourselves wondering about the legitimacy of Christian contact with modern art, we should stop to consider that we cannot run away from our own society, that we must face its art and values, and that the Bible itself insists on our contact with realism in art. We are left walking a tightrope between the extremes of total rejection and total affirmation. A sense of balance is what a Christian needs. People who are inclined either to immerse themselves in modern art or to avoid it completely probably need to check their inclination.

A Checklist

To summarize the general drift of my comments about the necessity and dangers of modern art, I offer the following questions as a helpful checklist to guide a Christian's encounter with modern art:

1. Does this work of art call my attention to something about either reality or modern culture that I need to know?

2. What is the precise nature of the gulf between this work and my Christian beliefs and values?

3. Does my contact with this work have a negative effect on my Christian beliefs or on my moral behavior?

4. Does the overall cultural or intellectual significance of this work exceed in importance the offensiveness of some aspects of it? Can I minimize the impact of these negative aspects in order to appropriate the larger benefits of the work?

5. If I do not enjoy this work, is there a reason why I should encounter it anyway?

6. Does my contact with this work make me more capable or less capable of being God's person in the society in which he has placed me?

Notes

1. See Roger Lundin's review article, "Modern Poets, Modern Madness," *Reformed Journal* (June 1984): 16–20.

2. William York Tindall, "Exile," the opening chapter in *Forces in Modern British Literature, 1885–1946* (New York: Knopf, 1947), 3.

3. John Donne, "Meditation 17" in *Devotions upon Emergent Occasions.*

4. William Wordsworth, "Preface to Lyrical Ballads," 305.

5. Oskar Kokoschka, "On the Nature of Visions," in *Theories of Modern Art,* ed. Chipp, 172, 174.

6. Albert Gleizes and Jean Metzinger, "Cubism," as excerpted in *Theories of Modern Art,* ed. Chipp, 214.

7. Eugene Ionesco, as quoted in Martin Esslin, *The Theatre of the Absurd* (1961; reprint, Garden City: Doubleday, 1969), 5.

8. Hilda Graef, *Modern Gloom and Christian Hope* (Chicago: Henry Regnery, 1959), vii.

9. Edmund Fuller, *Man in Modern Fiction* (New York: Vintage, 1949, 1958), 83–84.

10. Roland M. Frye, *Perspective on Man: Literature and the Christian Tradition* (Philadelphia: Westminster, 1961), 64.

11. Madeleine L'Engle, *A Circle of Quiet* (New York: Farrar, Strauss, and Giroux, 1972), 168–69.

12. Calvin Seerveld, *A Christian Critique of Art* (St. Catharines, Ontario: Association for Reformed Scientific Studies, 1963), 52.

13. This phrase comes from J. R. R. Tolkien, "On Fairy-Stories" in *Essays Presented to Charles Williams,* ed. C. S. Lewis (Grand Rapids, Mich.: Eerdmans, 1966), 79.

14. Virginia Mollenkott, *Adamant and Stone Chips* (Waco, Tex.: Word, 1967), 81.

15. Frye, *Perspective on Man,* 84.

10

Violence in the Media

Donald E. Wildmon

C ompared with all other advanced societies, the United States is by
far the most violent country in the world. Our rape rate is many times
higher than that of the United Kingdom. We have more homicides in
Manhattan than all of England, Scotland, and Ireland combined. Our
homicide rate is ten times that of the Scandinavian countries. Presently, *crimes of violence* are increasing at four to five times the rate of
population growth.

This aggressive behavior is increasingly directed toward women
and young girls. Since 1933, the increase in the rape rate in the
United States exceeds 700 percent. This means that the chances of a
woman getting sexually assaulted are seven times greater now than
then. That clearly indicates a change in male attitudes about sexual
aggressiveness toward women. Why the change in male attitudes?
Many studies indicate that in TV programming, sex is commonly
linked with violence.

Dr. Victor Cline of the Department of Psychology, University
of Utah, in summarizing the relationship between TV violence and
violence in society, noted that there are twenty years of behavioral

DONALD E. WILDMON is a United Methodist Church minister and the
founder and president of the American Family Association. He is a well-
known media watcher who has told his story in *Don Wildmon: The Man
the Networks Love to Hate.*

studies linking exposure to media violence with violent behavior. Cline stated: "I do not think that any fair reviewer . . . can deny that the media are one important contributor to the violence problems in our society."

Cline went on to state that "repeated viewing desensitizes the observer. . . . We lose the capacity to empathize with the victim. Man's inhumanity to man (or woman) becomes a spectator sport we develop and cultivate an appetite for no different than in early Rome."

What does research tell us about television violence? In two separate studies by the University of Pennsylvania, children were asked, "How often is it all right to hit someone if you are mad at him?" The study showed that children who were heavy viewers of television responded more often that it is "almost always all right." This and other studies have given parents justifiable cause for concern over the violent content of today's network television.

A Legacy of Fear

The Foundation for Child Development made a survey of 2,200 children, ages seven to eleven. They found that children who are heavy TV watchers were twice as likely as other children to report that they "get scared often." Violence is a shoddy way for networks to get a rating at a low price. But the price society pays is costly—very costly. Studies show that heavy viewers of television are more likely than light viewers to answer questions about the real world in terms that reflect the world according to television. Heavy viewers are more inclined to be overly fearful of their own chances of becoming a victim of violence.

The National Coalition on Television Violence (NCTV) reported that aggressive behavior and an inclination to violence can best be predicted by two factors. First, children who are punished more harshly and rejected more often by their parents become more violent. Second, the more violence a child watches on TV, the more violent an adult he or she will become. These results came from the longest follow-up study ever done on human aggressive behavior. The researcher, Dr. Leonard Eron of the University of Illinois at Chicago, followed more than 400 third-graders first studied in 1960.

Research by Dr. Paul J. Fink of Thomas Jefferson University in Philadelphia found that children and adults who watch prime-time TV are more prone to hostility and to seeing the world as a dangerous place. According to the NCTV, more than 2,000 studies confirm the relationship between viewing violence and real violence.

A Question of Responsibility

The networks have a unique way of dealing with these studies. In the summer of 1983, NBC released what it called a "new study" on TV violence. The study found no causal connection between television violence and aggressive behavior in children. Three of the researchers were NBC staffers. This "new study" was conducted from 1970 to 1973!

In reporting the tension between TV executives and newspaper TV critics, *Advertising Age* says each group distrusts the other. Consequently, the networks try to avoid talking to the press. And the critics are fed up with contradictions that surface when the networks *do* talk. The article gave this example: "A network official will take great satisfaction in pointing out that an episode of 'Happy Days' in which the Fonz gets a library card apparently spurred thousands of children to do the same thing within days. But in almost the next breath, the same executives will say TV does *not* influence viewers' behavior. The stance is an effort to wriggle out of addressing questions on the impact that TV sex and violence have on viewers."

Networks have consistently refused to accept responsibility for crimes committed in imitation of graphic, gratuitous violence shown in their programs. Alfred R. Schneider, vice-president of ABC, told a group of Florida college students that violence was very profitable for his network and that ABC had no intention of changing its practice. An article reporting on Schneider's speech said that the financial returns in airing violent shows are a factor in deciding how much violence is too much. "I work for a company that has to have a profit," Schneider stated.

The Media Institute released the findings of a study concerning crime on television. Done by the research team of Drs. Linda and Robert Lichter of George Washington University, the study turned up some interesting information. The study found 1.7 crimes per show, more than two per hour. Murder was by far the most common crime on TV, with TV crime more than 100 times more likely to involve murder than real-life crime.

The study brought to mind a quote by comedian Red Skelton concerning the networks. "They sell violence," Skelton said. "Now they say this doesn't affect your mind in any way whatsoever, but if you can subliminally sell a product in thirty seconds, what does one hour of filth or violence do to your brain?"

Criminals Imitate TV Crimes

Frank Mankiewicz wrote a book called *Remote Control*. He said that he could not find a police chief in any major city in America who was not convinced that much of the crime with which he was dealing originated on television. He cited the example of Rod Serling who wrote a movie called *Doomsday Flight* in which a terrorist placed a bomb on an airplane which was set to go off if the plane dipped below a certain altitude. The skyjacker then broadcast his demands for ransom while the plane was in the air. While the movie was still in progress, a threat exactly like that on television was reported to police. Within the next few months, nine more similar threats were reported in major cities. Serling later said that he was sorry he had written *Doomsday Flight*.

In Bellevue, Kentucky, a teenager copied murder scenes from the movie, *Helter Skelter*. The young man told police that he "just wanted to know what it felt like to kill" because his girl friend had just left him. Consequently, he was charged with slashing to death a sixty-eight-year-old man and pouring acid over the body. He allegedly dragged the body into the apartment of his estranged girlfriend's sister. There he used lipstick to write "helter skelter" on the bathroom mirror. Then he used the victim's blood to write the same phrase on the bedroom mirror. A friend of the accused said they had watched the television movie *Helter Skelter* shortly before the murder. The movie tells the story of California mass murderer Charles Manson. When the movie first aired on network television, more than nine murders were traced to it.

Remember *The Executioner's Song* on NBC? It was the movie about Gary Gilmore. Following the program, twenty-year-old Jeffrey

Alan Cox shot his seventy-seven-year-old grandfather four times in the head (similar to a scene on the program). He then turned on his seventy-two-year-old grandmother and shot her four times in the head. Both were killed instantly. Family members and law officials said they feel the movie triggered Cox to kill. He had no previous record.

Topeka, Kansas, police detectives in the juvenile division concluded a case in which a thirteen-year-old boy molested a four-year-old girl. One detective said the action was inspired by curiosity and not for sexual or violent reasons. The boy had seen several sex scenes on cable television and wanted to find out what sex was about, the detective said.

Jeffrey Gurga admitted stabbing to death Kathleen Pearson and wounding her daughter Jeannine after breaking into their Chicago apartment. Gurga, a former assistant state's attorney in Illinois, said he did not know either of the women, but was acting out fantasies based on violent scenes he studied on video cassettes. A lawyer in private practice, Gurga would walk the streets at night armed with a knife and fantasize about stabbing the women he encountered. Finally, he decided to act out what he had seen.

The Link Between Pornography and Rape

The more pornography men and women are exposed to, the less they consider rape a serious crime, according to one study. Eighty male and eighty female college undergraduates were randomly assigned to one of three groups. Over the six weeks of the study, a "massive exposure" group saw thirty-six porno films, each about eight minutes long; an "intermediate exposure" group saw eighteen porno and eighteen nonporno films, also lasting about eight minutes each; and a "no exposure" group saw thirty-six nonporno films of the same length. The researchers asked members of the various groups to suggest an appropriate prison term in the case of a local man who had been convicted of raping a hitchhiker but had not yet been sentenced. Men who had watched the nonporno films recommended sentences averaging ninety-four months, nearly twice as long as the sentence recommended by the men who watched the porno movies. Women who watched the porno films recommended sentences of seventy-seven months; women who did not watch the porno films recommended 143-month sentences. The results verify that the more we become desensitized to pornography, the less we consider rape to be wrong.

Another study done by researchers at the University of Wisconsin and UCLA confirmed that violent films spur some males to sexually assault females. The authors said their research showed conclusively that viewing violence—especially sexual assault—will motivate some male viewers to violent acts toward women. About 35 percent of the men surveyed indicated they would consider assaulting a woman if they knew they would not be caught, the study reported. The study indicates that television has desensitized viewers to violent behavior and reinforced myths that women enjoy being sexually assaulted and that some women "are asking for it."

Dr. Neal Malamuth of the University of Manitoba sent hundreds of students to movies. One group watched *Swept Away*, a movie about a violent male aggressor and a woman who learns to crave sexual sadism, and a second film called *Getaway*, about a woman who falls in love with the man who raped her in front of her husband, and how the two of them taunt the husband into committing suicide.

A second group of students were sent to see two control films, *A Man and a Woman* and *Hooper*, each containing scenes of tender romance and nonexplicit sex. Within a week of viewing the films, an attitude survey was administered to all students participating. Dr. Malamuth found that exposure to the films portraying violent sexuality *significantly increased male acceptance of violence against women.*

Commenting on these findings, Dr. Victor Cline of the University of Utah stated four effects of repeated viewing of violent sexual presentations: (1) they stimulate and arouse aggressive *and* sexual feelings, especially in males; (2) they show and instruct in detail *how* to do the acts; (3) the acts are in a sense legitimized by repeated exposure; and (4) there is increased likelihood the individual will act out what he has witnessed. Common sense has been saying the same thing for centuries.

Alaska and Nevada lead all other states in readership of pornography per capita. They also have higher rape rates than all other states. Alaska is number one and Nevada is number two in both categories. These facts appeared in a carefully researched study by Murray Strauss and Larry Baron, sociologists at the University of New Hampshire. The study also found "an unusually high correlation between sex magazine readership and the rape rate" in other states.

A Minnesota program to treat sex offenders requires rapists to swear off hard-core pornography, which one psychologist there describes as being "like a shot of whiskey to an alcoholic." It is a proven fact that when people become addicted to pornography, they become more likely to commit sex crimes. Consider these examples:

- *From New Jersey:* A young boy, exposed to pornography by a man, became so aroused that he brutally raped and murdered a ten-year-old girl.

- *From New York:* Girls, aged nine and twelve, told police a bookstore owner showed them pornography, then abused one of them. Thousands of pornographic publications were found in the shop when the man was arrested.

- *From Texas:* A fifteen-year-old boy viewed his father's collection of pornography, became sexually aroused, then dragged a nine-year-old girl into the bushes and molested her.

- *From Ohio:* A rapist confessed that he had been reading pornography prior to his assault of a woman on her way to church.

- *From Iowa:* A man was convicted of kidnapping and murdering an eight-year-old girl, and kidnapping and raping a ten-year-old. He confessed that one of the girls reminded him of young girl he had seen in a pornographic magazine, which incited him to the sexual attack and, ultimately, the murder.

Charles Keating, founder of Citizens for Decency through Law (CDL), gave some sobering testimony before the Senate Judiciary Committee. "Police vice squads report that 77 percent of child molesters of boys and 87 percent of child molesters of girls admitted trying out the sexual behavior modeled by pornography," Keating said. In one group of rapists, 57 percent indicated they had tried out the sexual behavior they had seen depicted by pornography. One of the many specific examples Keating offered was of seven Oklahoma teenage males who gang attacked a fifteen-year-old female from Texas, forcing her to commit unnatural acts. Four of the teenagers admitted being incited to commit the act by reading pornographic magazines and looking at lewd photographs.

Two brothers, aged seven and nine, in St. Petersburg, Florida, sexually assaulted an eight-month-old girl, who died in the attack. The testimony stated that the sexual abuse of the infant, with a pencil and coat hanger the boys picked up in the bedroom, mimicked acts seen in porno magazines their mother kept around the house. The mother acknowledged she kept pornographic magazines and that the boys could have had access to them. The infant was found on the floor in a bedroom where the two young boys were sleeping. She died shortly afterward. Medical examiner Joan Wood testified that the cause of death was "blunt trauma" to the chest and abdomen. She said it was consistent with one of the boys kneeling on the baby.

Stories similar to these can be repeated again and again. Police files are filled with such cases. Innocent people are victims of pornography. Still, otherwise respectable companies keep selling pornography because it brings in money. According to police sources, in the Los Angeles area alone pornography made more money than Sears & Roebuck made nationwide. The *Los Angeles Times* reported that some law enforcement officials estimate organized crime pockets about half of the $6 billion porn purse. Robert L. Niklaus in *Religious Broadcasting Magazine* wrote that pornography is now the mob's third greatest money-maker, behind narcotics and gambling.

The Rise of Child Pornography

Child pornography has, in recent years, become a malignant cancer in the life of American society. According to Dr. Shirley O'Brien, University of Arizona human development specialist, child pornography flourishes, though it is illegal. O'Brien's findings are reported in a book aptly and simply titled *Child Pornography*. Dr. O'Brien reports being shocked at the magnitude of the problem and says that, because it is such a lucrative industry, it will be difficult to stamp out. In her book Dr. O'Brien considers child pornography anything that relies on sexual exploitation and abuse of children used as models or actors. Informed estimates of their numbers range up to 600,000 nationwide. That includes boys and girls as young as three years and as old as eighteen, but mostly ten- to sixteen-year-olds.

"These children are too young to know what they are getting into," she says. The harm done to the child, even if not physical, is real and long-lasting. That harm was the basis for a U.S. Supreme Court decision which upheld a New York State law against child pornography. The decision allows states to use a different free-speech standard for child pornography than they use for other material.

The trend toward visualizing children as potential sex partners is visible even in commercial advertising. Brooke Shields was fifteen years old when she started advertising jeans. But more recent Jordache jeans ads feature girls nowhere near their teens wearing lipstick, eye makeup, and sexy hairstyles. In their December 1983 edition, *Harper's Bazaar* presented a photo spread entitled "Fabulous Christmas Fantasies: Tiny Treasures." Four full-page photos feature a beautiful little girl—perhaps six years old—in provocative poses. The cherubic child stares mournfully from the four-page spread, her golden hair frizzed and piled high in adult styles, her sad eyes framed with adult makeup, her lips painted in garish hues of red, no hint of clothing in the chest-up photos. Her tiny fingers caress bottles of popular perfumes, each sensually described in the accompanying copy. *Harper's* writers chose such suggestive phrases as "the first feminine impulses that lead to a woman's delight" and "fragrances to express romance . . . seduction with just a hint of innocence."

Ann Wolbert Burgess, a researcher in the field, says that the public is becoming desensitized to the thought of youngsters as sex objects. Burgess is associate director of nursing research for the Boston Department of Health and Hospitals. In an address at the third annual Sexual Abuse Conference, she cited two examples of child pornography in advertising. According to the Fort Worth, Texas *Star-Telegram,* Burgess told the conference that a recent issue of *Gentlemen's Quarterly* showed a nude six-year-old girl in a shirt advertisement. Burgess asked what is it about the ad that would sell a shirt? *Gentlemen's Quarterly* is aimed primarily at the affluent professional man. It covers a wide range of subjects of interest to men, but is not normally comparable to men's pornographic magazines. It causes one to wonder exactly why the editors (and the advertiser) chose to exploit a nude child to sell shirts to men of upper social class.

A law enforcement task force on child pornography, child prostitution, and the kidnapping and selling of children has shown that the United States is the world's leader in using children for sexual exploitation and abuse. FBI agent James Murphy stated that children from three years old and up are being kidnapped for sex services and pornography. "You can order a child by height and weight," Murphy stated. According to the CDL Reporter, many of the children are murdered by the pornographers after they are finished with them so that they cannot testify. And if all this isn't enough, consider this: The Federal Bureau of Investigation data indicates that one of four twelve-year-old girls in the United States will be sexually assaulted during her lifetime.

Cliched Arguments

Those who get involved in the battle for decency will sooner or later run into some or all of the following arguments. We hope that these suggested answers will prove helpful in your fight for decency. (Some arguments and answers are adapted from material supplied by *Morality in Media,* an organization headed by Father Morton Hill that deals primarily with pornography and related issues.)

What right do you have to tell me what I can watch on television?

The question is faulty. Only the networks and local stations decide what is going to be on television. The proper question is, "What right do you have to become involved in the process of deciding what is to be shown on television?" And we have every right. Each local station is licensed by the government to broadcast in the public interest. The Federal Communications Commission encourages the public to become involved in the broadcasting process. Even the National Association of Broadcasters, in its code of ethics, encourages individuals and parents to become involved and make their views known to the broadcasting industry. We have been told to become involved in the process by our government and by the broadcasting industry itself. Would you deny us that right?

Some people like to see violence and sex and hear profanity on television. Shouldn't they have the right?

Some people would like to see child pornography on television. Shouldn't they have that right? That some people would like to see something on television is no reason for it to be on television. Television programming should make a positive contribution to our cultural, social, mental, emotional, and spiritual well-being, not appeal to and exploit our prurient interests.

Do you believe in censorship?

When asked this question, simply throw it back to the one who asked it. "Do you believe in censorship?" (The usual answer is, "No, I do not.") Follow up by asking, "Do you believe it is OK to show child pornography on television?" Unless totally devoid of morals, taste, and common sense, this person has climbed into his or her own trap.

Ever since communication began, there has been censorship. Every word ever printed, every word or scene ever aired has been censored. It all depends on who is doing the censoring. Are we for government censorship of usual programming? No. We are for corporate responsibility on the part of the networks as well as by the sponsors.

If you don't like what is on, turn off the television. That will solve the problem.

Would you also say to me if you don't like crime in the streets, stay in your house? Would you say to me if you don't like drunk drivers, stay off the highways? We are a society, not a group of isolated individuals.

To illustrate this: A mother and her young daughter in California watched an exceptionally good movie on television entitled *Born Free*. When the same network carried a movie entitled *Born Innocent*, the mother and daughter thought it might be the same type of movie and began to watch. Very early in the program was a graphic scene of a young girl being raped with a plumber's helper. The mother immediately got up and turned off the set. Two days later, her nine-year-old daughter was raped with a beer bottle by a gang of children and youth. The children and youth were imitating the movie they had seen on television. Turning off the television is noninvolvement, and problems are never solved that way.

Do you presume to have the right to tell an advertiser which programs he can help sponsor?

We don't tell an advertiser which programs he can help sponsor. The advertiser makes that decision. We cannot tell him where to spend his money because it is his money to spend. But we have an equal right to spend our money where we desire just as that advertiser does. And if the advertiser wants to put his money into low-quality, immoral, or anti-Christian programming, then we certainly have the right to spend our money with other advertisers and to encourage our friends to do the same. In fact, we have a responsibility to spend our money where it will do the most good.

Don't you think television should deal frankly with reality? After all, violence, sex, and profanity is a part of the world in which we live.

Yes, television should deal with the real world. But love, truth, compassion, beauty, and other positive values are also a part of the real world. Why should television dwell primarily on the ugly and ignore that which is beautiful?

Watching television has never corrupted anyone; neither has a book ever corrupted anyone.

Then watching television has never helped anyone, and reading a book has never helped anyone. If that is true, we should do away with all our schools because they aren't doing any good. No, the truth of the matter is that all television is educational television.

What is television currently teaching? It is teaching that sex has no morals attached, that violence is a legitimate way to solve conflict, and that profanity is acceptable language. Television too often ridicules those values which made our country strong and which we have long held as worthwhile to pursue. This can only have a detrimental effect on our society.

Pornography is harmless; a presidential commission report said so.

The Majority Report of the Presidential Commission on Obscenity and Pornography was called a "scientific scandal" by many in the scientific community. It was rejected by the U.S. Senate by a vote of sixty to five. The Hill-Link Minority Report of that commission was read into the record in both houses of Congress as a "responsible position on the issues." The Hill-Link Report cited numerous instances where evidence was suppressed when it went counter to the predetermined "findings" of the majority report. The Hill-Link Report and the chapters by Dr. Victor B. Cline in *Where Do You Draw the Line?* exposed the majority report for what it was. In addition, studies in the Hill-Link Report show linkages between exposure to obscene material and sexual deviancy, promiscuity, affiliation with criminal groups, and more. However, extremists who want obscenity laws repealed (as the majority report recommended) began a campaign in early 1977 to have the report resurrected and considered a valid study.

The Supreme Court in *Paris Theatre v. Slaton* (June 1973) said: "The sum of experience, including that of the past two decades, affords an ample basis for legislatures to conclude that a sensitive, key relationship of human existence, central to family life, community welfare, and the development of human personality, can be debased and distorted by crass commercial exploitation of sex."

You can't legislate morality.

On its face, this cliche is absurd because every law legislates morality. Every law sets some standard for its citizens, and every citizen must ultimately make the moral decision to obey or disobey. Private morals are private; public morals are the business of the entire community; and the officers empowered by the community are to defend the welfare of the community against the willful minority. Commercial obscenity is public business. It is public morality that obscenity laws are designed to safeguard, not private morality.

Obscenity is in the eye of the beholder. What is obscene to you may not be obscene to others.

This implies that obscenity is subjective. It is not. It is the description or depiction of specific sexual activity, the description or depiction of which is prohibited by law to protect the common good. It is as objective as stealing or murder.

I'd rather see people make love than see violence. War, poverty, hunger, and violence are the real obscenities. Sex is not obscene.

Of course sex is not obscene. It is the design and creation of God. It is the debasing abuse of sex that is obscene. Today, as in the past, the judiciary definitely specify certain abuses of sex as obscene. And violence is inherent in pornography. There is no love in pornography. It is totally loveless, debasing women, children, and humanity in general.

Freedom of expression is protected by the First Amendment.

It most certainly is. But the Supreme Court has always held that obscenity is not protected by the First Amendment. It is not a protected expression, any more than libel or slander are. Obscenity is not a First Amendment issue. It is a crime, and most of the traffic in hard core pornography in the country is controlled by organized crime.

Who are you to tell me what I can see or read? You are imposing your morality on me.

The United States Supreme Court has said that what you do in the privacy of your home is your own business. But your privacy right does not extend to the marketplace. Nobody can tell you what to see or to read. But the community can tell you what movies and literature can and cannot be sold or distributed. The community sets up standards for itself and has a right to legislate to protect those standards. No one person is imposing their morality on anybody. It is the consensus of the community that determines the standards of public decency.

Obscenity is a victimless crime.

There is no such thing as a "victimless crime." In every crime there is a seller or seducer, and a purchaser or seduced. That person is the immediate victim, and society is the ultimate victim, for with each seduction the moral fabric of society is diminished. The "victimless crimes" theory is an insidious attack on almost all laws dealing with public morality, maintaining there is "no victim" when "consenting adults" indulge in drugs, prostitution, obscenity, homosexuality, adultery, incest, gambling, etc. For centuries, civil communities have maintained laws against such behavior as detrimental to the public health, morals, and welfare.

When "consenting adults" go to see a dirty movie, no one is being harmed.

Regarding so-called consenting adults, the United States Supreme Court said in its *Paris Theatre* decision: "We categorically disapprove the theory that obscene films acquire constitutional immunity from state regulation simply because they are exhibited for consenting adults only. Rights and interests other than those of the advocates are involved. These include the interest of the public in the quality of life, the total community environment, the tone of commerce and, possibly, the public safety itself." (If we followed the "consenting adults" theory, we would have never outlawed dueling in this country.)

If pornography were allowed to flow freely, people would get bored and the problem would take care of itself.

The boredom or satiation theory is invalid. Heavy users of pornography do not get bored. They go deeper and deeper into more and more bizarre forms of it. Pornography is addicting.

Denmark is often brought up when the boredom theory is espoused. Denmark legalized pornography, the argument goes, and porn profits dropped because people got bored. Denmark's porn profits are falling, but not because of boredom. Underworld infiltration of the porn industry, gangland violence, and tie-ins with traffic in narcotics forced Copenhagen police to close down dozens of smut dens, and all live sex shows have been outlawed.

How do you define obscenity?

How I define obscenity is not the issue. The Supreme Court has defined obscenity to the satisfaction of most. It said obscene materials are those which "taken as a whole appeal to the prurient interest in sex, which portray sexual conduct in a patently offensive way, and which, taken as a whole, do not have serious literary, artistic, political, or scientific value."

But the Supreme Court left it to communities to decide what is obscene.

This is an oversimplification, and a misleading one. Community standards are not the only test for obscenity, but part of the test. In 1973 the Court said: "The basic guidelines for the trier of the fact must be: (a) whether 'the average person, applying contemporary community standards' would find that the work, taken as a whole appeals to the prurient interest . . .' (b) whether the work depicts or describes, in a patently offensive way, sexual conduct specifically defined by the applicable state law," etc. It is the "trier of the fact," a jury or a judge who decides what is obscene under the guidelines.

Why bother enforcing the law? The adult bookstores and porno movie houses keep operating, while their owners are in the courts.

Continuous, vigorous enforcement of the law is the answer. When arrests and prosecutions begin, the sex industry is put on warning. Prison sentences, fines, and legal fees will put the pornographers out of business. Atlanta, Jacksonville, and Cincinnati have rid their cities of a great deal of pornography through vigorous, continuous enforcement of the law. And experts say that with aggressive enforcement of federal law, the back of the porno industry would be broken in eighteen months.

But I want to see cableporn in my home, and I pay to see it. If you don't want it, you don't have to subscribe to it.

You might pay for it, but once the cable operator transmits pornography through that wire, it is released to the community. It becomes the community's business, and the community can legislate against it. And the law is aimed, not at you, but at the cable operator who transmits the cableporn to you. You might also want heroin in your home and pay for it, but it is against the law for the seller to sell it to you.

A law prohibiting cableporn would interfere with the First Amendment rights of the cable operator, with the free flow of information.

There is already a federal law prohibiting the broadcasting of the obscene, indecent, and profane, and it has never interfered with the free flow of information in broadcasting. Cable casting, the U.S. Department of Justice has decided, does not come under the purview of the broadcasting law because it is transmitted through wires. There is almost no regulation on cable TV and there should be. There should be the same regulation of cable as there is of broadcasting. Different technology or not, it comes through the same instrument, the TV set, into the home.

Godfrey Ellis, professor of family relations at Oklahoma State University, says the sexually explicit shows on cable TV may be billed as adult entertainment, but children are frequently the viewers. He thinks children who watch adult programs may become sexually precocious or aggressive. In a sample study of 450 sixth-graders who watch cable, Ellis found 66 percent of the children watched at least one program a month that contained nudity, violence, or heavy sexual content.

In addition, there have been complaints from many areas of the country that the signals of cableporn channels are "bleeding" over onto the sets of people who don't subscribe to them. Audio signals are clear and unscrambled; video signals fade in and out clearly. There is no lock box that is a match for a child's curiosity.

11

The Facts on the Family

Gary L. Bauer

A few years ago social analyst and commentator Ben Wattenberg wrote a book that I don't believe received enough attention. It was titled *The Good News Is the Bad News Is Wrong.* Wattenberg argued that in spite of the headlines to the contrary, America was really in much better shape than most people believed. I believe that Wattenberg, in his enthusiasm, overstated his optimistic case. But in many ways he was very close to an important truth.

No one denies that we must confront some difficult challenges. A lot has gone wrong in recent years. A tremendous amount of work will have to be done if we are to rebuild our homes and neighborhoods, stabilize our families and get economic growth going again. But lost in all of the negative statistics and headlines of despair are the hopes, solid values, faith, and the love for hearth and home that have always motivated our people and formed the foundation for the nation. These great national resources can, and must, be replenished in each generation.

Bill Bennett has often observed that we are a traditional people. Put some Americans on an uninhabited planet, and we will do what

---

GARY L. BAUER is president of the Family Research Council, Inc., a Washington, D.C., based center that advocates family values in public policy. He is coauthor of the best-selling book, *Children at Risk,* with Dr. James C. Dobson, president of Focus on the Family.

the early colonists did. First, we will build some houses for the safety of our families and try hard to turn them into homes. We will build a church to give thanks for our blessings and ask for the Lord's protection. Finally, we will build a school, hoping that somehow we can give our children a better shot at life than we had by helping them to know more. We are traditional, and we are looking for ways to put those values back to work.

One of my great frustrations during the time I served in government was the inclination of bureaucrats and social scientists to spend all their time dwelling on what was not working. All the attention and resources are focused on the dysfunctional family, the failed school, and the declining neighborhood. Wouldn't it be better for us to examine what works, and to build on those strengths to solve the pressing problems we know we must confront?

As it turns out, there is a lot of good news. Away from the unreality of Washington, D.C., and the fake glitz of Madison Avenue and Hollywood, the same rock-solid values prevail in the heartland of America.

Political analyst and commentator Fred Barnes has observed that,

> Families who hold to traditional values get scant media attention, and the little they get is often scornful. Still, their values thrive—not in trendy restaurants and boutiques, but all over America in homes with children. The old virtues are quietly exalted in suburbs and rural areas and urban residential neighborhoods where families live.

Everywhere, even in the wreckage of our modern culture, there are signs of life that seem to point to an overwhelming desire to return to basic values. A Massachusetts Mutual Life Insurance Company study discovered that Americans were placing increasing importance on family values and were turning away from materialism as a guiding principle in their lives.

There has also been a significant increase in the percentage of Americans who said that respecting one's parents and respecting one's children are their most important values. And in a dramatic shift of attitudes since 1989, 84 percent of adults strongly agreed that "family is the place where most basic values are instilled"—a rise of 22 percentage points.

Perhaps the best news of all is that we are rediscovering the joys of family life and of children. For most of this century the trend lines have been against the values of hearth and home. More mothers entered the work force, more infants were placed in child care, more boys and girls became latchkey children, more marriages failed, and more couples chose careers over nurturing. Often these decisions had good reasons. Many couples couldn't pay for their basic necessities without two incomes, a new emphasis on equality opened opportunities in the work force for women who weren't there before, and some marriages ended because the women in them would no longer tolerate physical abuse. No one is in a position to second-guess these decisions, but a price has been paid in the overall health of our children.

"From the child's point of view, the break-up of the family has been very unambiguously unhappy," says Karl Zinsmeister of the American Enterprise Institute. "The data are monolithically worrisome. None of these circumstances—divorce, single-parent families, step-parent families—are healthy. There is no precedent for what has happened in any other time, in any other place."[1] Now, increasingly, Americans are looking for ways to return to a strong family life and put children first.

Mom Rediscovered

A few years ago at a conference on children, best-selling author Sylvia Hewlett shared a story about her successful effort to convince a national accounting firm—Arthur Anderson—to begin a day-care program at work. The day-care center was necessary because many of the women at the company put in sixty-hour weeks after the birth of their children.

This solution was no doubt good for Arthur Anderson. But the story prompted one analyst to ask, "What kind of human society urgently encourages its new parents to hold sixty-hour-a-week jobs as if nothing changed when their child was born? . . . Is tax preparation and figure juggling (or any other paid occupation) really so urgent and noble an undertaking as to justify sacrificing the welfare of our children?"[2]

There are now signs that a growing number of women are deciding that children come first. In fact, a new consensus is emerging on the importance of maternal care in the raising of children.

- A 1989 *Washington Post*/ABC News poll found that eight out of ten parents with children under age fourteen believe it is best for children to be cared for by a mother at home.
- A 1989 University of Michigan study found that most employed mothers opting for care by family members do so out of preference rather than necessity.
- A 1989 *USA Today* survey found that 73 percent of all two-parent families would have Mom stay home full time with the children if money were not an issue.

This parental preference for care by family members is widely shared by the public at large. For example:

- A 1989 Lou Harris poll found that 82 percent of the American public believes care by parents or other family members is superior to care by nonrelatives.
- A 1989 poll commissioned by the Massachusetts Mutual Life Insurance Company found that Americans believe parents having less time to spend with their families is the single most important reason for the decline of family values in our society.
- A 1989 Gallup poll found that by a five-to-two margin, Americans believe it is better for families to make economic sacrifices so that children can be cared for by a mother at home than to maximize family income to improve their economic standing.

Back to the Home

The increase in the proportion of Americans concerned about children in day care is only one indication that the work-and-family pendulum is beginning to swing back toward home. According to surveys taken by the Yankelovich, Clancy, and Shulman polling firm, the proportion of all employed women who would consider giving up work indefinitely if they no longer needed the money shot up eighteen percentage points (from 39 to 57 percent) between 1989 and

1990. Similarly, the proportion of teens who told the American Chicle Youth Poll that they want their mothers to stay home jumped from 34 percent in 1986 to 48 percent in 1990.

Most surprising of all, 23 percent of employed baby boom women, the major recipients of the new equality of opportunity in the work force, say they plan to quit work *altogether* within five years. If it happens, this would be an extraordinary shift in attitude.[3]

Even professional feminists are conceding that the pendulum is swinging. Feminist philosopher Betty Friedan now admits, "In the first stage of modern feminism there was a defensiveness which was probably necessary against defining women only in terms of their child care and family roles." But now, "It's time to change the rhetoric and admit that many women want nothing more than to stay home with their children."[4]

Nearly 30 percent of working women polled last year in the Yankelovich survey responded that "wanting to put more energy into being a good homemaker and mother" was a good enough reason to consider giving up work entirely. This is the highest figure in more than twenty years and an 11 percent increase over 1989.

My colleague, William R. Mattox, Jr., director of policy analysis at the Family Research Council, has reviewed all of the research and polls and reached a startling conclusion: "During the past two to three years, there has been nothing short of a dramatic change in the way in which women and men view questions of work and family. The pendulum appears, at least at an attitudinal level, to be swinging back in the direction of home. Men and women, in large numbers, are expressing concern about not having enough time for their children."[5]

It is unlikely that many women in the '90s will abandon the work force permanently. Economic pressures alone will probably prevent that. But many women are looking for alternatives.

Working at Home

With the advent of more convenient technology from FAX machines to home computers, an increasing number of mothers are finding ways to work from home. This almost ideal approach can help provide badly needed income while also making it possible to be there when children come home from school.

Other women do appear to be taking a new look at "sequencing"—going in and out of the work force to accommodate their family situation at the time. The idea of being a superwoman who can hold down a full-time job, keep a home, nurture children, and then go out for a night on the town with her husband is increasingly seen by many women as an unrealistic lifestyle.

Sequencing is not a new concept. Arlene Rossen Cardoza, the author of a book entitled *Sequencing,* has pointed out some pretty well-known examples of women in public life who took time out from their careers to nurture children, including former British Prime Minister Margaret Thatcher, former United Nations Ambassador Jeane Kirkpatrick, and U.S. Supreme Court Justice Sandra Day O'Connor.

Countless women who are not household names are doing the same thing. As our family grew, Carol shifted from working full time, to working part time, and finally to being a full-time homemaker. I suspect when our children are older Carol will reenter the job market. In the meantime, we are fortunate to be able to get along financially without a second paycheck. Not every family can. Millions of women who don't want to be away from their children have been forced into the workplace—and that is a national tragedy.

Family Time Famine

Changing attitudes are at least partly rooted in a growing perception that parents today do not spend enough time with their children.

This perception is based on reality. A recent Family Research Council study found that parental time with children has declined roughly 40 percent since 1965. Americans also increasingly sense that unfriendly cultural changes have made unhurried parental time with children even more important today than it was a generation ago. Whereas June and Ward Cleaver's biggest worry was that their sons might get caught up in some of Eddie Haskell's schoolboy pranks, today's parents have to contend with much weightier fears: drugs and guns in schools, sex abuse in day care, teen pregnancy, AIDS, and youth suicide.

In confronting such problems, however, parents today have fewer allies. A generation ago, parents looked to the schools, youth organizations, and even the media to reinforce the values they wanted transmitted to their children. Far from being allies, these social institutions today are often viewed by parents as part of the problem rather than part of the solution. Thirty minutes of the Fox Network's "Married . . . with Children" and a trip to the school-based condom dispensary help to explain why.

It is too early to tell just how much the growing concern about America's family time famine is affecting parental behavior. There is some recent evidence that the decades-long rise in maternal employment has stalled and may even be receding a bit. These trends may continue. A lot of young people have grown up without much parental attention. They are now part of the twenty-something generation that is entering young adulthood and preparing for careers and families of their own. There are some indications that this generation intends to commit more time to family and children than their parents did.

They're not thinking just about so-called quality time either. Chicago's Leo Burnett ad agency has studied the mood and tastes of the twenty-something generation. It discovered "a surprising amount of anger and resentment about their absentee parents." Burnett's research director said, "The flashback was instantaneous and so hot you could feel it."[6] Nearly 65 percent of this generation is saying that they will spend more time with their children than their parents spent with them. "My generation will be the family generation," says Mara Brock of Kansas City. "I don't want my kids to go through what my parents put me through."

Here Comes Dad

It is not just mothers who are rediscovering the job of raising children to responsible adulthood. Many fathers, too, are beginning to reevaluate their priorities. As James Levine, director of the Fatherhood Project, a nonprofit clearinghouse, says, "Fathers are beginning to talk about the same issues that working mothers are struggling with. They are trying to figure out ways to cut down from their 12 hour work days. They're leaving the office early enough to eat dinner with their kids and then they're working at home for a few hours."[7]

The *Wall Street Journal* has highlighted this trend, although it has focused on highly paid executives who have more leeway to rearrange their priorities than do many working-class families. One executive who took a 50 percent cut in pay so he could spend more time with his family was quoted as saying, "I used to be on the train to work before they were even awake, but now I can get them off to school. And I have memories I never would have had—like seeing my daughter's face light up when I meet her at the school bus. That's become more important to me than power and prestige."[8]

Hollywood and Home

Even in jaded Hollywood, the land of quick divorce and avant-garde lifestyles, there seems to be the stirrings of a renewal of hearth and home. Sigourney Weaver, the star of the *Alien* movies, has publicly talked about how her priorities have changed with marriage and children. Speaking of the challenges in raising her daughter Charlotte, she said, "I've much more patience and energy than I would have predicted as someone who never really was interested in children. It's what do you want at the end of your life? Do you want to have 50 films? . . . Or do you want pictures of your grandchildren? It's great women have to face that dilemma.

"When people talk about the power list, a lot of us (women) who could be on it have better things to do. Which is taking care of our kids and families. And that's a lovely thing to do with your life."[9]

Harrison Ford can boast of starring in three of the five all-time box office hits. He has an eight-hundred-acre spread in Wyoming, a home in Los Angeles, and an apartment in New York. But when asked about his accomplishment and his wealth, he talks instead about his two young children, Malcolm and Georgia. "It seems like all I've been doing for the last 25 years . . . I realize that what's most sustaining is having kids."[10]

The reordering of priorities can be seen in the movies coming out of Hollywood, too. It is no coincidence that three well-received movies in 1991 had this as a central theme—*City Slickers, Regarding Henry,* and *The Doctor.*

These Hollywood stars are not leading the way, however. They are just reflecting the changes in attitude that are taking place in many communities and neighborhoods. We have seen it among our own circle of friends in the "go-go" world of Washington, D.C. Many mothers are switching to part-time work in order to have more time with their children. Some of my male friends have made conscious decisions to be home earlier and forgo weekends at the office. It is more than being burnt out; it is a renewed awareness of what life's richest rewards are and where they are to be found. Family bonds are never "junk."

This shift didn't occur overnight. *Newsweek* magazine reported several years ago that Americans were ready to choose family over money. The Gallup poll captured the mood when it asked, "Which do you feel is more important for a family these days: to make some financial sacrifices so that one parent can stay home to raise the children or to have both parents working so the family can benefit from the highest possible income?" A parent at home won handily by 68 to 27 percent.

In fact, given a choice of two career paths—one with flexible full-time work hours and more family time on a slower career track—the other with inflexible work hours on a faster career track—78 percent chose the slower, family-oriented career path.

Rabbi Harold Kushner, the author of *When All You've Ever Wanted Isn't Enough* believes the '90s and beyond will witness a significant change in attitudes:

> We are going to see a more idealistic America, where career professionals are going to say, "My integrity is more important than my income, my family is more important than my job title, watching my daughter in her ballet performance or watching my son in his Little League game is more important to me than working late at the office."[11]

Kushner contends that for a long time we bought into three myths:

- Doing something that makes money is more valuable than doing something that shapes people's souls.
- Working with numbers is more valuable than working with human beings.
- Dealing with adults is more valuable than dealing with children.

But now we see the myths for what they are. Now home and family beckon.

Not by Bread Alone

I am not suggesting that economic growth is not important. A vibrant economy enables families to care for their children, buy a house, and provide for the future. The steady economic growth of the '80s resulted in more than 18 million new jobs. When that growth stopped in the early '90s, there was real pain and suffering.

But more of us seem to understand that the biggest assets we have cannot be readily tallied in a financial statement. By the same token, the most important resources a nation has cannot be computed in its gross national product. There is nothing wrong with wealth, but things alone are not enough to make life worth living.

It is a poor man who has never fallen in love nor held a crying child, regardless of what his bank statement says. There are many individuals of modest means, even poverty stricken, who are rich with friends.

Instinctively, most of us know these things even though our culture sometimes entices us down a dead-end road in the pursuit of power, fame, and money. For many of us it takes a crisis to get our priorities in line. For some, unfortunately, the truth is discovered too late.

Lee Atwater, in the final months of his life, wrote movingly about life and love. I knew Lee personally. He had a reputation as a tough competitor, and he was. We had our share of disagreements. When you took on Lee, you always knew when it was over that you had been in a fight.

On March 5, 1990, Lee's world abruptly changed. When he got out of bed that morning he was on top of the world. In 1988, at the age of thirty-seven, he had managed George Bush's winning presidential campaign. He was rewarded with the chairmanship of the Republican party—thus realizing one of his lifetime goals. His delightful wife, Sally, was pregnant with their third child. Lee was nailing down plans to cut a rhythm-and-blues album with B. B. King, one of his idols, fulfilling another dream. As Lee put it himself, "I was one cocky guy."

Later that day he was giving a major fund-raising speech in Washington. He was delivering the speech with his usual enthusiasm, when suddenly his left foot started to shake. Lee tried to press ahead with his remarks, but then the whole left side of his body began to move uncontrollably. Eventually he collapsed and was rushed to George Washington University Medical Center. By that evening he had been given the devastating news that he was suffering from a brain tumor and was in a fight for his life.

In the months that followed, Lee fought the killer inside him and he also fought to understand what was really important in life. Suddenly walking in the corridors of power didn't seem so significant. Lee confessed that he "felt guilty about the degree to which my career and my illness had robbed me of critical time with my children." He was able to reconcile with his father, who was also fighting cancer. He came to know God and spent long hours in conversation with friends who could help him develop his faith.

In one of the last articles Lee wrote, he talked about the acquisition of wealth, power, and prestige. Then he confessed, "What power wouldn't I trade for a little more time with my family? What price wouldn't I pay for an evening with friends? It took a deadly illness to put me eye to eye with that truth, but it is a truth the country can learn on my dime."

Not many of us can name the top ten corporate executives in America, or ten leading U.S. senators. Few, except for political junkies, can name the members of the Bush cabinet or the biggest Wall Street high rollers. But all of us can name our best friends and the people who love us. Our own experiences tell us what is really important.

The Family That Eats Together

Even the family meal is making a comeback! A *New York Times/ CBS News* poll found that eight out of ten people had eaten dinner with their family the night before. And the experts are now conceding that such time together is of great importance. William Mattox of the Family Research Council has written,

> One of the things that makes the family strong is the tendency to gather together for regular rituals and routine activities that everyone is part of. The meal is the most routine and the most symbolic. It's a rich time for social interaction between family members and a time when emotional needs are nourished.

When I worked at the White House I often infuriated some of my colleagues by my insistence on being home for dinner whenever possible. It was worth the heat I took.

Don't misunderstand me. If dinner at your house is anything like dinner at mine, it is not all sweetness and light. It is around that table that I often hear from Sarah for the first time about a spelling test that didn't quite work out or a long explanation from Zachary about why he wasn't a good boy today. Victories and good news are brought to that table, and so are childhood hearts broken by a first love. In that brief hour together we shed the load of worries we have been carrying all day and help tend to each other's wounds.

Carol always fixes a healthy meal, but the real sustenance received is not on our plates, but in the words that pass between us. There won't be that many more years when the Bauer family will be able to routinely gather around the table together at the end of a long day for a meal "well talked over." Elyse, our oldest, is only a few years away from college. I will miss these simple times when we, as a family, renew our souls as much as our bodies.

Call Me Old Fashioned But . . .

The daily papers are filled with stories about child abuse, drunkenness, violence, and family disintegration, but these are still the exception, not the rule. According to the Times Mirror Center for the People and the Press, 86 percent of us agree with the statement, "I have old-fashioned values about family and marriage." Nearly as many (70 percent) agree that "there are clear guidelines about what's good or evil that apply to everyone regardless of their situation." So much for the situation ethics that are being taught in many of our elementary and secondary schools, as well as on our university campuses. Most of us just don't buy it!

Baby boomers, usually thought of as liberal and hostile to traditional values, now appear to be leading the charge back home. When they were asked whether the country was better off or worse off because of recent changes in our culture, 59 percent of the boomers chose worse off because of more permissive attitudes on sex, 67 percent said worse off because of increased single parenting and 72 percent selected worse off because of less religious training for children.

Being a boomer myself, I am not surprised by these results. In my own circle of friends and acquaintances, I have seen tremendous tragedy, most of it due to the breakdown in values. It is among my generation that illegitimacy has skyrocketed and venereal diseases have gone wild. Many of my peers have relearned the old lessons of life the hard way—by suffering the consequences of breaking those rules.

I believe these hard knocks are reflected in the way many in my generation are now raising their own children. The conventional wisdom thought these liberal younger Americans would reject the so-called old-fashioned approach. But when *Rolling Stone* magazine posed that question, they were surprised to find that nearly half of the baby boomers now embraced the same child-rearing values that their parents emphasized. They wanted their children to experience a strong family bond, religion, duty, responsibility, and accountability. They wanted them to believe in the work ethic and honesty and to have good manners. Another 32 percent were emphasizing discipline and respect for authority as they raised their own children.

When Carol and I were newly married it was easy to be theoretical about how we were going to raise our children before we had any. But there is nothing like a toddler to give you a little perspective on the need for discipline. And there is something about the admiring glance of a fourteen-year-old boy in the direction of your oldest daughter that gives you a whole new outlook and concern about old-fashioned ideas like virtue and chastity.

Parent Gap

In recent years we have heard a lot about the generation gap, the division between young and old, and the gender gap, the differences of opinions between men and women. But increasingly the defining division of our time may be the family gap. Married people with children have decidedly more conservative views on a host of issues than do single adults and even those who are married with no children. The very act of raising a child, of trying to bring another human being who is dependent on you to responsible adulthood, profoundly alters the way we think about the issues and events of our time.

Carol and I have experienced the transformation in our own lives. Getting married changed some of our youthful attitudes. But it wasn't until Elyse came along, and then Sarah and Zachary, that the changes became pronounced. In college it was easy to engage in purely abstract discussions about drug legalization or theories of child raising. But once you hold a newborn in your arms—your child, flesh of your flesh, blood of your blood—theory recedes and the long arduous task of nurturing and protecting begins.

Youthful Wisdom?

The evidence of the growing shift toward hearth and home is also apparent among the young. A generation that has experienced the trauma of divorce, the absence of parents, and a culture heavily laden with sex and violence may now be ready to look for a more traditional approach.

In fact, Irma Zandl, a "trend predictor" who specializes in working with children, believes that is exactly what is happening. Her work is unearthing a tremendous shift in attitudes among the young.

Zandl reports that many teenage girls are rejecting the role of superwoman trying to balance family and career. Instead they say they want families first with careers to follow later.

She believes these youthful attitudes are a reaction to the trends in the '80s. Many of these young people were latchkey children, and now "they want to come home to a warm house instead of an empty house. . . . They have very positive core values. Family, friends and children are taking a pre-eminent place in their lives." Zandl predicts that these teenagers will start getting married younger and start their families younger—reversing the trends of the last thirty years.[12]

The more conservative trend is apparent in other ways too. A poll released by *USA Today* on sex, morals, and AIDS asked this question: "Does the safe-sex message trouble you because it might condone casual sex?" Fifty-four percent of adults agreed that the safe-sex message was dangerous, but a whopping 63 percent of the teenagers surveyed said they thought it was. When was the last time young people had more conservative attitudes about sex than their elders did? Apparently our children understand the moral implications of this issue even better than some of their parents.

Most young people place a high value on such goals as having children and a happy family life and living closer to parents and other relatives. Significant majorities of adolescents also express agreement with the values of their parents, and generally the number doing so in 1990 is higher than the number in 1975. Over time, young people are likely to reflect the changes taking place in the generation that went through the 1967 Summer of Love and is now enduring the 1992 Winter of Their Discontent and all its second thoughts about the value of the sex-and-drugs revolution.

Aging is itself a conservatizing process, as is marriage, but becoming a parent causes the biggest change of all. (As someone once remarked, "A conservative is a liberal with a teenage daughter.") But the apple, even when young, does not fall far from the tree. In 1990, 71 percent of young people told researchers from the University of Michigan that they agree with their parents about what to do with their lives; 69 percent agreed with Mom and Dad about religion; and 86 percent about the value of education. Admittedly, the numbers for "politics" and "what is permitted" on a date were somewhat less impressive, just under 50 percent. But I predict time will bring those numbers more in line, too.

As young people mature, however, the tendency to return to the nest, emotionally and in every other way, is strong. Just four years after high school, the percentage of young men and women who say that being successful at work and having lots of money are important declines sharply (the latter to under one-third for men and one-fifth for women). The percentages saying it is very important to have a happy family life soar to 87 percent for men and 88 percent for women. No gender gap here! The figures suggest that the vast majority of young people do "go home" in their lifetimes. It's vitally important, of course, that someone be there to greet them when they do.

That Old-Time Religion

At one time or another, roughly two-thirds of the baby boomers dropped out of organized religion, but in recent years more than one-third of the dropouts have returned. More than 80 percent of the boomers consider themselves religious and believe in life after death.

198 • Salt and Light

In fact after thirty years of increased secularization of our public life, most Americans have had enough and appear to be yearning for a return to that old-time religion. Overwhelming majorities believe that voluntary Bible classes and prayers should be permitted in public schools, and 55 percent of us believe that religion has too little influence in American life. Sixty-three percent of us are willing to take our views into the ballot box by not voting for a presidential candidate who does not believe in God.

In the intellectual precincts occupied by our cultural elite the influence of religion on public life is still seen as dangerous. The Supreme Court provided the latest evidence of this foolishness on June 25, 1992 when it struck down as unconstitutional nonsectarian prayers at high school graduations. This was only the latest in a long stretch of cases that seek to separate Americans from our most deeply honored traditions. Justice Antonin Scalia spoke for a minority of the Court but for the majority of the American people when he referred to the Court's reasoning as senseless.

As I listened over dinner with my family to this case being announced on the evening news, I couldn't help but think back to 1962. That was the year of the first Supreme Court decision that struck down prayer to begin the school day. I was a sophomore in high school at the time.

I was so angered by the decision that my classmates and I organized a protest. We plastered signs objecting to the ruling on the walls at Newport High School. We held rallies and led students who agreed with us to local churches for prayer *before* school. More importantly, at the age of sixteen, I decided that I would devote my life to fighting in the public arena for the values of family and faith.

Thirty years have gone by and the Court still has not found its bearings. Few things in life are certain, but this one is: These rulings will be challenged. The traditions of faith, family, and freedom are too deeply interwoven in the fabric of our history for the ruling in this case to endure. Three decades after the Supreme Court's first assault on the religious tradition of communities, the American people still overwhelmingly support the role of religious values and religious observance in public life. The roots of that tradition run too deep, its branches are raised too high, for the Court's mistaken judgment to stand.

On issues of religious liberty, the Supreme Court continues to scrape against the bedrock of the American spirit. It's an awesome conflict to watch, but in the long run I have no doubt that it is the spirit of the people that will prevail.

Some of the most important moments in our home are built around prayer. Our two girls pray on their own now when they turn in for the night. But I usually slip into Zachary's room in the evening to pray with him before bedtime just as my father used to do with me. On the wall of our son's room there hangs a beautiful print of a father praying over his son while an angel bars the window from the evil lurking outside. Not all that long ago I probably would have thought the picture was melodramatic, but now as I tuck in my own flesh and blood and ask God to keep him safe, the evils of the world outside seem very real.

In our universities many young people are taught that when you become "educated" you shed silly, irrational things like faith, religion, and prayer. But in the real world, when life is about begetting and getting through the day, we learn anew that it is faith that gets us to the finish line.

The popular culture still ridicules religion and often treats it like the plague, but that will change too. Even normally secular *Time* magazine believes that the separation of church and state has gone too far. In a special report at the end of 1991, *Time* concluded,

> For God to be kept out of the classroom or out of America's public debate by nervous school administrators or overcautious politicians serves no one's interests. That restriction prevents people from drawing on the country's rich and diverse religious heritage for guidance, and it degrades the nation's moral discourse by placing a whole realm of theological reasoning out of bounds. The price of that sort of quarantine, at a time of moral dislocation, is—and has been—far too high. The courts need to find a better balance between separation and accommodation—and Americans need to respect the new religious freedom they would gain as a result.[13]

That's what the numbers are showing. Poll after poll, study after study, are all pointing to a rediscovery of family values, hard work, religious faith, and a rejection of materialism and hedonism. But polls reflect people's attitudes; they don't always tell us what is actually happening. We may claim to believe one thing while we continue to do another. What about the real world of our day-to-day lives? Are there signs of renewal there? Thankfully the answer is yes.

Notes

1. Karl Zinsmeister, "Raising Children in a Difficult Age," in *Who Will Rock the Cradle?* ed. Phyllis Schlafly (Dallas: Word, 1990), 27.

2. "Whose Values?" *Newsweek,* 8 June 1992, 20.

3. Brad Edmondson, "Burned-Out Boomers Flee to Families," *American Demographics* (December 1991): 17.

4. "Trouble at the Top," *U.S. News & World Report,* 17 June 1991, 42.

5. Terri L. Darrow, "The Sequencing of Motherhood," *Kiwanis Magazine* (March 1992): 35.

6. "Proceeding with Caution," *Time,* 16 July 1990, 58.

7. Michael Kaplan, "You Can Go Home Again," *Ad Week,* 7 May 1990, 14–15.

8. Carol Hymowitz, "Trading Fat Paychecks for Free Time," *Wall Street Journal,* 5 August 1991, B1.

9. Stephen Schaefer, "Weaver, Performing Strong," *USA Today,* 20 May 1992, D1.

10. Tom Green, "Patriot Star Settles Far from L.A.," *USA Today,* 5 June 1992, D1–2.

11. Sarah Ban Breathnach, "Living in a Lower Gear," *Washington Post,* 31 December 1991, C5.

12. "Prognosticator Plugs into Teens' Thoughts, Dreams," *USA Today,* 22 January 1992, D3.

13. "America's Holy War," *Time,* 9 December 1991, 68.

Crisis in American Education

William J. Bennett

*I*n 1983 the National Commission on Excellence in Education released the landmark report *A Nation at Risk,* the closest thing we have had to a national education grievance list. It cited among other problems, poor performance by American students on a variety of international education tests; a decline in scores on most standardized tests; and a decline in student knowledge in crucial subjects such as English and physics. It gave voice to the growing public sense of crisis about our children and their schools. "The educational foundations of our society are presently being eroded by a rising tide of mediocrity that threatens our very future as a nation and a people," the report said. "We have, in effect, been committing an act of unthinking, unilateral educational disarmament." Countless reports since 1983—some issued by me—have further documented a performance that can only charitably be described as mediocre. "American education is to education what the Soviet economy is to the economy," according to Chester E. Finn, Jr., one of the most insightful commentators on American education.

WILLIAM J. BENNETT is currently a John M. Olin senior fellow at the Hudson Institute, Distinguished Fellow, Cultural Policy Studies at the Heritage Foundation, and a senior editor of *National Review* magazine. He has served as U.S. Secretary of Education and as director of the Office of National Drug Control.

Our students score last in math and science in comparison with students of other industrialized nations. A 1989 international comparison of mathematics and science skills showed American students scoring at the bottom and South Korean students scoring at the top (South Korean students perform at high levels in math at four times the rate of U.S. students). Ironically, when asked if they are good at math, 68 percent of American students thought they were (the highest percentage of any country) compared to 23 percent of South Korean students (the lowest percentage of any country), which demonstrates that this country is a lot better at teaching self-esteem than it is at teaching math.

According to the 1991 National Assessment of Educational Progress (NAEP) study, 72 percent of our fourth graders can do third-grade math, only 14 percent of our eighth graders can do seventh-grade math, and only 5 percent of our high school seniors "showed an understanding of geometry and algebra that suggested preparedness for the study of relatively advanced mathematics," i.e., for college-level math.

Math and science aren't the only subjects where American students are left in the backwaters of education. Finn and Diane Ravitch, authors of *What Do Our Seventeen Year Olds Know?* have shown that 43 percent of our high school seniors could not place World War I between 1900 and 1950. More than two-thirds of them did not know even the half-century in which the Civil War took place. And more than 75 percent were unable to say within twenty years when Abraham Lincoln was president.

According to an NAEP-based survey of 21-to-25-year-olds conducted in 1986, fewer than 40 percent were able to interpret an article by a newspaper columnist. And the situation is worse among minorities; just one in ten black young adults and two in ten Hispanic young adults can satisfactorily interpret the same newspaper column. In 1989, *National Geographic* did a survey of geography knowledge. Americans aged eighteen to twenty-four finished *last* among ten countries, including Mexico.

Unfortunately, much of the education establishment, which includes the unions and other "professional" educational organizations, opposes every common-sense reform measure: competency testing for teachers, opening the teaching profession to knowledgeable individuals who have not graduated from "schools of education," performance-based pay, holding educators accountable for how much children learn, an end to tenure, a national examination to find out exactly how much our children know and parental choice of schools. These are reforms most Americans endorse.

With big money pouring into education and with the rise of unionism, the special interests began to control American education. The teacher unions (especially the NEA) and the professional associations increasingly began to show their muscle. Power was slipping away from parents and individual schools and toward them, which was fine as far as the unions were concerned. According to reporter Robin Wilson of *The Chronicle of Higher Education*, the NEA "has attacked parents' moves to gain more control, saying that they have gone overboard and that teachers cannot be effective under parental veto power."

Some of the largest education interests also increasingly aligned themselves with the political philosophy of the left, with the notion that education problems, like most other social issues, were amenable to solutions from Washington. This meant ever more and ever larger programs created and controlled by Washington, and guided and fine-tuned by those who "knew best" the education establishment itself.

The modern-day NEA is primarily a political action organization. It routinely takes liberal and even left-wing stands on political candidates and on many national and international affairs. In recent years, the union's Representative Assembly went on record in favor of teacher strikes; school-based clinics dispensing contraceptives; a nuclear freeze; gay rights; the Equal Rights Amendment; D.C. statehood; and Jimmy Carter, Walter Mondale, and Michael Dukakis for president. It has voted against merit pay for teachers; parental choice; voluntary school prayer; state takeovers of bad schools; home schooling; English as the official language; drug, alcohol, and AIDS testing; nuclear power plants; aid to the Nicaraguan resistance; the nomination of Judge Robert Bork to the Supreme Court; and Ronald Reagan and George Bush for president. And at the 1991 NEA convention, while adopting a measure calling on its members and union publication to monitor attacks on First Amendment rights such as freedom of speech, the NEA invoked a separate policy adopted by the board of directors which ousted the Boy Scouts of America from the convention exhibition hall. Some delegates were also prohibited from displaying anti-abortion material.

Asked to explain this contradiction, NEA president Keith Geibert said it was a "paradox." "I don't apologize for it," he said. "I don't try to explain it."

The record then is clear: the NEA is an organization embodying the philosophy of modern-day liberalism. When power is seized by, or ceded to, an organization of this political and philosophical temperament, it has consequences.

In my visits to schools all over the country, I met and saw many fine teachers; some were members of the NEA who felt that the increasing politicization of their union was doing a tremendous disservice to their profession. Many teachers do not want to get involved in politics in general and liberal political activism in particular, but they feel powerless to resist it. According to C. Emily Feistritzer, director of the National Center for Education Information, "In recent years . . . the NEA's agendas have seemed to veer further and further away from representing the interests of teachers. It is spending millions of dollars annually to support political positions and candidates representing views that increasingly seem at odds with those of teachers."

Defining the Goals of Education

Because of the effects that the guiding philosophy of the NEA and other large education organizations have had on traditional American educational practices, many of our schools lost their focus, their confidence, and a clear sense of their mission. This helped open the way for an all-out assault from the Far Left, and our schools were systematically, culturally deconstructed. Many of the things which mattered most in our schools were removed, and they were set adrift. As a result, today many schools (and many education spokesmen) are no longer able to answer the basic institutional, existential questions: Who are we? Why are we here? And where are we going?

My view, to put it simply, is that the purpose of school is to make students both smarter and better, to develop intellect and moral character. When the American people are asked what they want from our schools, they consistently put two tasks at the top of their list: first, teach our children how to speak, write, read, think and count correctly; and second, help them to develop reliable standards of right and wrong that will guide them through life.

What, then, to do? We must give greater attention to a sound common curriculum emphasizing English, history, geography, math, and science. To do this we have to understand why these subjects were thrown out or weakened in the cultural deconstruction of our schools of the last twenty-five years. In the late sixties and seventies we saw a sustained attack on traditional American values and the place where those values had long had a comfortable and congenial home—the school. Many of the elite correctly understood that civilization's major task is the upbringing of children; if they could alter the ways we raised children by changing the way we teach them, they could then alter American society to suit their view of the world. Academics provided much of the intellectual heavy artillery—citing how endemically corrupt and sick America is. Once the traditional teachings were discredited and then removed, the vacuum was filled by faddish nonsense, and the kids lost.

The gradual watering down of the high school curriculum was one result of this then-fashionable elite critique of America. Schools, like so many other institutions of our society, were seen as "repressive, coercive" institutions, the curriculum as an instrument of oppression, and their students as little better than prisoners. This attitude was summed up by the then liberal critic Neil Postman, who co-authored a book in the late 1960s, *Teaching As a Subversive Activity*. At the time he believed, "The institution we call school is what it is because we made it that way. If it is irrelevant; if it shields children from reality; if it educates for obsolescence; if it is based on fear; if it induces alienation; if it punishes creativity and independence"and Postman dearly believed at the time that it did all these things "it must be changed." (Postman later wrote another book, *Teaching As a Conserving Activity*, in which he recanted his original views.)

According to this view, it was wrong to make students do things they didn't want to do, whether math, homework, or other distasteful pursuits like sitting quietly in a classroom. Testing "dehumanized" students and reduced them to mere "statistics." Basic courses gave way to trendy courses; homework was thought to be outdated and unnecessary.

Too few adults stood their ground to answer the challenge, and to answer the question "Why?" Why, for example, are English, history, math, and science important subjects? Adults sitting on school boards or state boards of education became reluctant to articulate what was academically important and what was not, and lost clarity about what we expected our schools to do.

This confusion and diffidence had particularly damaging effects on school curricula, effects we still feel today. According to *A Nation at Risk:*

> Secondary school curricula have been homogenized, diluted, and diffused to the point that they no longer have a central purpose. In effect, we have a cafeteria-style curriculum in which the appetizers and desserts can easily be mistaken for the main course.

English, history, math, and science gave way to a curriculum lacking substance, coherence, or consistent structure; it was replaced by faddish, trivial, and intellectually shallow courses. If you give the average fifteen-year-old the choice of trigonometry or, say, "Rock and Roll as Poetry" and "Baja Whale Watch," many will opt to take the latter—not because they're stupid or bad kids, but simply because they're teenagers. So schools became laboratories, and students guinea pigs. If there was a bad idea in the land, often the first place it was tried was in the school. If we had problems of order in the classroom, the solution was an open classroom and no order at all. If our students weren't learning history, the solution was not to teach them history but to teach them social studies, often a sloppy amalgam of half-baked, "politically correct" sociological theories.

Increasingly, parents became alienated or disenfranchised from their schools and yielded to the cult of "expertise," the authority of superintendents, "education judges," or administrative bodies. And, as the teachers tell us, more and more parents dropped their children at the doorstep of the school and were gone to pursue their own interests. So parents disenfranchised themselves. When serious teachers are asked the single most important improvement that could be made in education, they invariably say greater involvement and cooperation on the part of parents.

A Question of Excellence

The fundamental problem with American education today is not lack of money; we do not underspend, we underproduce. The American people have been remarkably generous in their contributions to our schools. In 1990 we spent $414 billion on education, roughly $140 billion more than on national defense. In the international competition on education spending, the United States wins the gold medal. In absolute terms we spend more on education than any other nation in the world. And expenditures keep climbing. In 1950, we spent (in 1989 dollars) $1,333 per student. In 1989, we spent $4,931. As John Silber, the president of Boston University, has written, "It is troubling that this nearly fourfold increase in real spending has brought no improvement. It is scandalous that it has not prevented substantial decline." During that period we probably experienced the *worst* educational decline in our history. Between 1963 and 1980, for example, combined average Scholastic Aptitude Test (SAT) scores—scores which test students' verbal and math abilities—fell 90 points, from 980 to 890.

Improving American education requires not doing new things but doing (and remembering) some good old things. At the time of our nation's founding, Thomas Jefferson listed the requirements for a sound education in the Report of the Commissioners for the University of Virginia. In this landmark statement on American education, Jefferson wrote of the importance of calculation and writing, and of reading, history, and geography. But he also emphasized the need "to instruct the mass of our citizens in these, their rights, interests, and duties, as men and citizens."

Jefferson believed education should aim at the improvement of both one's "morals" and "faculties." That has been the dominant view of the aims of American education for over two centuries. But a number of changes, most of them unsound, have diverted schools from these great pursuits. And the story of the loss of the school's original moral mission explains a great deal.

The Abdication of Values

Starting in the early 1970s, "values clarification" programs started turning up in schools all over America. According to this philosophy, the schools were not to take part in their time-honored task of transmitting sound moral values; rather, they were to allow the child to "clarify" his own values (which adults, including parents, had no "right" to criticize). The "values clarification" movement didn't clarify values, it clarified wants and desires. This form of moral relativism said, in effect, that no set of values was right or wrong; everybody had an equal right to his own values; and all values were subjective, relative, personal. This destructive view took hold with a vengeance.

In 1985 *The New York Times* published an article quoting New York area educators, in slavish devotion to this new view, proclaiming that "they deliberately avoid trying to tell students what is ethically right and wrong." The article told of one counseling session involving fifteen high school juniors and seniors. In the course of that session a student concluded that a fellow student had been foolish to return one thousand dollars she found in a purse at school. According to the article, when the youngsters asked the counselor's opinion, "He told them he believed the girl had done the right thing, but that, of course, he would not try to force his values on them. 'If I come from the position of what is right and what is wrong,' he explained, 'then I'm not their counselor.'"

Once upon a time, a counselor offered counsel, and he knew that an adult does not form character in the young by taking a stance of neutrality toward questions of right and wrong or by merely offering "choices" or "options."

In response to the belief that adults and educators should teach children sound morals, one can expect from some quarters indignant objections (I've heard one version of it expressed countless times over the years): "Who are you to say what's moral and what's important?" or "Whose standards and judgments do we use?"

The correct response, it seems to me, is, are we really ready to do away with standards and judgments? Is anyone going to argue seriously that a life of cheating and swindling is as worthy as a life of honest, hard work? Is anyone (with the exception of some literature professors at our elite universities) going to argue seriously the intellectual corollary, that a Marvel comic book is as good as *Macbeth?* Unless we are willing to embrace some pretty silly positions, we've got to admit the need for moral and intellectual standards. The problem is that some people tend to regard anyone who would pronounce a definitive judgment as an unsophisticated Philistine or a closed-minded "elitist" trying to impose his view on everyone else.

The truth of the real world is that without standards and judgments, there can be no progress. Unless we are prepared to say irrational things—that nothing can be proven more valuable than anything else or that everything is equally worthless—we *must* ask the normative question. This may come as a surprise to those who feel that to be "progressive" is to be value-neutral. But as Matthew Arnold said, "the world is forwarded by having its attention fixed on the best things." And if the world can't decide what the best things are, at least to some degree, then it follows that progress, and character, are in trouble. We shouldn't be reluctant to declare that some things—some lives, books, ideas, and values—are better than others. It is the responsibility of the schools to teach these better things.

At one time, we weren't so reluctant to teach them. In the mid-nineteenth century, a diverse, widespread group of crusaders began to work for the public support of what was then called the "common school," the forerunner of the public school. They were to be charged with the mission of moral and civic training, training that planted its roots in shared values. The advocates of the common school felt that the nation could fulfill its destiny only if every new generation was taught these values together in a common institution.

The leaders of the common school movement were mainly citizens who were prominent in their communities—businessmen, ministers, local civic and government officials. These people saw the schools as upholders of standards of individual morality and small incubators of civic and personal virtue; the founders of the public schools had faith that public education could teach good moral and civic character from a common ground of American values.

But in the past quarter century or so, some of the so-called experts became experts of value neutrality, and moral education was increasingly left in their hands. The common sense view of parents and the public, that schools should reinforce rather than undermine the values of home, family, and country, was increasingly rejected.

There are those today still who claim we are now too diverse a nation, that we consist of too many competing convictions and interests to instill common values. They are wrong. Of course we are a diverse people. We have always been a diverse people. And as Madison wrote in *Federalist* No. 10, the competing, balancing interests of a diverse people can help ensure the survival of liberty. But there are values that all American citizens share and that we should want all American students to know and to make their own: honesty, fairness, self-discipline, fidelity to task, friends, and family, personal responsibility, love of country, and belief in the principles of liberty, equality, and the freedom to practice one's faith. The explicit teaching of these values is the legacy of the common school, and it is a legacy to which we must return.

People often say, "Yes, we *should* teach these values, but *how* do we teach them?" This question deserves a candid response, one that isn't given often enough. It is by exposing our children to good character and inviting its imitation that we will transmit to them a moral foundation. This happens when teachers and principals, by their words and actions, embody sound convictions. As Oxford's Mary Warnock has written, "You cannot teach morality without being committed to morality yourself; and you cannot be committed to morality yourself without holding that some things are right and others wrong." The theologian Martin Buber wrote that the educator is distinguished from all other influences "by his *will* to take part in the stamping of character and by his *consciousness* that he represents in the eyes of the growing person a certain *selection* of what is, the selection of what is 'right,' of what *should* be." It is in this will, Buber says, in this clear standing for something, that the "vocation as an educator finds its fundamental expression."

As Education Secretary, I visited a class at Waterbury Elementary School in Waterbury, Vermont, and asked the students, "Is this a good school?" They answered, "Yes, this is a good school." I asked them, "Why?" Among other things, one eight-year-old said, "The principal, Mr. Riegel, makes good rules and everybody obeys them." So I said, "Give me an example." And another answered, "You can't climb on the pipes in the bathroom. We don't climb on the pipes and the principal doesn't either."

This example is probably too simple to please a lot of people who want to make the topic of moral education difficult, but there is something profound in the answer of those children, something educators should pay more attention to. You can't expect children to take messages about rules or morality seriously unless they see adults taking those rules seriously in their day-to-day affairs. Certain things must be said, certain limits laid down, and certain examples set. There is no other way.

We should also do a better job at curriculum selection. The research shows that most "values education" exercises and separate courses in "moral reasoning" tend not to affect children's behavior; if anything, they may leave children morally adrift. Where to turn? I believe our literature and our history are a rich quarry of moral literacy. We should mine that quarry. Children should have at their disposal a stock of examples illustrating what we believe to be right and wrong, good and bad—examples illustrating that what is morally right and wrong can indeed be known and that there is a difference.

What kind of stories, historical events, and famous lives am I talking about? If we want our children to know about honesty, we should teach them about Abe Lincoln walking three miles to return six cents and, conversely, about Aesop's shepherd boy who cried wolf. If we want them to know about courage, we should teach them about Joan of Arc, Horatius at the bridge, and Harriet Tubman and the Underground Railroad. If we want them to know about persistence in the face of adversity, they should know about the voyages of Columbus, and the character of Washington during the Revolution and Lincoln during the Civil War. And our youngest should be told about the Little Engine That Could. If we want them to know about respect for the law, they should understand why Socrates told Crito: "No, I must submit to the decree of Athens." If we want our children to respect the rights of others, they should read the Declaration of Independence, the Bill of Rights, the Gettysburg Address, and Martin Luther King, Jr.'s "Letter from Birmingham Jail." From the Bible they should know about Ruth's loyalty to Naomi, Joseph's forgiveness of his brothers, Jonathan's friendship with David, the Good Samaritan's kindness toward a stranger, and David's cleverness and courage in facing Goliath.

These are only a few of the hundreds of examples we can call on. And we need not get into issues like nuclear war, abortion, creationism, or euthanasia. This may come as a disappointment to some people, but the fact is that the formation of character in young people is educationally a task different from, and prior to, the discussion of the great, difficult controversies of the day. First things first. We should teach values the same way we teach other things: one step at a time. We should not use the fact that there are many difficult and controversial moral questions as an argument against basic instruction in the subject. After all, we do not argue against teaching physics because laser physics is difficult, against teaching biology or chemistry because gene splicing and cloning are complex and controversial, against teaching American history because there are heated disputes about the Founders' intent. Every field has its complexities and its controversies. And every field has its basics, its fundamentals. So too with forming character and achieving moral literacy. As any parent knows, teaching character is a difficult task. But it is a crucial task, because we want our children to be not only healthy, happy, and successful but decent, strong, and good. None of this happens automatically; there is no genetic transmission of virtue. It takes the conscious, committed efforts of adults. It takes careful attention.

Three Steps toward Sound Education

Americans know that we have problems; the issue is on the table. We must regain control of our schools so that they can serve their time-honored purpose of educating children. I believe that to be effective, reform should attack three fundamental flaws in public education: a soft curriculum, a general lack of accountability for results, and a lack of parental choice.

Step One: Strengthening the Curriculum

We have recently begun to make some progress in the curriculum. *A Nation at Risk* recommended in 1983 that every high school graduate have at least four years of English, three of math, three of social studies and three of science. In 1982, only 13 percent of U.S. high school graduates could meet these *bare minimum* requirements. In 1987, we were up to 29 percent. But this is still a dismally low percentage for graduating seniors.

Solid and meaningful years of study means the study of the essentials of these disciplines. Acquiring "skills" should not come at the expense of acquiring knowledge. Students should finish high school knowing not just the "method" or "process" of science or history; they should actually know some science and history. They should know fractions and decimals, and percentages and algebra and geometry. They should know that for every action there is an equal and opposite reaction, and they should know who said "I am the state" and who said "I have a dream." They should know about subjects and predicates, about isosceles triangles and ellipses. They should know where the Amazon flows, and what the First Amendment means. They should know about the Donner party and slavery, and Shylock, Hercules, and Abigail Adams, where Ethiopia is, and why there was a Berlin Wall. They should know how a poem works, how a plant works, and the meaning of "If wishes were horses, beggars would ride." They should know the place of the Milky Way and DNA in the unfolding of the universe. They should know about the Constitutional Convention of 1787 and about the conventions of good behavior. They should know what the Sistine Chapel looks like and what great music sounds like.

Our students should also know our nation's ideals and aspirations. We believe in liberty and equality, in limited government and the betterment of the human condition. These truths underlie our society, and though they may be self-evident, they are not spontaneously apprehended by the young.

These are things we should want all our students to know. We should not hold some students to lesser goals, pushing them into educational backwaters while everyone else is advancing upstream. Albert Shanker once asked a class of average and less than average students: "What should we ask you to read?" After a pause one student raised his hand. "Mr. Shanker," he asked, "what do the smart kids read?"

Not all students have the same abilities, so it is up to our teachers to adapt good material to the level of the student. Good teachers will vary the pedagogy, of course, but they will also retain the substance. Whatever the pedagogy (books, tapes, films, or stories), they must not lose the substance. In certain places in America, there has sometimes been a great zeal to remove certain topics from study. We need to match that zeal for exclusion with a zeal for inclusion.

Step Two: Making Teachers Accountable

A second key education reform is providing for much greater accountability. Today, *there are greater, more certain, and more immediate penalties in this country for serving up a single rotten hamburger*

than for furnishing a thousand schoolchildren with a rotten education.
In fact, there's actually a perverse incentive not to succeed, because if
a school district performs poorly, it usually gets more money based on
the argument that it's doing poorly because it lacks money.

American education and its educators need good, palpable reasons to avoid failure and good, palpable incentives to strive for success. If we are to improve our schools, we must have ways of
identifying and rewarding schools that work, methods that work, and
principals and teachers who work. We should give superintendents
greater authority to run their districts; give principals greater autonomy to run their schools, and teachers greater authority to run
their classrooms; and then hold them all accountable for the results
they achieve. We must have ways of identifying and, if necessary,
moving out those who fail to do their jobs and of identifying and rewarding those who do their jobs well. As the nation's governors put it
in their 1987 report, *Time for Results,* "Someone has to pay a penalty
for continued failure, but it should not be the students." To determine results we must have true reliable national standards. Students
must be tested to those standards and the results (by state, district,
and school) should be made public.

Step Three: Parental Involvement and Choice

A third key education reform is parental choice—full, unfettered
choice over which schools their children will attend. In a free market
economy, those who produce goods and services are ultimately an-
swerable to the consumer; if quality is shoddy, the consumer will buy
someone else's product. It doesn't work that way in public education,
though. Even when armed with adequate information about school
quality (which they rarely have), parents in most places around the
country are not permitted to transfer their children from a bad school
to a good one.

As I told the National Catholic Educational Association in 1985:

All parents, regardless of income, should be able to choose
places where they know their children will learn. And they
should be able to choose environments where their own values
will be extended instead of lost. It's possible that there are

some public schools nobody would choose. They are so bad that they might suddenly find themselves without any students. But I have no idea why we should be interested in protecting schools like that from competition—or any schools from competition. Our worst schools are our non-competitive ones, and that's no coincidence.

The philosophy behind the choice proposal is that we need to break the monopoly currently exercised by state-run schools and allow all schools including private and religious schools to compete for public dollars. A full-scale voucher program would promote a healthy rivalry between public and private schools, as well as among public schools. This is why full-scale choice was, and remains, the linchpin of sound education reform.

Critics of full choice for American parents in the selection of schools argue that choice isn't right: public money should go only to public and not religious schools, and so full choice would amount to a violation of the separation of church and state. They have it wrong. Voucher bills have been proposed, including the one we advanced to Congress in 1986, that are fully constitutional. Most of our critics conceded it to be so. Public money goes to Catholic and Jewish hospitals to care for the public, and public money supports fire and police forces that serve religious institutions. Public money should be for the education of the public, and a child in Catholic, Methodist, or Jewish school is every bit as much a member of the public as a child in a state-supported school.

There's another issue associated with choice as well—social justice. At present, our most affluent families do exercise choice, by buying a home in the neighborhood of their choice, or by sending their children to private school. The poor do not now have that kind of choice. In contrast to the dismal report of the Chicago public schools, Chicago's Catholic schools are graduating 85 percent of their children at a cost of about $2,500 a year and with a fraction of the administrators per student (only 32 central-office administrators for more than 160,000 students). Since many Chicago public school teachers, knowing the relative strengths, choose private schools for their children, shouldn't others be given the same choice? It is a question of social justice.

The critics of elementary and secondary school choice should also acknowledge the inconsistency and even hypocrisy of their position.

The fact is, we already have a system of choice in American higher education and people don't object to it. When we give out billions of dollars every year for students to go to college, with their Pell Grants or their Stafford Loans, they can take them to Indiana University, Notre Dame, Yeshiva, or Liberty Baptist. Indiana University isn't diminished because Notre Dame is a fine school; Liberty Baptist isn't daunted because Notre Dame is a fine school. Broad choice in higher education hasn't hurt public higher education; on the contrary, greater competition has helped it and helped students. Why, then, do we not allow it at the elementary and secondary levels, which are so much more important and formative?

There is an additional benefit to choice. If we invite parents to choose their schools, it can be a good first step in the critical effort of reenfranchising them. Choice among schools is a first involvement in the schools, a critical investment, and it may lead to further involvement, which is something teachers long for. If parents know the results by school of tests with national standards, they will choose more wisely. The more we can do to involve (or reinvolve) parents, the better.

The scholastic success of many Asian-American children has reminded us all of the importance of parental involvement. A few years ago, in the Asian-American community in Riverdale, New York City, teachers and principals were puzzled that their textbooks were being sold at a rate much faster than the number of children registered in classes could account for. They wanted to know why. After doing a little investigating, they discovered that most Asian-American families were buying two sets of textbooks. One set was for the child, and a second set was for the mother, who could better coach her child if she worked during the day to keep up with the lessons. These teachers said that Asian-American children entering school in the fall with no English ability finished in the spring at the top of their classes in every subject. At the Department of Education we repeatedly said that the parent is the child's most important teacher, the child's all but indispensable teacher.

Facing the Future

I believe the ideas I have outlined will work. They're the same ideas we put forward to the Congress during my tenure as Secretary of Education, but almost without exception the Congress rejected these far-reaching reform proposals—not on their merits, not because they wouldn't improve American education, but because our proposals were a direct challenge to the power of the education establishment. The political clout of the NEA and its brethren remains considerable. With few exceptions, Congress does the bidding of the education establishment and not of the general public.

American schools are a long way from where they need to be. Today the battle lines are being drawn over what to do, how to do it, and who gets to decide how to do it. It is a battle over who will control the schools—the educrats who gave us the educational disasters of the sixties and seventies, or parents, taxpayers, and a sizable number of dedicated and able principals and teachers? The fact is, we know what to do; we know what works; we know what we should expect.

The issue, then, is whether we have the political courage and the will to do the job. The future of American education depends on how we answer these questions: Are we willing to reward excellence (merit pay for outstanding teachers and principals)? Are we willing to penalize failure (terminate the contracts of incompetent teachers and bad principals)? Are we going to give parents more say in which schools their children attend (full parental choice)? Are we willing to "deregulate" the teaching profession by making room for men and women of energy, intelligence, and broad backgrounds (alternative teacher certification)? Are we going to insist on high standards (making the receipt of federal student aid or receipt of a high school diploma contingent on passing a qualifying test with real national standards)? Are we willing to get the litter out of the curricula and put the basic subjects back in? Are we going to return to homework? And are we going to stop accepting lame excuses for low performance?

The American people have to answer the tough questions; they have to lead the revolution; they have to take back our schools, for the sake of our children.

13

Rescuing the Earth

Tony Campolo

Facing an Environmental Disaster

*T*he world is becoming dirty and ugly, and it's time to do something about it. In America, more than 7 million cars are junked every year. In New York alone, there are over 70,000 abandoned cars on the streets. We throw away 40 billion metal cans, 26 billion bottles, and 65 billion bottle caps annually. Indestructible plastic appears everywhere. Oil spills pollute our beaches, and chemical rain and expanding industry destroy our rain forests.

Sooner or later we will all get caught up in the environmental movement, because sooner or later we will all get hurt by what is happening to nature. I suppose that becoming a grandfather has heightened my concern about the destruction of the beauty and ecological balance of our planet. I wonder what kind of world will be waiting for my grandchildren when they come of age. Will I have to tell them about whales because there are none for them to see? Will there be no more mountain gorillas in Africa? Will the trees be devoid of singing birds?

TONY CAMPOLO is professor of sociology at Eastern College in St. Davids, Pennsylvania, and also founder and president of the Evangelical Association for the Promotion of Education. He is the author of a number of books including *The Kingdom of God Is a Party* and *Growing Up in America*.

In the midst of such speculations, I cannot help but ask myself, *What is so important for me to have that I am willing to sacrifice the future of my children and grandchildren in order to get it?* Do I so desire to maintain my affluent, wasteful lifestyle that I do not care if my heirs have to live in a cancer-causing, filthy environment? Am I so in love with the things that the media convinces me I want that I am indifferent to the devastation to the environment that results from their production?

In 1962, Rachel Carson published her now famous book *Silent Spring.* In that book, she sounded an alarm that caught the attention of millions. For the first time, large numbers of people became aware of the fact that DDT and other chemicals used to fight insects and to treat the soil poisoned birds and other animals. Carson made it clear that unless we took some drastic steps to change things, entire species of birds and other animals that add beauty, music, and joy to our lives would become extinct.

Smog alerts are becoming increasingly common in cities across the country. Exhaust from automobiles and soot from industrial smokestacks render the air so putrid that it becomes dangerous to breathe. People with respiratory problems are warned to stay inside, preferably in air-conditioned rooms. There are frequent deaths that result from simply breathing the air on "bad" days. Anyone who regularly flies recognizes the unmistakable brown layer of smog hovering over such cities as Los Angeles and Denver.

Something has gone wrong with the weather. It is getting slightly warmer with each passing decade due to the "greenhouse effect." Soda pop cans and styrofoam containers trash our once-beautiful beaches. The bacteria count in the water has become so great that beach closings are now common. Along the New Jersey shore, sewage, pharmaceutical containers, and other forms of medical waste dumped into the ocean wash up regularly on the sand.

A list of impending ecological disasters is readily available, yet there has been little response from the church. And studies indicate that Christian people are the least likely to be concerned about the environment. Evangelical Christians seem to show the greatest indifference. In the face of this catastrophe, there are still Christians who think that being committed to saving God's creation is something that goes with being a bit offbeat. Worse than that, when some of us talk about saving planet earth, some church people whisper under their breath, "I think our friends are slipping away from true Christianity."

Contemporary researchers have discovered that the more theologically conservative church members are, the less likely they are to show any interest in saving our planet from what is certainly an impending ecological holocaust. We are going to have to ask ourselves why. This is an especially important question since the most often quoted verse in the Bible, John 3:16, tells us clearly that "God so loved the *world,* that He gave His only begotten Son" (NKJV) to rescue it from the effects of sin and corruption.

There are those who try to escape from what this verse has to say to us about the environment by claiming that when the gospel of John tells us that "God so loved the world" the word *world* only refers to human beings. Their particular interpretation of John 3:16 implies that God has no deep and abiding concern with what happens to other living creatures or to our physical environment. The salvation of God, they claim, is only meant for *homo sapiens.*

This twisting of John 3:16 belies the fact that in the original Greek, the word for *world* is *kosmos.* And as any lexicon makes quite dear, *kosmos* refers to anything and everything that is in the universe, including the animals, flowers, insects, and fish—God loves them all. It also includes the land and the oceans and the air we breathe. Of course, God loves us humans most of all. But we must not allow his great love for us to obliterate the fact that he loves all of his creation.

To be a Christian is to be concerned for this planet and for those creatures, great and small, which inhabit it along with us. Faithfulness to the Word of God should make us "green Christians"—those whose concern for the environment arises out of biblical imperatives.

Green Christians remind the rest of the church that God, after he created this world, looked on all that he had created and called it "good" (Genesis 1:31). Furthermore, they declare that this same God is brokenhearted over what has happened to us and to our world because we sinfully abused his gift of creation. They know that it was God's heartfelt concern for us and for planet earth that moved him to send his Son into history with the mission to rescue his cosmos and to make it new again (Revelation 21:5). Green Christians are those whose hearts resonate with the heart of God and share a burden with him for his sick and dying creation.

Destructive Chain Reaction

One of the primary arguments for becoming involved in efforts to preserve God's creation lies in the growing awareness that those who are most prone to suffer the consequences of environmental irresponsibility are the poor. As changes in the climate and erosion of the soil through deforestation result in diminished food production, the poor go hungry. As the temperature on the earth's surface edges upward and the world's drinkable water supply becomes more and more depleted, the poor will go thirsty.

Already the poor and weak are suffering the consequences of the exploitation of nature. In the Amazon, the precious rain forest is being systematically destroyed. Every minute a parcel of the jungle, the size of a football field, is leveled. Every year an area of the jungle, the size of the state of Massachusetts, is devastated. The reason is simple. More land is needed for grazing cattle. As the annual consumption rate of beef soars in nations like Japan, Germany, and the United States, cattlemen raze the forests to make room for raising cattle.

The rain forest of the Amazon has been the home of preliterate tribes who lack the means to defend themselves against the encroachment of "civilized" peoples who want their land. These poor and defenseless indigenous people are no match for those who use guns and tractors to take away and to destroy their natural habitat. So innocent people are pushed off their land, lose their homes, and are driven to extinction, all to ensure the beef supply for people who would be a whole lot healthier if they didn't eat so much of it.

There is an even worse consequence of the devastation of the Amazon rain forest—an ongoing famine in Africa. In the Sahel region of Africa, climate changes are making drought and famine inevitable. The rain that makes life viable in this part of the world comes from the rain forests in Brazil. The moisture from the jungle forms rain clouds that float across the Atlantic to fall upon the parched soil of such countries as Mauritania, Senegal, and Mali. But, because the rain forests have been depleted, the rain clouds, so essential for the survival of life in the Sahel, have become increasingly rare. Less rain has resulted in more than a drought; it has created a permanent climate change in the Sahel—a climate change that will mean starvation and death for millions of Africans. It's all connected, you see. We eat hamburgers here; they cut down the jungle in Brazil, and there's a climate change that kills people in Africa.

The chief of a nomadic tribe living along the south bank of the Senegal River told me that for centuries his people herded sheep and goats from place to place throughout the semiarid region. But things changed. The animals died. The chief said that his people were hungry and despairing about the future.

The chief and his people had known many droughts over the years, but he knew that what was happening now was more than a drought. Somehow he knew that this was a climate change. He knew that his people, who had survived centuries of droughts, would soon be no more. He told me with a deep sadness, which defies description, that he was facing the beginning of the end of the history of his tribe.

Something had gone wrong with nature. The elements turned against him, and he did not know why. All he knows is the wind does not feel the same when it blows on his face, and the Senegal River has changed. Rivers do not talk to me, but this chief told me that the river had spoken to him and said that it was dying. He showed me his people, and I saw women trying to nurse their infants from dried up breasts. I saw children with stomachs swollen from malnutrition. There was the feeling of death in the air. What little water was available was being pumped to the capital city so that residents would have enough to drink.

Some of us say that what is happening to this tribe is sin. For the sake of justice, the rain forest must be saved. It is not right in the eyes of God that some people should live in such a way as to cause people in far and distant lands to suffer. If justice is to roll down for those who cannot defend themselves against the power of the rich nations of the earth, the people of God must try to put an end to this oppression.

But you don't even have to be a Christian committed to social justice to get upset over the destruction of the rain forests of Brazil. Consider the fact that the destruction of the Brazilian rain forest is in all probability destroying some special forms of plant life that hold the cures to some of the most terrible diseases and sicknesses in the world today. Most of us have paid little attention to the fact that many of the medicines we use in the treatment of illnesses are compounds derived from plants. Plants develop unique properties that cannot be duplicated with chemicals in laboratories. Often special plants are the only sources of the essential organic pharmaceuticals, the wonder drugs hailed by those who practice medicine. As we destroy the jungles of Brazil, we are destroying thousands of rare plants that have as yet undetermined curative properties for many of the sicknesses that torture us, our families, and our friends. There is no way of telling whether or not, at this very moment, the cure for cancer or for AIDS is being wiped from the face of the earth.

Consider the story told by Jay D. Hair, president of the National Wildlife Federation:

> About four years ago . . . my older daughter Whitney was very ill with cancer. She literally came within a few days of death. She is here today, and she is a beautiful, fourteen-year-old, healthy, completely cured young lady. Why? The drug that saved her life was derived from a plant called the rosy periwinkle. The rosy periwinkle was a plant native to the island country of Madagascar. The irony of this story is that 90 percent of the forested area of Madagascar has been destroyed. One hundred percent of all native habitat of the rosy periwinkle is gone forever. And just at a time when we're learning about the marvels of biotechnology. We are losing entire genetic stocks of wild living resources at a time when we're learning about the potential medical marvels of some of these plants, like the one used to cure my daughter. We are destroying them and their potential values forever. This is a tragedy with incredible consequences to the future of global societies.

Who Is to Blame?

In 1967, Lynn White published an article in *Science* magazine that blamed Protestant Christianity and, more specifically, Calvinism, for the orientation toward nature that has led to ecological disaster.[1] There is no doubt that John Calvin—the prime creator of the reformed theology that has so strongly influenced the development of Protestant Christianity in the industrialized, capitalistic societies of the Western world—had what might be called "a utilitarian view of nature." However, I contend that contrary to

White's understanding, Calvin had more than a utilitarian view of nature. I must point out that in that same commentary on Genesis to which White refers in his article, Calvin also urges us to be good stewards of God's creation. While Calvin may tell us, in accord with his understanding of the Bible, that we have the right to subdue nature and exercise dominance over it, he also tells us to assume responsibility for God's creation. Stewardship over creation means that we should treat creation with the same loving care as Jesus would if he were in our place.

When students of the cultures of Native Americans read a book such as *Black Elk Speaks,* they often blame biblical religion and the attitudes generated by the Judeo-Christian tradition for the loss of the awe and reverence people once had for the natural world. But I believe the sense that animals, flowers, and trees have a spiritual value, which makes them worthy of care, was not lost because of a worldview generated by biblical Christianity. Actually, Christians worship a Jesus who could talk to the wind and the waves (Matthew 8:23), who considered lilies to be more filled with "glory" than anything we humans might create (Matthew 6:28–29 NKJV), and who is a spiritual presence through whom everything in the universe is held together (Colossians 1:1–17). The preachers of biblical revelation, even those in the Protestant tradition, are not the culprits behind the loss of spiritual mystery about the world. It is those hard-nosed scientific rationalists who have taken the life out of everything. They are the ones to blame.

Max Weber, the famous father of German sociology, contended that because of scientific rationalization, man has become disenchanted with his world. Erich Fromm, one of the prime figures in the Frankfurt School of Social Science, makes a similar point in his writings in psychoanalysis.

Fromm said human beings, under the influence of science, have undergone a process of emotional separation from the rest of nature; and therefore we no longer believe we can have any kind of feeling of "oneness" with nature. Even Karl Marx, the sociologist who reduced everything in time and history to material forces, bemoaned the fact that humanity, under the influence of science, had become alienated from the rest of nature and that people had become strangers in their own world.

None of these social scientists considered themselves to be religious. And in the case of Marx, the more blame that could be dumped on religion the better. Yet all of them blamed science, not religion, for the negative and "unspiritual" attitudes people had toward nature.

The loss of mystery and awe about nature and the sense that we alone in all of creation have subjective feelings, these have contributed to the mind-set that accepts the destruction of the environment as a necessary evil. Science has brought on a loss of emotional affinity, and that has caused trouble.

Only people who do not consider the feelings of animals can kill them for fun. Only those who sense nothing "holy" about the forests and the plants can destroy them with little concern. Only those who do not sense the stars and galaxies declaring the glory of God can be indifferent to the pollution that hides them from view.

A world without God is not viewed with a sense of awe. A universe in which his presence is not felt is doomed to abuse. Such a world is primarily the creation of science—or more specifically, a particular kind of science.

The science generated by Descartes and other children of the Enlightenment is to blame. The rationalistic approach to nature fostered in the Enlightenment did the damage. This approach taught us to use what ever we could find in our environment to further our own selfish interests without regard to the consequences. It led us to forsake "creation-care," and to abandon the stewardship which God asked us to exercise when he entrusted this planet into our hands.

Having tried to defend Calvin against White's "bum rap," I think it is far more important to acknowledge that the real cause of our problem lies elsewhere. In the final analysis, it accomplishes very little for scientists and Calvinistic clerics to point fingers at each other. Deep down inside, I think we all know the truth. And that truth is that there is something radically wrong with human nature. There is an innate sinfulness at the core of our being that lies at the base of all of our troubles. The condition called "original sin," is what makes us unwilling to adopt a more socially and environmentally responsible lifestyle.

We live in a time when people seem unable to regulate their own behavior. Most people cannot control their desires even when self-destruction is the result. Appetites for alcohol, tobacco, and cocaine have come to dominate their lives. Sexual drives seem out of control as people risk families and reputations to gratify their hungers.

Selfishness and greed have reached epidemic levels. People seek to get what they want when they want it. We have abandoned moral norms. No one expects us to show loving concern for others. The world is out of control, and all of creation is suffering from the consequences. It is this uncontrolled selfishness that has motivated the destructive behavioral patterns that have polluted and corrupted our natural habitat.

However, the forces that keep us from giving nature some time to recuperate are demonic. We are not simply up against some bad habits that we can overcome through an effective educational program. The problem is more serious than that. The problem is spiritual. We are not fighting against flesh and blood, as Scripture so perfectly explains; we struggle against principalities and powers. We are up against rulers in high places (Ephesians 6:12). Consequently, this flaw in our personality cannot be overcome by good intentions or even by sheer determination of the will.

The ruined world, which begs for a chance at renewal, comes from a sinful lifestyle that is not likely to be abandoned by those who have become accustomed to its comforts. Only the miracle wrought by our repentance and willingness to yield to the work of the Holy Spirit offers any real hope.

The character of people must change. And that can happen only as the result of God's work in our lives. Our values and our definitions of what constitutes "the good life" must radically change, and that can only occur when God breaks through our cultural system and gives us a glimpse of his kingdom and of his righteousness.

Too often, when I read the books or listen to speeches of environmentalists who are not Christians, I recognize a basic shortcoming. Too frequently, they build their pleas for temperance and self-control on enlightened self-interest. Adopting a more environmentally responsible lifestyle, they point out, is the only reasonable thing to do if we know what is good for us. But much more than that is needed. We ourselves have to become completely different people.

An enlightened plea won't work. If we are ever going to change the world, our basic consciousness must be transformed and our essential selves converted.

I believe that a repentant people who have yielded their lives to Christ will find the strength to exercise the kind of self-control that the world needs. In him, we will be able to escape the bondage to the culturally prescribed consumeristic lifestyle that has brought us to the brink of environmental disaster. I believe that in him, we will be able to reject the comforts which we wrongly believe are both necessary and desirable. I believe that in his power, we will be able to opt for a thoughtful, careful way of living which will make concern for others and a sensitivity to God's creation the basic motivations for all that we will and do.

Those who would save the environment must themselves be saved. Those who would see a new heaven and a new earth that is full of his beauty and glory must, themselves, be filled with his beauty and glory.

Warnings to Keep Us Out of the New Age Movement

If we're serious about leading our society in a commitment to saving the environment, we will have to work with people outside the church and that means we will inevitably end up in dialogue with New Agers. They are everywhere. It is almost impossible these days to go to a conference dealing with ecological issues without meeting them. They wrote many of the books on the environment. And what they say and how they say it is often attractive enough to seduce the unprepared into a mind-set estranged from biblical Christianity. This has happened time and time again. Some of the most prominent thinkers in the New Age movement started off as rather traditional Christians, seeking ways of thinking about nature that might raise the church's consciousness on environmental issues and concerns.

The increasing affinity that the New Age movement has with the environmental movement has made many evangelical leaders suspicious of anyone who is involved in creation-care concerns. They have seen too many cases in which involvement with environmental issues was the first step into the strange, cultic world of New Age thinking.

Obviously we cannot abandon a cause that is so central to the biblical message about the kingdom of God simply because it has been joined by some who are anti-Christian. Otherwise, off-the-wall religious groups could drive us out of almost any worthwhile enterprise or movement simply by joining it. We must get smart enough to figure out where, when, and how dangerous ideas creep into our worldview. That is why I need to present some warnings here and now. That is why I must run up some red flags.

We ought to remember that in the world of ancient Israel the Jews often flirted with and were seduced by the religion of the Canaanites. They found the worship of nature and the mystical relationships with the earth espoused by their Canaanite neighbors very attractive.

This pagan worship of nature led the Jews away from God and made them idolaters. I am afraid that in some respects history is repeating itself. I see signs in certain quarters of contemporary Christianity, even as there were in ancient Israel, that people are looking to pagan religions for inspiration and guidance. Environmental concerns can easily pave the way for all of this. Without a biblically based theology of creation, Christians who want to understand nature in spiritual terms can all too easily find themselves involved with pagan religions.

There is a vast difference between sensing a unity with nature and advocating union with nature. The call to *union* with nature, which New Age gurus advocate, is part of pagan religion and is also a major emphasis of Eastern religions. To sense ourselves as part of God's creation and to be able to recognize a certain unity with the rest of nature as we worship God is a good thing. But to treat nature as some kind of spiritual personality with whom we can merge through meditation and psychic surrender is a serious mistake. God breathed his own breath only into the human race. Only we are created in God's image.

Humans have a level of consciousness that makes them transcend the rest of nature. We must not treat nature as some kind of spiritual entity, as though we owe it homage and surrender. Any talk of yielding ourselves to the forces of nature so as to experience union with it is certainly outside Christian thinking.

Christianity is about getting to know and worship God as he has expressed himself in Jesus Christ. The God who confronts us as a person is our salvation. To him and to him alone, we surrender.

As we come to Christ in praise and love, we can join with nature, which also was destined to worship him. But even as we participate with nature in glorifying God, we do so in a way that is qualitatively different. Just as God's ways are not our ways and his thoughts are not our thoughts (Isaiah 55:8), so our ways are not nature's ways, and our thoughts are different from any kind of thinking that goes on in the biosphere or ecosphere of creation.

Furthermore, salvation comes not when we yield to *Gaia* (the "in" term for Mother Earth among ecologists). It comes in knowing and yielding to the person of Jesus Christ. Union with a universe which is defined as a spiritual deity is far removed from the Christian belief that there is only one God, and that he is transcendent over all he created.

God uses nature, and through it he gives us messages which offer us inklings and hints of his power and majesty. But he uses nature like we use telephones, as an instrument through which he speaks to us. Just as we are separate from the telephones we speak through, so God is separate from the creation through which we sometimes receive messages. Thinking that we should become unified with nature just because God sometimes whispers messages through it makes as much sense as some romantic lovingly giving himself to a plastic telephone simply because the sounds of his sweetheart are sometimes heard through the thing.

We must not think that all life is of equal value. Evangelical Christianity rejects any such belief system. While we sense something sacred in all of life, because we claim that all life is sustained by God, we nevertheless hold to a belief in what Arthur Lovejoy has called "the great chain of being"; we believe that there is a hierarchy in God's creation.[2] At the top of the hierarchy is Jesus, whose name is above every other name and whose standing gives him preeminence over all the rest of God's creatures, both in heaven and on earth.

Any theology or mystical philosophy that levels that hierarchy is contrary to the will of God and should be regarded with more than passing questioning. Christian orthodoxy requires the hierarchy prescribed by Scripture. All life is not of equal value. Did not Jesus himself say:

> Are not two sparrows sold for a copper coin? And not one of them falls to the ground apart from your Father's will. But the very hairs of your head are all numbered. Do not fear therefore; you are of more value than many sparrows.
> Matthew 10:29–31 NKJV

As God works through his church, we should recognize that there is more to saving his creation than what he does through us. The church is his first and primary means of working to rescue the world from corruption and decay. But insofar as the church does not heed his call to be his rescuers of creation, he will use instruments outside the church to accomplish his will. I believe that because of the slow response of the church to environmental concerns, God is even now using groups like Greenpeace, the Audubon Society, the Sierra Club, and the National Wildlife Federation to carry out his renewal plan for our small planet. Furthermore, we have this warning in Romans 9–11 that if the church refuses to do his will and carry out his mission, then he will abandon the church as his prime instrument for salvation even as he once abandoned Israel for its refusal to carry out his mission in history. We in the church must be about the tasks God has given us to do lest the privilege of doing them be taken from us.

My concern is that if we fail to develop a *biblically based* theology of nature that fosters feeling for nature, then other religions and New Age gurus will move in to offer alternative systems that do. If the church cannot teach the citizens of our century how to enter into the sufferings of creation, those false prophets who play with the occult will. Then charlatans will be the only ones to offer people a spiritual basis for being pro-actively responsible for their environment.

In the struggle for the minds and hearts of this generation, we cannot yield anything to Buddhism or any version of the New Age movement. We cannot give ground on this incredibly pertinent issue. If some kind of empathy with nature is essential to the development of a mindset that can rescue dying creation, then we must show that the biblical message meets this need. We must, therefore, carefully develop the implications of what we know about how Jesus related to nature. And, until we come up with some more solid alternatives, the perspective of St. Francis ought to provide some of the inspiration for our preaching.

Environmentalism as the Fruit of the Spirit

Spirituality and creation-care are tied together. To be properly committed to the one should lead us inevitably to commitment to the other. If there is anything that becomes clear as you read the writings of those Christians who have stood historically as models of spiritual maturity, it is that along with their deepening awareness of

God came a growing sensitivity to nature and a profound sorrow about its sufferings.

To know God is to care. More specifically, it is to care for all that concerns God. That means, of course, that first and foremost we will be concerned about God's people and their salvation. As we take on the mind of Christ (Philippians 2:5) through prayer and meditation, the desire to see his salvation extended to all of his creatures will become very much a part of our thinking. As we grow in Christ, we cannot help but become concerned about all the living things of the world.

A genuine devotional life will lead the Christian into a special consciousness of creation, which is the best basis for environmental responsibility. Being spiritual, we will discover, leads increasingly to a demonstration of what the apostle Paul calls the "fruit of the Spirit"—"love, joy, peace, longsuffering, kindness, goodness, faithfulness, gentleness, self-control. Against such there is no law" (Galatians 5:22–23 NKJV).

Most of us know that the evangelical social reformer William Wilberforce was a primary force in England for the abolition of slavery and that he worked day and night to protect children by helping to pass child labor laws. But not many of us realize that this great Christian reformer also was a primary force behind the founding of the Royal Society of the Prevention of Cruelty to Animals. Not many know that the same Holy Spirit who gave Wilberforce a deep compassion for slaves and for children also gave him a bleeding heart for suffering animals. Wilberforce believed that humans should show goodness and kindness toward animals. The Bible teaches that goodness and kindness must be shown toward the rest of creation too.

We *must* teach children tenderness toward animals because, for children, animals are usually the only creatures more vulnerable and helpless than themselves. Children learn how to treat those who have less power than they do as they relate to these innocent creatures of God.[3]

Getting the Church Involved in Environmental Concerns

I believe that the church is the "now" body of Christ. Two thousand years ago, the eternal Christ incarnated himself in Jesus of Nazareth. In that mortal body, Christ spoke and acted in the midst of our world; he did his Father's will on earth.

In today's world, the body of Christ is the church. Through the church, God's contemporary work on earth is accomplished. The eternal Christ chooses to speak to our world through the church. And if this world is to hear God's message about creation-care, it will be through the church.

Most churches require potential members to undergo a training period, usually through some kind of discipleship class. Here would-be new members learn what the church believes and what is expected of them as members. These classes provide an ideal opportunity to sensitize Christians to their responsibilities to care for the environment and to respect the lives of all God's creatures. The pastor, or whoever else is teaching the class, might secure audiovisual materials that will tell the story of how all of this fits into the Christian lifestyle. The Mennonites have provided some excellent material for just this purpose.[4]

We must make it clear to those who come into the church that being a Christian is much more than just giving intellectual assent to propositional truths. We need to let them know that it involves even more than living lives of personal holiness and spiritual purity. We must help them to understand that being a Christian requires a commitment to social justice. In that context, ample time and teaching should be given to environmental concerns.

It must be recognized that in the end the evils that have befallen the environment, primarily at the hands of those who live in industrially developed nations, will only be eliminated as individuals opt for a new, responsible Christian lifestyle. The church must demonstrate not only to its own members but to those outside of the church just what this new lifestyle is all about. Over and against the selfish consumerism that is the hallmark of our times should stand Christians who bear witness to their Lord by living lives of responsible nonconformity. What we Christians buy, what we use, and what we throw away should demonstrate that we care about God's world. New church members must see that Christian living requires that we go far beyond the simple pieties of the past. They must learn that being Christian determines all that they say and do.

The Bible tells us that "whatever you do in word or deed, do all in the name of the Lord Jesus" (Colossians 3:17 NKJV). Certainly this applies to our consumer habits. Here are a handful of things each of us can do that will make a difference:

- Plant a tree. If every American would plant a tree, more than a billion pounds of "greenhouse gasses" would be removed from the atmosphere every year.[5]

- Cut down on junk mail. Just cutting down on the junk mail that you alone get over the course of a year would save one and a half trees.[6]

- Use a clean, low-phosphate or phosphate-free detergent. Phosphates fertilize algae to the point where it grows out of control, using up vast amounts of oxygen needed by other plants and marine life. The result is that lakes and ponds across the nation are dying.

- Use latex paint. As much as 60 percent of all hazardous waste dumped by individuals comes from oil-based paint or paint products.

- Make sure that your tires are properly inflated (more than 50 percent are not). If all Americans did this, we would save up to two billion gallons of gasoline a year.

- Cut down on the use of batteries. Batteries contain heavy metals that contribute to hazardous wastes. You can make the world a better place by using rechargeable batteries whenever possible. You'll save a lot of money too.

- Save water. Put a rock in every water tank attached to every toilet in your home. Don't use a brick; it can break apart and clog your system. Take short showers. Install a low-flow shower head. Make sure that there are good washers on all the faucets in your home. One drop per second wastes more than 24,000 gallons per year. Wash your car as seldom as possible. Do not run your dishwasher or washing machine unless you have a full load.

- Do an environmental audit at church.[7] Are church newsletters and stationary printed on recycled paper? Are cleaning products environmentally safe? Are the church buildings used efficiently, and are they properly insulated?

Communicate ecological responsibility to other congregations through proposing resolutions at denominational gatherings, calling Christendom to ecological responsibility.

I finalize this list by stating the most practical thing of all—*pray*. Prayer changes things! We should not only have special prayers on special occasions in which we hold environmental concerns before the Lord. I am suggesting that prayer for the environment be part our everyday personal devotions.

First of all, we should pray for forgiveness. What we have done to wreck God's creation is sinful, and we should repent. We should confess how our consumer lifestyles have contributed to the pollution of the rivers, lakes, oceans, and the air we breathe. Having confessed, we should repent and ask the Lord to guide us into more careful living.

Second, ask God to intervene in matters related to the environment that are in the news. Reports of environmental catastrophes are part of everyday life. They include stories of oil spills, destruction of the ozone layer of the atmosphere, and destruction of the rain forests. All of these matters should be put daily before the Lord.

Lastly, we should be praying for the church, that God might awaken its people to their responsibility to care for his creation and be his agents for renewing what has been devastated by uncaring humanity.

What I find intriguing is that children find nothing strange about thanking God for nature and praying for his protection of the animals that are dear to them. The prayers of the little girl at her bedside thanking God for flowers and birds, and of the small boy at the table asking God to bless his puppy and to make his sick cat well again, these seem like natural prayers. What I am asking is simply that we all become like little children in order to be part of God's kingdom.

Creation is a trust from God. When Christ returns, he will ask what we have done with it. He will want to know if we watered it, nurtured it, and encouraged its fruitfulness, or if we abused it, forsook it, and ignored its needs.

God expects us to take what he has given us and do more than just return it to him the way we received it. He expects us to care for his creation, to bless it, and to make it more fruitful. He expects us to be faithful servants who attend to his creation.

One day, God will call us before his judgment seat, and we can be certain that he will ask us to give an account of what we have done to the world which he has entrusted into our hands (Matthew 25:130).

Notes

1. Lynn White, Jr., "The Historical Roots of Our Ecological Crisis," *Science,* 10 March 1967, 1203–7.

2. Arthur O. Lovejoy, *The Great Chain of Being* (Santa Fe: Bear and Co., 1983).

3. See *The Animal Voice,* a magazine published by People for the Ethical Treatment of Animals.

4. See Jerry L. Holsopple, *Whole People Whole Earth: Shalom Lifestyles* (Harrisonburg, Va.: Mennonite Media Productions).

5. See Linda Kanamine, "Budget Crises Fell Urban Tree Programs," *USA Today,* 13 November 1991, 10a.

6. To stop your name from being sold to most large mailing list companies, write to: Mail Preferences Service, Direct Mailing Association, 11 West 42nd Street, P.O. Box 3861, New York, N.Y. 10163-3861

7. Tim Cooper, *Green Christianity* (London: Hodder & Stoughton, 1990), 252–57.

14

AIDS and Public Policy

William E. Dannemeyer

For the past several years AIDS has occupied an increasingly important place in the American consciousness. In fact, today the American
people regard the disease as the greatest single health problem in the
nation. Certainly they are right. The number of cases is now increasing at an alarming rate. The number of dead continues to keep pace,
despite new medications that seem to retard the progress of the disease. And there is solid evidence that the virus has made its way into
the heterosexual community. A recent study suggests that there are
almost twice as many cases of undetected AIDS in the United States
as the Centers for Disease Control has projected, and that many of
these cases will be found among heterosexual teenagers. Virtually
everyone is in agreement on one point: things are going to get much
worse before they get better.

But why this grim prediction? Or, to put the question in even
more pertinent terms, why have we allowed this disease to rage out of
control, when we first diagnosed it almost a decade ago in no more
than a handful of homosexuals? The answer to this question can be
found in the attitude adopted by the homosexual leadership and the

WILLIAM E. DANNEMEYER is a United States Congressman (R) representing the thirty-ninth district of California. He serves on the Energy and
Commerce, and Budget committees. He is a leading conservative spokes-
man in Congress, addressing such subjects as the pro-family issue and the
AIDS epidemic.

enormous influence that this small group has exerted on public policy at every level.

Clearly, from the outset AIDS has been a primary threat to the American homosexual community. Indeed, when the disease was first diagnosed in this country, it was probably confined to that particular segment of the population. Had public health officials quickly and effectively adopted traditional methods for dealing with sexually transmitted diseases, there would have been no AIDS epidemic and tens of thousands of people now dead would still be alive—most of them homosexuals.

But the homosexual activists—the officers and members of organizations like the National Gay Task Force—were intent on advancing a "gay rights" agenda and consequently made it difficult for indecisive public officials to root out the disease.

In a very real sense the homosexual community was faced with a choice at the moment AIDS first appeared in this country. They could either insist that they be allowed to continue their sexual practices undisturbed by public health officials, or they could submit themselves to the restrictions and procedures historically employed in treating sexually transmitted diseases and give up the idea of absolute sexual freedom, at least until the disease was eradicated. They chose to defend and advance their sexual revolution, even though to do so meant to risk the lives of tens of thousands of their own constituency.

It is true that the choice did not seem so obvious and so absolute at first. Only later, when the spread of AIDS had already reached epidemic proportions, could they fully understand the threat that uncontrolled and unmonitored sexual intercourse posed to the very survival of their community. Yet even then they chose to risk death rather than to accept discipline. With few exceptions the leaders of the homosexual movement have continued to fight every proposal to identify AIDS carriers and to curb dangerous behavior. Their attitude is clear: Give us liberty and give us death!

Let me illustrate what I mean. In San Francisco, where the AIDS virus was particularly prevalent, the homosexual bathhouse was a central gathering place for the most promiscuous homosexuals, those who engaged in countless sex acts with multiple partners. Some men had as many as ten sexual encounters in a single night, and in some cases their various partners numbered in the hundreds over the period of a year. At these bathhouses every conceivable perversity was practiced, but particularly anal intercourse, the most dangerous of all homosexual behaviors. A man would lie naked on his stomach, a can of vegetable shortening beside him, and wait for some stranger to enter. He would turn his head and nod, and the stranger would sodomize him. Typically, no conversation would take place, and the stranger would quickly leave. Then another would enter. And another. Such scenes would be taking place almost around the clock in the homosexual district.

Yet when San Francisco authorities tried to shut down the bathhouses as a health menace, the homosexual leadership hauled them into court and won an injunction to keep the bathhouses open—thereby ensuring that the AIDS virus would be passed from man to man in increasing numbers. Many California bathhouses are still open and are still the breeding grounds of the AIDS epidemic. Even today after a law was finally passed forbidding bathhouses, the suggestion that the bathhouses should be closed is met with stern opposition.

The same is true of other traditional health measures. Homosexual spokesmen insist that once-standard public health practices such as testing and contact tracing are foreign to the idea of freedom. Surprisingly, many commentators and public officials accept this version of American history without investigating its validity.

In fact, for generations the American public health community has routinely tested people for syphilis. At one time, most states mandated premarital testing, and many hospitals automatically tested all people entering for whatever reason. In addition, during the late 1930s and early 1940s there was widespread testing in American industry involving literally millions, testing by federal agencies, testing by states (everyone between fifteen and fifty in Alabama), and testing by the Selective Service of all draft registrants during World War II (tens of millions of young men). The result of this anti-syphilis program: hundreds of thousands of cases were diagnosed and cured, and the number of total cases was reduced to a fraction of what it had once been. (It is ironic that following the discovery of penicillin, many of these public health measures were relaxed or abolished, and now infectious syphilis is on the rise and has once again become a serious health problem.)

But in the past the health care community did not confine its activities to mere testing. They also reported cases of syphilis to public health departments and traced all sexual contacts of the infected patient, informing them of their risk, testing them, and also taking their recent sexual histories in order to identify additional infectious people. Almost every physician over fifty remembers such policies, even if they are no longer in force. Perhaps this is why an *MD* magazine poll revealed that a great majority of practicing physicians disagree with their colleagues in the U.S. Public Health Service, who have taken the homosexual position in arguing against routine testing and contact tracing for AIDS.

Of course, the homosexual leaders have argued that routine testing and contact tracing serve no useful purpose in dealing with a disease for which there is no cure. "Who cares if he has been infected with the AIDS virus?" they argue. "Better not to know, if you're going to die anyway." This attitude was preached by the Reverend Troy Perry to his United Fellowship of Metropolitan Community Churches flock, the largest homosexual organization in the country. As Troy explains it, he does not want his members to be additionally burdened with the knowledge that they are HIV infected when they already have enough troubles to weigh them down.

No argument better illustrates the psychological warp of the homosexual community, its intense and overarching self-preoccupation. This viewpoint is perfectly valid *as long as the only person you consider is the homosexual with AIDS.* But what about his future sexual partners? Don't they deserve every consideration that society can reasonably afford them? Isn't it valid to assume that at least some of the homosexuals who find themselves HIV infected will refrain from further sexual liaisons? Or restrict sexual activities to less-risky behavior? Or at least inform a prospective partner of the infection so that both people involved can make a realistic assessment of the dangers inherent in the sex act? Few husbands would want to submit their wives to the danger of infection if those husbands knew they were AIDS carriers. I would like to believe that many homosexuals would reject the self-centered policies of their leadership, if only because, in the end they are not really defending the homosexual community but in fact contributing to its ultimate annihilation.

Let me put it another way. If all of the homosexuals who are now dying of AIDS could be given the opportunity to turn back the clock to 1981 and dictate public policy toward AIDS, would they order the bathhouses to remain open and allow the federal and state public health services to avoid testing and contact tracing at a time when only a few homosexuals were HIV infected? Or would they say, "Let's move to stop this thing in its tracks, so that a few years from now I won't contract the disease and end up in a hospice, my body covered with cancers, my lungs filling up with fluid."

Yet the situation has not changed. Those homosexuals who are still uninfected can join with those of us who want to reinstitute traditional health measures in order to save the remaining population from the virus. They can acknowledge that the measures we advocate are not only proven deterrents to the spread of sexually transmitted diseases but also, if applied immediately, would be of primary benefit to homosexuals, because homosexuals are currently the chief transmitters and therefore the chief victims of the disease.

Yet those who advocate conventional health care measures are regarded by the homosexual leadership as "homophobes." Ironically, anyone who genuinely hates homosexuals has an easy course to follow these days: simply give the "gay activists" everything they want. They are determined to lead their constituency to early graves.

Obviously, then, we must listen to someone other than the homosexual community if we are to adopt the best policies for meeting the AIDS crisis; and the most likely source of guidance is the U.S. Public Health Service, which has historically led the way in the prevention and containment of contagious disease. Yet federal authorities have not acted in the wise tradition of their predecessors. Instead of applying such proven methods as testing and contact tracing, they have sometimes been the chief opponents of these measures.

For example, in his 1986 *Report* former Surgeon General Dr. C. Everett Koop said that the use of condoms is a "measure" sufficient "to safely protect you" from the HIV virus, even though your partner is infected by the virus.[1] At the time he issued this report, some of us warned that well-known studies of condoms showed a 10 to 18 percent failure rate in the prevention of pregnancy and that at least one study published in Britain indicated a failure rate of up to 50 percent in anal intercourse. But for a long time he refused to acknowledge that his *Report* had overstated the efficacy of condoms. It has become clear that government health policies extolling "safe sex" have been wrongheaded and dangerous.

The first evidence came in a study conducted by Dr. Margaret Fischl of the University of Miami. Dr. Fischl, monitoring married couples where the male partner had AIDS, reported that after eighteen months of condom use, three of eighteen previously uninfected women had contracted the virus from their husbands. The failure rate, then, was about 17 percent over a year and a half.

Early in 1987, the FDA began to look more closely at the condom industry as the result of the Public Health Service statements stressing their efficacy. At a time when experts were saying that condoms were adequate to safely protect users from the HIV virus, the FDA was telling my researcher that they didn't know how effective condoms were in preventing disease, that they could not specify the degree to which current testing procedures could answer such a question.

We discovered that the mechanical test the condom industry used—taking random samples, filling them with water, and seeing whether or not they leaked—allowed a failure rate of up to four condoms per thousand. That meant that in every 250 condoms you might well find one that was punctured or broken, allowing sperm or the HIV virus to penetrate.

One out of 250 was the permissible level of failure in the industry-administered test. When the FDA moved in to make certain that the industry was living up to even those standards, they found out something very disturbing: about 20 percent of the condom batches—approximately one-fifth—*didn't even measure up to the standards.* So they had to recall literally millions of condoms, almost two million in one batch.

At this point some of us became concerned, and so did some reasonable people in the Department of Health and Human Services. The public was also nervous, since the FDA released the news of the condom recall to the general public. As a consequence of this growing concern, the National Institute of Child Health and Human Development (NICHHD) commissioned a study, to be carried out at UCLA and USC, that would attempt to answer the essential question: Do condoms really prevent AIDS?

In this study, the pregnancy figures of the past would be discarded. No one would rest with the knowledge that water would not squirt through a tiny hole. One phase, we were told, would involve attaching an electronic charge to an HIV virus and then seeing if it could penetrate a latex membrane. Another phase would involve monitoring two groups of human subjects, one using condoms, one without—or so the later reports would say. Very little about the mechanics of the study was revealed, only that it was intended to clear up doubts about the degree to which condoms could protect against HIV.

But it seemed as if the study was doomed from the beginning. First, the condom industry began to pressure the NICHHD to issue a "stop-work order" and shut down the project. The *Los Angeles Times* reported that the condom manufacturers were "motivated by industry concerns that the research might conclude that no American-made condom is currently able to consistently prevent the spread of AIDS."[2]

While the industry disputed this explanation, it demanded, among other things, that the UCLA-USC researchers use only those standards used by the condom makers themselves, and that American manufacturers should be allowed to supply selected batches of condoms "especially screened for this." (The team had planned to use prophylactics purchased from retailers to be sure they were getting a representative sample of what was actually being used.)

That was in August of 1987. In late January of 1988, the study again made the pages of the *Los Angeles Times*. This time, in violation of their own secrecy procedures, the UCLA researchers informed the FDA that they had discovered a batch of condoms so failure prone that they needed to be taken off the market. The discovery had first been made in November. The FDA had been informed, and the agency had in turn contacted the manufacturer, who reported that the entire batch had already been sold to unsuspecting customers. Yet in January of 1988 the researchers still found the same defective condoms on the shelf. These "rogue condoms" were so bad that some broke when they were being removed from the package, while others burst even before they were inflated to the required pressure.

By July of 1988 the National Institute of Health withdrew support from the UCLA-USC study. Why? Because the federal government feared that those homosexuals who were using condoms in the study would be infected by the AIDS virus. As the *Los Angeles Times* reported it, ". . . the NIH now fears that the risks of condom failure and subsequent AIDS transmission to study volunteers were unacceptably high."

So a little more than two years after the *Surgeon General's Report* was hailed by homosexuals and by the press, and less than three months after the Department of Health and Human Services mailed a pamphlet in which condoms were recommended to every household, the federal government's AIDS policy seemed to be in shambles. You no longer heard responsible health officials talking about "safe sex" or even "safer sex."

Now that the nation is without an AIDS policy, we offer these suggestions in hopes that whoever is in charge will listen. Here is my own list of priorities, with supporting evidence that these measures can form the basis for a sound AIDS policy. What I am recommending are steps that could have been adopted years ago and saved thousands of lives. But they can still be put into motion today, perhaps to save millions.

Step One: Widespread Testing

Widespread testing for the HIV virus is desperately needed, and for three basic reasons.

First, testing will ensure the best available medical diagnosis and treatment for infected persons. Recent studies indicate that early treatment slows progression of the disease. Studies in animals strongly suggest that current drugs can effectively block the AIDS virus, especially if a person is treated soon after exposure to the virus. Antiviral agents, such as AZT, coupled with drugs that boost the immune system, have proven successful in stopping the progress of the HIV virus in attacking the immune system. Widespread testing would result in tremendous benefits for those who are infected with the virus, giving them a decided edge in the struggle to survive.

Second, a national testing policy would be beneficial to those who are not infected by the virus. For one thing, those who have engaged in high-risk behavior and who test negative would be reassured and could take steps to make certain they did not expose themselves again. But perhaps more important, if we are able to identify those who are HIV carriers, then we can persuade them to avoid exposing those who are as yet uninfected.

And third, a substantial national sampling is needed if we are ever to determine just how many Americans are infected with the virus. No one knows the extent to which AIDS has spread throughout our increasingly promiscuous society. A couple of years ago CDC experts "guessed" that the total number of infected persons was about

1.5 million—a frightening figure. They came to this conclusion by estimating that the number of asymptomatic people carrying the virus was probably fifty times the number suffering from the advanced symptoms of the disease. At the time, the CDC had identified around 30,000 cases of full-blown AIDS. Today that figure is up to over 250,000, yet the estimate of asymptomatic carriers still stands at 1.5 million. We need to *know* the extent of infection in order to make plans for the future.

Perhaps the most widely debated epidemiological question is the extent to which AIDS has spread into the heterosexual community. There is substantial disagreement among experts, and this disparity between estimates is not a minor squabble. If the higher estimates prove to be accurate, then as a nation we are totally unprepared for the catastrophe about to overtake us, the magnitude of which is beyond current comprehension. We must drastically revise our long-term medical planning. We must quickly develop a fiscal policy for dealing with such enormous expenditures. And we must frame a legislative program that will cut our losses while at the same time guaranteeing that in a time of dire national emergency our nation can retain its traditional atmosphere of freedom and compassion.

Those who oppose routine testing argue that voluntary testing will be just as useful. But voluntary testing has not worked. Less than 2.5 percent of HIV cases discovered in the military came to light as the result of "self-referral," and less than 2.5 percent were identified after admission to a clinic. That means that more than 95 percent of all HIV-infected cases in the U.S. Army were identified as the result of one of the army's mandatory screening programs.

According to Dr. Robert Redfield, an AIDS researcher at Walter Reed Hospital, "Self-requested testing is a discriminatory and limited approach, offering the opportunity to be tested only to those who are reached by education programs and who understand the importance and benefits of such knowledge. Routine testing provides equal opportunity to all. . . . This approach enables the majority of Americans to be informed of their infection status independent of education or social background."[3]

If we are to have routine testing, then who should be tested? For reasons that will become apparent, I would suggest that the following groups be included in any comprehensive testing program.

A. *Persons Convicted of Intravenous Drug Use, Prostitution, or Sexual Assault*

Such people should be tested to protect potential "customers," cohorts, and victims. We also need to determine the rate of infection among such groups in order to assess the need for greater law enforcement efforts and additional legislation.

Intravenous (IV) drug users have been considered a high-risk group from the outset of the epidemic. Currently, they account for 17 percent of all cases, and another 8 percent are cases of male homosexuals who also use IV drugs.

Prostitutes have recently been singled out by the FDA as a "high-risk group," and for good reason. In a study conducted by Howard University, thirteen out of twenty-six prostitutes tested were found to be infected with the HIV virus. In a CDC study, researchers found that one out of nine prostitutes tested nationwide was an HIV carrier. A Miami study found 58 percent of all prostitutes tested were positive for HIV. These figures more than justify the classification by the FDA.

Persons convicted of sexual assault and related crimes should be tested because they have placed their victims in jeopardy. In addition, the results of these tests should be made available to the victim so that he or she will be reassured or else informed about infection in order to take all steps available to minimize the dangers involved. Currently, many states refuse to perform the HIV test on those convicted of sexual assault, and some states that do perform such tests will not release the results to victims. In my opinion, such a policy is shortsighted and inhumane and favors the criminal rather than the victim of the crime.

B. *Persons Receiving Treatment or Services for Family Planning, Tuberculosis, Drug Abuse, or Sexually Transmitted Disease*

Persons receiving treatment or services for family planning have committed no crime, so why test them for HIV? Actually there is a good epidemiological reason for doing so. Evidence suggests that an increasing number of younger women will become infected with HIV, either as a result of IV drug use or through heterosexual transmission of the virus. Title X, a federally funded program, annually provides family planning services to 4.3 million sexually active women. Most of these women (about two-thirds) are below the age of twenty-five, many are members of minority groups, and 85 percent are members of low-income families. For this reason, Title X clients closely resemble the population of women thought to be at risk for HIV infection. Thus, in testing these women we can help those who are infected (see above) and at the same time learn more about this particular population of women in order to assess the spread of AIDS into the heterosexual community.

Persons receiving treatment for tuberculosis are more and more likely to be AIDS victims as well. Tuberculosis (TB) is the latest of the known diseases associated with the HIV epidemic. Unlike other opportunistic infections, however, TB is an airborne disease and seems to be contracted more easily than other opportunistic diseases.

The heightened threat posed by TB is illustrated by the case of twelve Urbana nurses who tested positive for TB after caring for two patients suffering from both AIDS and TB. This outbreak, which occurred at the Carle Foundation facility, was described by a resident physician as an "epidemic."

This case illustrates the wisdom of testing all patients with TB for HIV as well. But there is also another reason: a positive HIV test can change the recommended treatment for TB. According to the American Thoracic Society, "The presence of HIV infection in a person with tuberculosis alters the management of TB and should make the physician alert for other opportunistic infections."

Persons receiving treatment for drug abuse, as noted above, are especially at risk for HIV infection and need to be diagnosed and treated for the AIDS virus, which is as deadly as a drug habit.

Persons receiving treatment or services for sexually transmitted diseases (STDs) are also a high-risk group. It is estimated that a minimum of two million people annually are diagnosed with a sexually transmitted disease or treated for such a disease. Statistics indicate that persons being treated for STDs are not only at high risk for infection, but in many cities may already be infected. It is crucial that we test this population as expeditiously as possible in order to determine the infection rate and begin intensive counseling about the potential for transmission.

C. Premarital Applicants

Premarital applicants are not any more at risk than other members of the population at large, but testing couples before marriage can be justified for two reasons.

First, a large number of couples seek marriage licenses each year, and therefore this test would serve as a good random survey of the magnitude of infection in the United States.

Second, the potential spouse of a person who has been exposed to AIDS has the right to know if that person is HIV positive. Such knowledge is essential to making decisions concerning sexual relations and procreation. Indeed, a major goal of premarital testing is to protect unborn children. Recently the mother of an AIDS-infected child was quoted as saying that she would never have married had she known her husband was infected. She said, "I do not regret having him and I would not have had an abortion, but doing this to a baby is like holding a gun to a child's head."

D. Hospital Admittees between the Ages of Fifteen and Forty-nine

Routine screening of this group over a one-year period would result in the testing of 37 to 39 million people and would provide the large base of statistical data necessary to determine the extent of the epidemic.

In the past, critics of this proposal have made the hyperbolic argument that the cost per positive test would run as high as $18,000, assuming that children and old people would be tested. But limiting the sample to this age group would reduce the cost to $150 per positive test, a worthwhile expenditure if we could determine the extent of the AIDS epidemic and at the same time identify and treat large numbers of AIDS sufferers.

The American Medical Association has recommended voluntary testing instead of routine testing. But many medical authorities disagree with the AMA and are taking steps to institute a more sensible testing policy. Despite pressure from the AMA and other groups, surgeons at the Medical College of Wisconsin initiated a policy of mandatory testing for surgery patients in October 1987. Dr. Robert Condon, chairman of surgery, said that "sometimes the right to privacy has to be counterbalanced against society's needs . . . the risks are low, but not zero." He went on to say that physicians in Wisconsin feel "it is appropriate to reduce the risk." The policy calls for denying surgery to those who refuse testing, but so far no one has refused.[4]

In February 1988, Parkland Memorial Hospital in Dallas tested 709 emergency room patients without their knowledge. Approximately 1 percent tested positive for the HIV virus, and these were informed of the results. The AMA was swift in its condemnation of Parkland, stating that the hospital's conduct was unethical. But Parkland's president defended the tests, saying, "The only patients who were tested were severely injured and needed their blood drawn for other tests. Blood samples were coded to protect the patient's identity." He also added, "The AMA would be happier if we did not notify people who tested positive. We could let those people go and infect their loved ones, but we feel obligated to the patients."[5]

Finally, inpatients should be tested for HIV so that hospital personnel can be informed about the dangers they face. For example, in September of 1987, the CDC reported three cases of transmission to health-care providers. In the first, a nurse held a catheter in place for a comatose AIDS patient with the tip of her ungloved finger and became infected with HIV. In the second case, a woman who had small cuts and eczema on her hands was infected while caring for a man in his home. The third case involved a woman who contracted HIV while caring for her child, who had been infected as the result of a blood transfusion. In view of the proven risk of transmission by blood, hospital personnel should know the infection status of all patients.

In summary, let me say that we should have established a testing program of considerable scope when we first discovered the nature of the virus in the early 1980s. I am convinced that we would have done so had AIDS been a predominantly heterosexual disease. Routine testing has always been standard procedure in dealing with such infections as syphilis and tuberculosis. And it is important to note that when, during the Roosevelt administration, testing for syphilis reached its most intense level, the stigma of venereal disease was far greater than the stigma of AIDS or homosexuality today. To argue to the contrary is to admit a radical ignorance of the past.

Yet the homosexual activists, through a campaign of intimidation and misinformation, have convinced a large segment of the American population that there is something new and sinister about testing people in order to check a disease that has killed tens of thousands already and will kill millions before it runs its course. Somehow we must recover our good sense, if not our memory, and reinstitute the kind of testing program that helped to stamp out syphilis within the lifetime of millions of Americans.

Step Two: Reporting

We must also institute a national policy of reporting HIV infection just as we report other communicable diseases, including full-blown AIDS. Such a policy would allow us to obtain more accurate statistics on the numbers of people infected with the virus. Also, a system of reporting would enable us to locate HIV-infected persons and counsel them about their condition.

A large number of medical authorities have subscribed to the policy of mandatory reporting. Opponents of mandatory reporting of HIV argue that such a policy would force those in high-risk groups underground, that they would no longer consult physicians who might obey the law, that leaders and public health officials have taken this line. Present statistical evidence does not support such an assertion.

Step Three: Contact Tracing

Once HIV carriers are identified through testing, it is important to begin contact tracing (or, as public health officials now like to call it, "partner notification"). This is traditional medical practice, particularly in the prevention of sexually transmitted diseases.

Homosexual activists and some public health officials have consistently opposed contact tracing, arguing that it is a violation of the individual's right to privacy and that it is an ineffective and costly way to identify AIDS-infected persons. As far as I know, the courts have never ruled that contact tracing is unconstitutional; until they do, there is no "civil right" to infect others or even to remain ignorant of one's own infectiousness. The health of the public has always outweighed the individual's right to freedom of association, particularly if "association" means sexual intercourse with persons other than a spouse.

Needless to say, contact tracing has *always* been a "confidential procedure." Even in the heyday of Thomas Parran, when the eradication of syphilis was the chief mission of the U.S. Public Health Service, the names of sexual contacts were never made public. Like private physicians, public health officials were bound by ethical codes, and there is no reason to believe that these codes were ever breached.

It is also obvious that infected persons *always* surrender the names of contacts voluntarily, though some patients may require more persuasion than others. The government has never employed force to discover the identity of sexual partners, and no one has ever advocated such measures. Most people, presented with the obvious benefits of revealing names, eventually do so voluntarily. Clearly, however, any individual has the option of refusal—and always did, whether the disease was syphilis, gonorrhea, or typhoid fever.

Step Four: The Restoration of Laws against Sodomy

According to legal historian Charles Rice, every state in the Union outlawed sodomy until 1961. These laws were based on ancient legal tradition and derived from our society's roots in the Judeo-Christian ethical and moral tradition. In recent decades, homosexual activists and organizations like the American Civil Liberties Union have mounted an assault against such legislation on the state level. One by one, state legislatures repealed these laws, usually with little fanfare, justifying their actions by saying that the statutes were "unenforceable" or "unnecessary" or "probably unconstitutional," despite the fact that the Supreme Court has consistently upheld the right of states to pass and enforce anti-sodomy laws.

At last count only twenty-four states and the District of Columbia still carried such statutes on the books. Yet it is important that our legal system reflect what we believe about matters that have perennially been regarded as moral. We have laws on the books outlawing rape and child molestation because we believe these things are wrong. We should likewise reaffirm our belief in the immorality of sodomy by putting anti-sodomy statutes back on the books in those states where they have been dropped.

In reaffirming this belief, we will also be strengthening our commitment to the American family and its central place in our society.

The union of a man and woman in marriage is the single most important social institution in Western civilization. Since Genesis and the *Odyssey*, tribes, cities, states, and nations have been based on the bedrock of family. A Greek child was called by his father's name in addition to a given name. Rome was a city of families, each with its patriarch or *pater familias*, who spoke for the rest of his people in the councils of the empire. The twelve tribes of Israel were regarded as nothing more than extended families. And Christianity, with its emphasis on the Holy Family as a model for all human conduct, has extended and broadened the meaning of family to cosmic proportions.

Only in a modern ideological state like Nazi Germany or Soviet Russia has the family unit been denigrated or replaced in the interest of totalitarian regimentation. At least such has been the case until very recently, when—for reasons that should be obvious—homosexual activists have begun to attack those ancient social arrangements, either charging that the family has been the crucible of bigotry and intolerance or else redefining the family to include cohabiting for sexual purposes by members of the same sex. Homosexual organizations, bolstered by such allies as the National Organization for Women, are demanding that (1) they be given the same tax breaks as traditional families, (2) they be given equal consideration in the adoption of children, (3) their sexual arrangements be taught as valid "alternative lifestyles" in public schools, and (4) private institutions, such as businesses, give them the same fringe benefits (insurance, bereavement leave, etc.) that they offer to married people. Lesbians have even begun, through artificial insemination, to give birth to their own children, sometimes sharing them with the homosexual sperm donor.

These demands endanger the very survival of the family as we know it, and the only way to make certain that such recommendations are not put into practice is to reinstitute laws against sodomy in all states. By so doing we would settle the question of rights and prerogatives now in dispute, saying emphatically that homosexuals per se have no rights other than those they enjoy by virtue of being citizens of the United States.

In passing such laws, we would also affirm a normative way of life for all Americans: that they are born and nurtured in traditional families where children have both mothers and fathers and hence learn to understand the marvelous union of man and woman that continually leads to the rebirth of life and love and hope on earth.

As we have seen in the case of AIDS, widespread homosexual behavior is a formidable threat to public health. Their sexual practices expose them to a range of infections that normal people do not encounter. For example, anal intercourse is unhealthy in more ways than one. In addition to exposing both partners to HIV infection, this unnatural behavior frequently spreads hepatitis B, a killing virus that is frequently found among homosexuals and that, like HIV, has polluted the bloodstream and caused the death of innocent transfusion recipients, including comedian Danny Kaye. Hepatitis B attacks the liver and can cause cirrhosis as well as other potentially fatal complications. It is so dangerous that most health-care workers are routinely vaccinated against it. The general population, however, is at the mercy of the virus if exposed.

In addition to hepatitis B, perhaps the second most deadly of the predominantly homosexual viruses, there are four diseases that cause what doctors originally called "gay bowel syndrome" (GBS): hepatitis A, amebiasis, shigellosis, and giardiasis. GBS is a complex of symptoms (fever, diarrhea, etc.) that first occurred in a number of California homosexuals and later spread throughout the country, eventually infecting heterosexuals as well. More like a convention of infections than a single disease, a GBS sufferer is often invaded by at least two of the organisms and sometimes all of them. Each of these diseases, however, is devastating. For example, amebiasis causes dysentery and liver abscesses, while giardiasis can result in painful and chronic inflammation of the intestinal tract. Shigellosis is often fatal in children. Like typhoid, GBS can be transmitted by the handling of food, a fact that makes it particularly threatening to the community at large, since, according to the *New England Journal of Medicine*, in a heavily populated area like San Francisco, 10 percent of those infected with amebiasis, giardiasis, and shigellosis in 1980 were working as food handlers.

As noted earlier, AIDS patients, most of whom are homosexuals, increasingly contract tuberculosis, a disease that is still a killer in the United States, despite the complacency of the public at large. TB can be transmitted by sneezing and coughing; and while in the past the infection rate has been extremely low, there is some concern among medical authorities that TB may be more infectious in conjunction with HIV.

Another disease that goes hand in hand with HIV is cytomegalovirus (CMV). The incidence of CMV in AIDS patients is extremely high, close to 100 percent in some estimates; and while its symptoms are often negligible, it can damage unborn children. In fact, a nurse in California has charged that her son was born malformed because she contracted CMV while working with AIDS patients. She has also charged that the hospital where she worked refused to let her wear gloves and a mask out of concern for the feelings of the patients.

It is important to note that these diseases are contagious through casual contact, so the community at large is directly threatened with infection. This fact suggests that what people do in the privacy of their own bedroom is indeed the business of the community at large—if it threatens the lives and health of other people. To argue otherwise is to strike at the very idea of society.

In the past twenty years we have undergone profound changes, and for the first time we have begun to renounce our own wisdom and virtue as a people. In fact, if you examined only our sexual conduct during this period, you would have to say we have changed more in one generation than we did in the first 175 years of our history. Such changes are bound to affect the way we will fare as a nation, not only in the next 175 years but more immediately, in the next two decades.

Let us take a look at what has happened to nations whose histories parallel our own, remembering that thus far no society has outlived time.

The world is full of ruined monuments to the failure of civilization—or, to be more precise, the failures of numerous civilizations, each organized according to different principles, each brought to disaster in a different way. Some of them died slow deaths, stretching out over many centuries, like the Roman and the Chinese empires. Some were brought to sudden ruin, like Carthage. But in the greatest of civilizations, there is usually a common thread at the end, a corruption of spirit that leads to selfishness and preoccupation with pleasure, eventually to the exclusion of what is usual and normal. At that point, excess and perversion come into fashion, and after that—catastrophe. There are numerous examples of such decadence, and at the end of great civilizations you almost always find homosexuality—widespread, energetic, enormously proud of itself.

In Rome when the Emperor Nero was on the throne, Petronius in his *Satyricon* described the wild sexual excesses of the court, with particular emphasis on the practice of sodomy, which he treats as an amusing sport.

When the Spaniards came to Mexico in the early sixteenth century, the Mayan civilization they found was no longer the healthy, vital culture that had produced so much wealth and learning. It too had become decadent and self-indulgent. The pleasure-obsessed upper classes were sacrificing human beings, engaging in orgies, and practicing sodomy without shame.

By the seventeenth century, the once-powerful Venetian republic, one of the earliest European examples of representative democracy, had become worldly and sybaritic. Women were walking through the streets covered with jewels, their faces painted, their bare breasts exposed. Again homosexuality among men was widespread and unabashed, a symbol of the waste of sexual desire in a world that had lost all its meaning.[6]

Germany toward the end of the Weimar Republic was a society of economic chaos and moral bankruptcy. Perhaps the best interpreter of its perversity was popular composer Kurt Weil, whose cabaret songs and ironic musical plays depicted the cynical self-indulgence in a world in which homosexual intrigues take the place of normal sexuality for many of the jaded characters. Weil's Germany (which he eventually fled) was the nation that Adolph Hitler took over only a few years later.

And now some people are saying that the United States has come to the same point in its history, when its religious and moral traditions are held in contempt by increasing numbers of its people, when a growing segment of the population regards life as meaningless except during moments of self-gratification, when promiscuous sexual behavior is everywhere, and when once again homosexuality is not only accepted but applauded.

Are we going to be destroyed like the great civilizations of the past, because we no longer have the moral will to resist corruption? I don't really believe so, though sometimes I am ready to concede defeat. As Billy Graham was quoted as saying, "If God doesn't destroy the United States of America, he owes Sodom and Gomorrah an apology."

Step Five: The Rejection of Antidiscrimination Laws

Proposed AIDS antidiscrimination laws are popular these days because they make specious appeals to the best in Americans—their sense of fair play and their belief in tolerance. But these particular laws are wrongheaded attempts to force the community to accept homosexuality as a valid alternative to normal sexuality and to do so at the risk of the nation's health. At best they are irrational or inconsistent. At worst they are devious and perverse.

Are we saying to uninfected Americans that they must agree to work with HIV-infected individuals with infectious tuberculosis, transmitted through the respiratory system, and numerous other infectious opportunistic diseases because to discharge such individuals would be discriminatory?

Are we saying to the American people, particularly pregnant women, that they must consent to be exposed to cytomegalovirus (CMV), excreted by a person with ARC or AIDS and known to cause birth defects, because to fail to do so would be discriminatory?

Are we saying that pregnant nurses will now be required to take care of AIDS patients, notwithstanding certain exposure to CMV?

Are we saying to health care workers in America that they may not wear gowns, masks, and gloves at their own discretion in taking care of AIDS patients? Do the sensitivities of patients override the obligation of health-care workers to protect themselves from CMV, TB, and Epstein Barr syndrome, a precursor to mononucleosis?

Are we saying that persons with *curable* communicable diseases, whose status is routinely reported to public health authorities in confidence, will continue to be reported, but persons who are carriers of HIV, an *incurable* communicable disease, will not be reported? Are we willing to discriminate against the former to give special privilege to the latter?

In addition to asking these questions, I would make the following point: the three cities in America with the largest proportion of AIDS—52 percent of all cases nationwide—are New York, San Francisco, and Los Angeles. All three have antidiscrimination laws.

Currently we are a divided nation—divided in our understanding of what to do about AIDS, divided in our attitudes toward the toleration of homosexuality, divided in our commitment to a traditional public morality. Such a division has not existed in America since the

Civil War, and it will not be easily repaired. We have come to the moment, however, when we will have to decide which view of the future will prevail. In the next two to four years we will be forced by the further progress of this epidemic to commit ourselves irrevocably to one view or the other. Obviously, the choice we make will determine whether or not we survive as a people.

I am by no means certain what that choice will be. I believe that we have the moral will to restore traditional American morality, win the war against AIDS, and go on to create an even greater nation for our children and grandchildren. But I also think we have the capacity to make the wrong choice and plunge our people, and indeed the entire West, into a dark night of the soul that could last hundreds of years before the flame is again lit. It has happened before. It can happen again.

Notes

1. C. Everett Koop, in *Surgeon General's Report on AIDS* (Washington, D.C.: U.S. Department of Health and Human Services, 1986), 7.

2. Alan Parachini, *Los Angeles Times,* 28 August 1987.

3. Robert Redfield, Testimony before the Subcommittee on Health and Environment on Energy and Commerce (1 May 1987).

4. Associated Press, "Chief Surgeon Says AIDS Testing to Continue," 9 May 1988.

5. "Dallas Hospital Secretly Tested Patients for AIDS," *Washington Post,* 7 February 1988, 146.

6. Judith Cressy, "Empire of Reflection," *Arts and Antiques* (January 1988): 82.

15

I Have a Dream, Too

John Perkins

August 26, 1963. The drama unfolded against the backdrop of the Lincoln Memorial. Television cameras, broadcasting the historic event into millions of living rooms and offices throughout the nation, panned the expectant throng, over 200,000 strong. The occasion—the march on Washington.

The sun beat down and the afternoon wore on as a parade of speakers and singers issued impassioned pleas for liberty and justice for all. Then A. Philip Randolph, the march organizer, introduced the day's final speaker: ". . . a philosopher of the nonviolent system of behavior—Dr. Martin Luther King!"

The crowd erupted into a cheering, applauding, chanting, banner-waving mass of humanity. Dr. King had to wait a long minute before he could be heard above the crowd. Then his voice rang out with the now-famous words of this speech, "I Have a Dream," in which he proclaimed in part:

JOHN PERKINS is president emeritus both of Mendenhall Ministries, Mendenhall, Mississippi, and of Voice of Calvary Ministries, Jackson, Mississippi. He is founder and president Harambee Christian Family Center, Pasadena, California, and the John Perkins Foundation for Reconciliation and Development, which publishes the *Urban Family Magazine*. He is the author of *Land Where My Father Died* and *Let Justice Roll Down*.

I have a dream that one day this nation will rise up and live out the true meaning of its creed: "We hold these truths to be self-evident; that all men are created equal."

I have a dream that one day on the red hills of Georgia the sons of former slaves and the sons of former slaveowners will be able to sit down together at the table of brotherhood.

When we let freedom ring, when we let it ring from every village and every hamlet, from every state and every city, we will be able to speed up that day when all of God's children, black men and white men, Jews and Gentiles, Protestants and Catholics, will be able to join hands and sing in the words of the old Negro spiritual, "Free at last! free at last! thank God Almighty, we are free at last!"

In those words, Martin Luther King captured many of my own hopes and dreams. His dream was my dream too. Yet at that very time God was at work in my heart, shaping a dream bigger than the American dream, a dream rooted in the very gospel of Jesus Christ.

As our little congregation took shape, my faith was approaching a crucial test. Mechanization was displacing local sharecroppers, driving them even deeper into poverty. Racial tensions were rising. The problems plaguing our little community were so great, and we were so few. What could we do?

Did the gospel have the power to tear down evil traditions and institutions? Was there a faith stronger than culture? A faith that could burn through racial, cultural, economic, and social barriers?

I remember as if it were yesterday how I started searching the Scriptures for principles, for a strategy I could follow. God's answer came one day as I read the story of the woman at the well in John 4.

First, I noticed how Jesus approached the woman. *He came to her on her territory.* He chose to go through Samaria. Jews traveling from Judea to Galilee usually crossed over the Jordan River and went around Samaria because of their prejudice. A Jew meeting a Samaritan on the road would cross to the other side to keep even the shadow of the Samaritan from touching him. Jesus deliberately went through Samaria for one reason—he wanted to personally touch the lives of the people there.

Second, the Holy Spirit showed me this profound truth: *Jesus' love, his bodily presence in a community, could reconcile people.* A ray of hope appeared. Jesus had gone to Samaria and evangelized the Samaritans. He had burned through racial barriers! Here was a method we could use! If Jesus' bodily presence had overcome racial barriers in Samaria, his presence in Mendenhall as his body could burn through racial barriers here. We, the church, were his body. Through us, as us, he was just as present in our community as he had been that day in Samaria. Here was the key to reconciliation! The reconciliation we were powerless to bring, Christ could bring supernaturally through the presence of his body, through his people, the church!

Third, I saw how Jesus opened the conversation with the woman. *He let her felt need determine the starting point of the conversation.* She was at the well to get water; he asked for a drink. Notice that he didn't just talk about her need; he brought his own need. Her need was water; his need was water. And by asking her to give, by asking her to help him, he affirmed her dignity. Man's most deeply felt need is to have his dignity affirmed. He wants to feel his somebody-ness—to know that he is a person of worth. That is what the woman at the well needed to know. She needed to know that she was as good as a Jew.

Jesus not only affirmed the woman's dignity, he also empowered her to rise above her past. He offered her living water that would free her from her self-destructive lifestyle. So while he met her at the point of her felt need, he did not stop there. That felt need became the stepping-stone to his meeting her deeper need.

When we meet people at the point of their felt needs, we avoid the trap of arbitrarily defining their problems for them and imposing our "solutions" on them. If we respond to their felt needs not with a dependency-producing charity, but rather with identification with the need, with receiving as well as giving and with an empowering response that permanently lifts them above their past, then we help them to become all God has in mind for them to be.

Within these three principles lay the seed of a strategy for the church, a strategy we would come to call the "three *Rs*" of Christian community development.

The first *R* is *relocation.* To minister effectively to the poor I must relocate in the community of need. By living as a neighbor with the poor, the needs of the community become my own. I am no

longer isolated in a suburban community. Shared needs and friendships become a bridge for communicating the good news of Jesus
Christ and working together for better conditions in the community.

If we are going to be the body of Christ, shouldn't we do as he
did? He didn't commute daily from heaven to earth to minister to us.
Nor did he set up a mission compound that would make him immune
to our problems. No, he became flesh and lived among us (John
1:14).

The second *R* is *reconciliation*. The gospel has the power to reconcile people both to God and to each other. Man's reconciliation to
God through Jesus Christ is clearly the heart of the gospel. But we
must also be reconciled to each other. Reconciliation across racial,
cultural, and economic barriers is not an optional aspect of the gospel.
I need you and you need me. God commands us to love and forgive
one another. Our love for one another demonstrates to the world that
we are indeed Jesus' disciples (see John 13:35). We must be reconciled to both God and man.

The third *R* is *redistribution*. Christ calls us to share with those
in need. This calls for redistributing more than our goods. It means
sharing our skills, our time, our energy, and our gospel in ways that
empower people to break out of the cycle of poverty and assume responsibility for their own needs. We must organize business enter-
prises within the community of need that will be owned by a broad
base of people. This will mean using such methods as cooperatives,
mutual savings and loan associations, and credit unions. The goal of
redistribution is not absolute equality, but a more equitable distribution of resources.

A Time for Harvest

After Jesus' disciples returned to the well, Jesus looked up and
saw the Samaritans coming out to him from the city. To his disciples
he said, "Do you not say, 'Four months more and then the harvest'?
I tell you, open your eyes and look at the fields! They are ripe for harvest" (John 4:35).

The fields of America are also white, ready for harvest. The
needs will not wait. The problems will not go away. According to
Gallup polls, over 40 million Americans profess to be "born again."

The same polls, however, reveal that crime and immorality in America are rising to unprecedented levels. Religion is up and morality is down. Despite its growth, the church is not bringing healing to our nation. It is not penetrating our communities with a message that transforms.

Conditions in the black community are especially bleak. Though blacks make up only 11 percent of the population . . .

—70 percent of the U.S. prison population is black.

—In major American cities, more than 50 percent of all black children are born out of wedlock.

—46 percent of black families are single-parent families.

—In 1977 more blacks were killed by other blacks than were killed in the entire nine years of the Vietnamese conflict.

—The National Alliance for Family Life reports that half of all blacks getting married this year will be divorced within two years.

In light of these figures, the need for evangelism is critical. Our day calls for an evangelism that touches people where they live—one that speaks to their felt needs. Our day calls for a gospel that reconciles black and white. For unless we preach a gospel of reconciliation, we preach no gospel at all.

In the face of such spiritual and human need the church's flight to the suburbs cannot go unchallenged. How can we claim to be loyal to Christ's mission when we flee the mission field at our doorstep? When we forsake the inner city so that our lives will not be inconvenienced by the sufferings of the neediest among us? We flee the very mission fields we should be invading. We try to soothe our consciences with such token ministries to the poor as tracts and media—nice, safe "ministries" that do not require living or working among the poor, "ministries" that insulate us from sharing in their suffering.

The poor of America today are at the mercy of politicians' whims and philanthropists' charity. But neither politicians nor philanthropists can offer people what they need the most—the incarnate love of Christ. Unless the church fulfills its responsibility to proclaim by word and deed the "good news to the poor," the poor have no true hope. We, the church, bear the only true gospel of hope. Only through us can the power of Christ's love save and deliver them.

My dream is to see healing come to our nation through the power of the gospel with a strategy of relocation, reconciliation, and redistribution. "The harvest is plentiful but the workers are few. Ask the Lord of the harvest, therefore, to send out workers into his harvest field" (Matthew 9:37–38).

The Reconciled Community

To raise up a community of believers reconciled to God and to each other—that was our dream in 1975 in Jackson, Mississippi. We believed that if we would faithfully *be* the people of God in our neighborhood, we could make a positive difference in the lives of people enslaved by poverty and racism.

We wanted our church to be much more than a worshipping congregation: we wanted it to be the family of God, the body of Christ within our community. To really function as Christ's body, we would each have to recognize the unique spiritual gifts that each person brought to the fellowship. We would have to recognize that we could not truly operate as a body unless we used our spiritual gifts to minister to each other, to sharpen each other. And then we would have to blend our gifts together in reaching out into the neighborhood in a way that would meet the needs of people and bring glory to Christ.

We decided that our best strategy in Jackson was to have both a church—Voice of Calvary Fellowship—and a ministry organization—Voice of Calvary Ministries. The church would be the vehicle for the relationships. The ministry organization would direct the community development programs. By keeping the two separate, people from other churches could work with us in VOCM without feeling pressured to join our church. Through VOCM we hoped to draw many pastors and congregations into the work of reconciliation and community development.

Though Mississippi might not have offered any historical precedents for a reconciled fellowship, the book of Acts did. We drew inspiration particularly from the Antioch fellowship—a church that demonstrated both the possibility and the necessity of reconciliation within the body of Christ.

"In the church at Antioch there were prophets and teachers: Barnabas, Simeon called Niger, Lucius of Cyrene, Manaen (who had been brought up with Herod the tetrarch) and Saul" (Acts 13:1). This one verse reveals a lot about the church at Antioch. The leadership team included blacks—Simon called Niger—and whites—Gentiles like Lucius of Cyrene. It included Jews like Saul and aristocrats like Manaen, along with common men and women. The fellowship of Antioch transcended racial, cultural, and social barriers. Not only were all these groups represented in the congregation, they were its leaders. It seems the Holy Spirit spontaneously gifted those he chose and brought them together into a unified team.

Now that doesn't mean that the Antioch church was without its tensions. When the Jewish Christians first went there, they preached the gospel only to Jews. It was not until Christians from Cyprus and Cyrene—evidently converted at Pentecost—came to Antioch that the gospel was preached to the Greeks (see Acts 11:19–20).

Peter himself ignited racial tension. While he was visiting in Antioch, Jews from the circumcision party arrived. Fearing their criticism, Peter quit eating with the Gentiles. The rest of the Jews from that local fellowship followed Peter's lead. Even Barnabas gave in to the pressure.

Paul minced no words about the seriousness of Peter's sin. He said that Peter "was clearly in the wrong" (Galatians 2:11), that his act was "hypocrisy" (v. 13) and that the Jews were not "acting in line with the truth of the gospel" (v. 14). So severe was Peter's offense that Paul rebuked him before the whole church. For the Jews to hold themselves separate from the Gentiles when God had declared them one was to violate the very truth of the gospel.

And so it is today. When blacks and whites who have worked and shopped and studied and eaten side by side all week go to segregated churches on Sunday morning at 11:00 A.M., the gospel itself is betrayed. If the gospel doesn't bring you into relationship with God, then bring you into relationship with your fellowman, then make you want to bring other people into that relationship, I can't imagine what the gospel is for.

The only purpose of the gospel is to reconcile people to God and to each other. A gospel that doesn't reconcile is not a Christian gospel at all. But in America it seems as if we don't believe that. We don't really believe that the proof of our discipleship is that we love one another (see John 13:35). No, we think the proof is in numbers—church attendance, decision cards. Even if our "converts" continue to hate each other, even if they will not worship with their brothers and sisters in Christ, we point to their "conversion" as evidence of the gospel's success. We have substituted a gospel of church growth for a gospel of reconciliation.

And how convenient it is that our "church growth experts" tell us that homogeneous churches grow fastest! That welcome news seems to relieve us of the responsibility to overcome racial barriers in our churches. It seems to justify not bothering with breaking down racial barriers, since that would only distract us from "church growth." And so the most segregated racist institution in America, the evangelical church, racks up the numbers, declaring itself "successful," oblivious to the fact that the dismemberment of the body of Christ broadcasts to the world every day a hypocrisy as blatant as Peter's at Antioch—a living denial of the truth of the gospel.

Bearing One Another's Burdens

Black separatism and white exclusiveness often grow out of a fear of what interracial relationships might bring. Our exclusiveness is our attempt to avoid suffering and conflict. Whenever two different groups of any kind come together, there is conflict. For that conflict to be resolved, somebody has to take the heat. The work of reconciliation calls for a leader who can draw out that hostility, who can accept that hostility himself, and who can bring together the conflicting people or groups.

Jesus, the Great Reconciler, suffered the agony of all our sins—an agony far beyond our comprehension. Yet without that suffering there would have been no reconciliation. We would still be God's enemies. If we are going to share in Christ's mission, we must also share in his suffering. "For it has been granted to you on behalf of Christ not only to believe on him, but also to suffer for him" (Philippians 1:29). We cannot follow Christ without taking up our crosses (see Matthew 10:38).

James says, "Consider it pure joy, my brothers, whenever you face trials of many kinds, because you know that the testing of your faith develops perseverance. Perseverance must finish its work so that you may be mature and complete, not lacking anything" (1:2–4). I think James needed to think of a word other than "joy" because it's not going to be joyful. But it is going to be good and it's going to be healthy. We must not try to avoid the suffering and short-circuit this process. Even when we ask for physical healing our primary motive should not be to end the suffering, but rather to be able to throw our whole bodies back into God's work again.

We were under no illusion that the work in Jackson would be easy. Most blacks didn't want whites in their churches, and most whites didn't want blacks in their churches. What we were coming to establish, most people didn't want. To be reconcilers in a racist city, we would have to suffer the hostility of both blacks and whites.

The duty to "carry each other's burdens" (Galatians 6:2) takes on added meaning in an interracial fellowship. When a white brother comes to the community, he's bringing all his superiority and all his guilt that society has put on him. I must be able and willing to absorb that if we are to be reconciled.

And my white brother in the community must also recognize that I bring my history of being treated as inferior, of being told I am a nobody, a nigger. He must understand that I am trying to claim my worth as a person created in God's image. He must help bear the burden of all the bitterness and anger that grows out of my past.

To be reconciled to each other, then, we must bear the burdens created by each other's pasts. And to be reconcilers in the world, to bring others together, we must bear the burdens of both parties we seek to reconcile.

Strategies for Community Formation

Since we wanted our ministry to be to both blacks and whites, we chose a target neighborhood that was about 80 percent white, and turning black. At the rate it was changing over, it would be all black in four or five years. In establishing our community there, one of our goals was to transform the neighborhood into one where blacks and whites would live together in harmony.

We bought a big house in our target area and called it the Four C Center—the Center for Continuous Christian Community. The

Four C Center was seven blocks from the Jackson State University campus, a black university where we wanted to establish a ministry.

From the beginning we were convinced that the ministry had to be based in Christian community, because only that kind of intense interdependence—an actual sharing of our lives—could mold us into the kind of ministry team that could make a strong positive impact on our neighborhood. We needed to be a Christian community because only such a community would provide us with a laboratory in which we could work out the tough nitty-gritty of reconciliation.

In Jackson we did not define community, as some groups have, in terms of extended households, though our community does have extended households. We outlined a geographical area six blocks in radius within which the families in our community would live. I moved from our house in another part of Jackson and bought a house in our ministry area. We knew that to be effective we had to live among the people we were ministering to.

We started out by holding Bible classes in the Four C Center. Then in 1975 we started our church fellowship.

Our first community development program was People's Development, Inc. This ministry involves buying old houses, remodeling them, and selling them at reasonable rates. The starting capital for the business came from our personal incomes. The houses provided homes within our target area for people joining our community.

Worshiping in a house posed a problem. Black people don't like to go to church in a house; they like to go to a church building. So we started focusing our ministry on the kids, hoping to reach the parents through them. Our ministry started bearing fruit, and people from the community started coming to our church.

Our success, though, created a problem. People outside our community began to come to our church too. Now, we wanted people to join us in our ministry, but we also wanted our church to be much more than a place where we worshiped together. We wanted it to be a Christian community—a team of Christians deeply committed to God and each other and to a common task—reaching our neighborhood with a holistic gospel. We had a unique purpose—to serve the people who lived in our target area.

I encouraged everyone who did not live in our target community to join churches in their own neighborhoods. We were convinced that people who did not live in the target area could not really bear the burdens of those who did. They could not have the same kind of concern for the target community as those who lived there and whose children went to school there.

Several of these families then moved into our community. Some, of course, stayed where they were and found churches in their own neighborhoods. This decision, I believe, was crucial to our effectiveness in the neighborhood.

As the church grew, we created what we call household groups. These small groups met once a week for Bible study and sharing. Ideally we wanted these household groups to consist of people from the same neighborhood who would get to know each other by eating and playing and studying and praying together. This shared life, then, would strengthen their witness in their neighborhoods. Like most churches we have a choir, Sunday School, prayer meeting, and so on, but our main life together is in the household groups.

Ten elders lead our fellowship. They take turns speaking, they lead the household groups, and together they make decisions about the life of our fellowship. The elders take turns moderating meetings. The moderator leads the discussion and determines when a decision has been reached. Of course, the elders don't make all the decisions; any major decisions are made by the congregation as a whole—by consensus, not by voting.

The community structures I have described worked well, but they are not, in themselves, Christian community. Christian community is personal relationships. It is people loving each other. And no matter how perfectly we plan the community structure or procedures, as long as people are human, achieving and maintaining unity will never be easy. We rediscovered this fact when we began to build our community in Jackson.

Reconciliation: A Strategy for Here and Now

If the purpose of the gospel is to reconcile us to God and to our fellowman, if our mission is to be God's ambassadors of reconciliation (see 2 Corinthians 5:20), how do we fulfill that mission?

It's tempting for us to start out with a list of things to do. But that is not how the work of reconciliation begins. Before we can *do* the work of God, we must *be* the people of God—the believing fellowship, the body of Christ. We cannot achieve Christ's mission by working alone; we must work as a body, each one exercising his spiritual gifts as a part of the whole.

The believing fellowship must be a living demonstration of the love that God gives us for one another. Our invitation to others then becomes, "Come join us in this fellowship which we have with each other and with God" (see 1 John 1:3). But before we can invite others to join our fellowship, we must *have* a fellowship. So before we can do the work of the church, we must *be* the church.

To do the work of reconciliation, then, we must begin by being a reconciled fellowship, by being the body of Christ. We must model the kind of relationships into which we want to invite others. Our love for each other gives credibility and power to our witness. We must begin by *being*.

Being, though, is not complete until it results in doing. As James says, "Faith by itself, if it is not accompanied by action, is dead" (2:17). A faith that doesn't express itself in works is not a true faith. We often get volunteers who come to VOC with the goal of being reconciled to Christians of another race. Now that's good, but it's not enough. It's not enough to just be a reconciled fellowship, though that is where we have to start. We must be a reconciled fellowship on *mission*. And our mission is to bring others into fellowship with God and with ourselves. "We proclaim to you what we have seen and heard, so that you also may have fellowship with us. And our fellowship is with the Father and with his Son, Jesus Christ" (1 John 1:3). John continues, "We must write and tell you about it, because the more that fellowship extends, the greater the joy it brings to us who are already in it" (1:4 PHILLIPS). Many of the people in the Christian community movement seem to lack this vision. They reach out into their neighborhoods with social action programs, and that is great. That's part of the gospel; but it's not the whole gospel. The whole gospel speaks to both man's social needs *and* his spiritual needs.

If some communities make the mistake of trying to *be* without *doing*, other groups make the mistake of putting doing ahead of being. This is my tendency. When I see poverty, I remember my own background and feel "these people don't need to suffer anymore." So in my eagerness to help, I sometimes put my doing ahead of my being. And if you aren't careful, I may manipulate you into putting your doing ahead of your being.

I'm still trying to learn not to let my doing run ahead of my being; not to put my "ministry" ahead of people. It's not easy to learn to strike the balance between being and doing. On the one hand we must avoid just "being a fellowship," without ever getting on with the task of reaching out to others with a holistic gospel and bringing people to a saving knowledge of Jesus. On the other hand we dare not so emphasize doing that we forget that people are more important than programs. If our "ministries" ever become more important to us than people, we have forgotten what ministry is. We must learn to strike a balance.

We begin, then, by being reconciled to each other. Blacks and whites are equally damaged, equally in need of healing. Even when these attitudes are not conscious, even when there is a real love for those of other races, with rare exceptions these attitudes are still there. Sometimes blacks or whites coming together will say, "Oh, let's don't talk about race. We don't need to talk about it." But talking about it is just exactly what we *do* need to do. Only when we've talked about it openly can healing really begin to happen.

In coming together we must expect conflict and struggle. And we have to understand each other's gimmicks. The black gimmick is to blame, to create guilt in the white. And the white likes to accept the black's problems as being his fault. The problem with that is that it removes the black person's responsibility to change the situation and encourages a patronizing response from the white person. That kind of response won't work; we must *share* the responsibility for building a better tomorrow.

I get so tired of all the cop-outs I hear at VOC. A black girl comes up with all this cheap hate against a white coworker to get out of being efficient and committed. Or some white guy says to me, "I can't be all I want to be, because if I do I'll overshadow this black guy." I come back, "Don't give me that patronizing garbage! Be the best you can be! That's what it's going to take for you to help anyone." Community brings out the best in us. And the worst.

If the church is to be a racially reconciled community, it must be a fellowship where we are so secure in each other's love that we can share our feelings honestly without needing to fear rejection. We must create an environment where we can confess our sins to each other, ask each other for forgiveness, and administer God's forgiveness to each other as his priests. And we must be able to confront one another lovingly and be willing to be confronted with our own sins.

Reconciliation, you see, is not a warm feeling; it is love, and love always acts. Reconciliation is a unity of heart, mind, and purpose. Our reconciliation is revealed and completed as we work hand in hand to reach out to bring others into fellowship with God and with each other. If we sit around and talk until we see eye to eye on everything before we do anything, we'll never do anything. But the very act of working together toward our common mission encourages the process of reconciliation.

Getting Started

When a community such as this is just getting started, it is a good idea for its leaders to receive guidance from the elders of another church for a while. A new group being sent out by a parent church should remain a part of that parent body until two or three of its elders have gained sufficient leadership experience to guide the community. If zealous young people take over the leadership too soon, the community members may destroy one another (see 1 Timothy 3:1–6). Don't choose an elder who likes to lord it over others. An elder should derive his authority from his spirituality and his servant spirit.

The presence or absence of a Bible-teaching church with a community outreach may also affect your choice of a target area. Do you plan to work through an existing church? Then find a church led by indigenous leaders who live in the community they serve and who share at least some of your vision for the community's renewal. If that kind of church is ministering in your target area, join it. Don't duplicate their ministry. Don't compete with it. Join forces with it. Submitting yourself to indigenous leadership will give you quicker and wider acceptance in the community.

While the ideal situation is to be able to submit your ministry to indigenous leadership, not finding the "ideal" is no excuse for not going. Our mandate is to take the gospel. If we sit around waiting for the ideal missionary opportunity, we will never go.

What can the church you are in right now do to encourage reconciliation? One of the best possible responses is to send out a ministry team from your church to relocate into a needy area and start a new church there. The daughter church could have a rally one Sunday afternoon a month which the people from your church could attend. You would put your offerings into the collection plate then so they could use it for their ministry with no strings attached. You could combine the rally with a potluck dinner where you could get to know the people in the new church and build bridges between blacks and whites or people of other races.

Another approach would be for your church to adopt an existing ethnic church. Have the pastor speak in your church at least once a year. Designate the offering from that service to go to the adopted church. Hold work days where people from your church help with projects at the adopted church. Combine the resources of your church with those of the adopted church to meet community needs neither church could meet alone.

Once your church has established a strong relationship with the adopted church, ask their people to join you in reaching out to other needy people in the community. For example, you could join forces to help clean up a church building or homes damaged by a storm. When you invite the people of your adopted congregation to become your partners in reaching out, they become your equals.

You personally can do things to bring about reconciliation even if you can't move into the ghetto. Turn your home and your yard into a laboratory of reconciliation by inviting people of other races to come over for a cookout together. Invite kids from the ghetto to your house. One white lady I know enrolled in a black college, not only because she needed the classes but also to build relationships with blacks. She now is bringing her black friends and white friends together when she entertains in her home.

However we do it, we must find ways to affirm people's dignity and help them to become all God has in mind for them to be. You can be God's agent to bring together people now divided by sin-built walls. You can participate in God's plan to bring healing and wholeness to our land.

You can be a reconciler!

16

The Naked Public Square

Charles Colson

> The greatest question of our time is not communism versus
> individualism, not Europe versus America, not even the East
> versus the West; it is whether men can live without God.
>
> Will Durant

A recent *Time* magazine cover story titled "Ethics" raised many disturbing issues: "What's wrong? Hypocrisy, betrayal and greed un-
settle the nation's soul. . . . At a time of moral disarray, America
seeks to rebuild a structure of values."[1]

Yet even in the midst of this long-overdue national soul-searching,
the authors still hedged the issue. "Who is to decide what are the 'right'
values?" wrote a professor of education. "Does ultimate moral authority lie with institutions such as church and state to codify and impose?
Or, in a free society, are these matters of private conscience, with final
choice belonging to the individual?"[2]

What such experts do not see is that by raising such questions,
they are pointing to the answer. We live in a society in which all transcendent values have been removed and thus there is no moral standard by which anyone can say right is right and wrong is wrong. What
we live in is, in the memorable image of Richard Neuhaus, a naked
public square.

On the surface, a value-free society sounds liberal, progressive,
and enlightened. It certainly sounded that way to the generations of

CHARLES COLSON served as special counsel to President Richard M. Nixon
from 1969 to 1973. He is the founder and chairman of Prison Fellowship
Ministries in Washington, D.C. His books include *Born Again*, *Against the
Night*, and *The God of Stones and Spiders*.

the sixties and early seventies—probably many of the same people now wringing their hands on the pages of *Time*. But when the public square is naked, truth and values drift with the winds of public favor and there is nothing objective to govern how we are to live together. Why should we be shocked, then, by the inevitable consequences; why should we be surprised to discover that society yields what is planted?

Why are we surprised that crime soars steadily among juveniles when parents fail to set standards of right behavior in the home, when school teachers will not offer a moral opinion in the classroom, either out of fear of litigation or because they cannot "come from a position of what is right and wrong," as one New Jersey teacher put it?[3]

Why are we horrified at the growing consequences of sexual promiscuity—including a life-threatening epidemic—when sex is treated as casually as going out for a Frosty at Wendy's?

Why are we shocked at disclosures of religious leaders bilking their ministries of millions when they've been preaching a get-rich-quick gospel all along?

Why the wonderment over the fact that, for enough dollars or sexual favors, government employees and military personnel sell out their nation's secrets? As C. S. Lewis wrote forty years ago, "We laugh at honor and are shocked to find traitors in our midst."[4]

Why is it so surprising that Wall Street yuppies make fast millions on insider information or tax fraud? Without objective values, the community or one's neighbor has no superior claim over one's own desires.

Whether we like to hear it or not, we are reaping the consequences of the decades since World War II when we have, in Solzhenitsyn's words, "forgotten God." What we have left is the reign of relativism.

Humanity cannot survive without some form of law. "The truly naked public square is at best a transitional phenomenon," wrote Richard John Neuhaus. "It is a vacuum begging to be filled."[5] Excise belief in God and you are left with only two principals: the individual and the state. In this situation, however, there is no mediating structure to generate moral values and, therefore, no counterbalance to the inevitable ambitions of the state. "The naked public square cannot remain naked, the direction is toward the state-as-church, toward totalitarianism."[6]

This has already occurred in Marxist nations where the death of God has created a new form of messiah—the all-powerful state whose political ideology acquires the force of religion. The same is true, though not as extreme, in the West where traditional religious influences have been excluded from public debates either by law or Chesterton's "taboo of tact or convention." As a result, government is free to make its own ultimate judgments. Hence government ideology acquires the force of religion.

The removal of the transcendent sucks meaning from the law. Without an absolute standard of moral judgment backing government "morality," where is the protection for the minorities and the powerless? "When in our public life no legal prohibition can be articulated with a force of transcendent authority, then there are no rules rooted in ultimacies that can protect the poor, the powerless and the marginal, as indeed there are now no rules protecting the unborn, and only fragile inhibitions surrounding the aged and defective."[7]

With no ultimate reference point supporting it—no just cause for obedience—law can only be enforced by the bayonet. So the state seeks more and more coercive power.

But the most dangerous consequence of the naked public square is the loss of community.

A community is a gathering of people around shared values, a commitment to one another and to common ideals and aspirations that cannot be created by government. As Arthur Schlesinger observed, "We have forgotten that constitutions work only as they reflect an actual sense of community."[8]

Without commitment to community, individual responsibility quickly erodes. One vivid illustration of this was a Princeton student's protest after President Jimmy Carter proposed reinstating the draft registration in 1977. Newspapers across the country showed the young man defiantly carrying a placard proclaiming: "Nothing is worth dying for."

To many, these words seemed an affirmation of life, the ultimate assertion of individual worth. What they fail to reckon with, however, is the reverse of that slogan: if nothing is worth dying for, is anything worth living for? A society that has no reference points beyond itself "increasingly becomes a merely contractual arrangement," says sociologist Peter Berger. The problem with that, he continues, is that human beings will not die for a social contract. And "unless people are prepared, if necessary, to die for it," a society cannot long survive.[9]

In these last twenty years of the twentieth century, we are sailing uncharted waters. Never before in the history of Western civilization has the public square been so devoid of transcendent values.

The notion of law rooted in transcendent truth, in God himself, is not the invention of Christian fundamentalists calling naively for America to return to its Christian roots. The roots of American law are as much in the works of Cicero and Plato as in the Bible. But if fundamentalists are guilty of distorting American history, their critics are guilty of distorting the whole history of Western civilization.

Plato, in terms as religious as Moses or David, claimed that transcendent norms were the true foundations for civil law and order. He taught that "there exist divine moral laws, not easy to apprehend, but operating upon all mankind." He refuted the argument of some Sophists that there was no distinction between virtue and vice, and he affirmed that "God, not man, is the measure of all things."[10]

Cicero, to whom the American Founding Fathers looked for guidance, maintained that religion is indispensable to private morals and public order and that it alone provided the concord by which people could live together.[11] "True law," wrote Cicero, "is right reason in agreement with Nature; it is of universal application and everlasting; it summons to duty by its commands, and averts from wrong-doing by its prohibitions."

Augustine wrote *The City of God* to defend the role of Christianity as the essential element in preserving society, stating that what the pagans "did not have the strength to do out of love of country, the Christian God demands of [citizens] out of love of himself. Thus, in a general breakdown of morality and of civic virtues, divine Authority intervened to impose frugal living, continence, friendship, justice and concord among citizens."[12] Augustine contended that without true justice emanating from a sovereign God there could never be the concord of which Cicero wrote.

During the French Revolution, Edmund Burke acknowledged that the attempt to build a secularized state was not so much irreverent as irrational. "We know, and it is our pride to know, that man is by his constitution a religious animal; that atheism is against, not only our reason, but our instincts; and that it cannot prevail long."[13]

Religion has always been a decisive factor in the shaping of the American experience. According to one modern scholar, it was the Founding Fathers' conviction that "republican government depends for its health on values that over the not-so-long run must come from religion."[14]

John Adams believed that the *moral* order of the new nation depended on biblical religion. "If I were an atheist . . . I should believe that chance had ordered the Jews to preserve and propagate to all mankind the doctrine of a supreme, intelligent, wise, almighty sovereign of the universe, which I believe to be the great essential principle of all morality, and consequently of all civilization."[15]

Tocqueville, the shrewd observer of American democracy, maintained that "religion in America takes no direct part in the government of society, but it must be regarded as the first of their political institutions. . . . How is it possible that society should escape destruction if the moral tie is not strengthened in proportion as the political tie is relaxed? And what can be done with a people who are their own masters if they are not submissive to the Deity?"[16]

In considering such lessons from the past, historians Will and Ariel Durant cited the agnostic Joseph Renan, who in 1866 wrote, "What would we do without [Christianity]? . . . If rationalism wishes to govern the world without regard to the religious needs of the soul, the experience of the French Revolution is there to teach us the consequences of such a blunder." The Durants concluded, "There is no significant example in history before our time, of a society successfully maintaining moral life without the aid of religion."[17]

The supreme irony of our century is that in those nations that still enjoy the greatest human freedoms, this traditional role of religion is denigrated; while in nations that have fallen under the oppressor's yoke, the longing for the spiritual is keenest. In the West intellectuals widely disdain religion; in the Soviet Union they cry out for its return.

In a wave of recent articles, three popular contemporary Soviet writers, Vasily Bykov, Viktor Astafyev, and Chinghiz Aytmatov, have blamed Russia's moral degradation upon the decline of religion. "Who extinguished the light of goodness in our soul? Who blew out the lamp of our conscience, toppled it into a dark, deep pit in which we are groping, trying to find the bottom, a support and some kind of guiding light to the future?" asks Astafyev, a Christian, in *Our Contemporary*, a popular Moscow journal.[18] Though a Muslim, Aytmatov centers his writings on Christ, whom he admires as a greater influence than Mohammed. He and his fellow writers boldly attacked Communism for creating "an all-encompassing belief" that has plunged the Russian people into a moral abyss. Bykov, winner of every Soviet literary award, declares there can be no morality without faith.[19]

Yet our twentieth century has set itself apart as the first to explicitly reject the wisdom of the ages that religion is indispensable to the concord and justice of society.

Mankind now has three choices: to remain divorced from the transcendent; to construct a rational order to preserve society without recourse to real or imagined gods; or to establish the viable influence of the Kingdom of God in the kingdoms of man.

The first option invites chaos and tyranny, as the bloodshed, repression, and nihilism of this century testify. We are then left with the second and third choices. These opposing arguments were well presented by two of the great thinkers of the twentieth century: the eminent journalist, Walter Lippmann, and Nobel laureate, Aleksandr Solzhenitsyn.

Before writing *A Preface to Morals,* Lippmann concluded that modern man could no longer embrace a simple religious faith. For Lippmann, the goal was to create a humanistic view in which "mankind, deprived of the great fictions, is to come to terms with the needs which created those fictions." For himself, Lippmann came to a rather fatalistic conclusion: "I take the humanistic view because, in the kind of world I happen to live in, I can do no other."[20] Lippmann thus set about to extract the ethical ideals of religious figures from their theological and historical context. Man in his own rational interest, he believed, could sustain a man-made religion. Some religion, even if it was a religion that denied religion, had to be followed.

On the other side of the spectrum from this religion of humanism stands Aleksandr Solzhenitsyn, a lonely and often outspoken prophet. In his 1978 Harvard commencement address, Solzhenitsyn listed a litany of woes facing the West: the loss of courage and will, the addiction to comfort, the abuse of freedom, the capitulation of intellectuals to fashionable ideas, the attitude of appeasement with evil.

The cause for all this was the humanistic view Lippmann had embraced. "The humanistic way of thinking," thundered Solzhenitsyn, "which had proclaimed itself as our guide, did not admit the existence of evil in man, nor did it see any task higher than the attainment of happiness on earth. It started modern western civilization on the dangerous trend of worshiping man and his material needs . . . gaps were left open for evil, and its drafts blow freely today."

In American democracy, said Solzhenitsyn, rights "were granted on the ground that man is God's creature. That is, freedom was given to the individual conditionally, in the assumption of his constant religious responsibility."

Solzhenitsyn lamented that two hundred years ago, as the Constitution was being written, or even fifty years ago, when Walter Lippmann was trying to preserve the husk of Western virtue, "it would have seemed quite impossible . . . that an individual be granted boundless freedom with no purpose, simply for the satisfaction of his whims. . . . The West has finally achieved the rights of man, and even to excess, but man's sense of responsibility to God and society has grown dimmer and dimmer."[21] Solzhenitsyn was saying that nothing less than spiritual renewal could save Western civilization.

If we reject the nihilism that denies all meaning and hope, we must believe human society has purpose. We are forced to choose, therefore, belief in man, faith in faith, hope in hope, and the love of love; or we must look for a point beyond ourselves to steady our balance.

The view that man in his own rational interest can sustain a man-made religion is voiced regularly on op-ed pages, on television specials, even from church pulpits. It remains fashionable because it offers a positive view of human nature, filled with hopeful optimism about man's capacities. But it ignores the ringing testimony of a century filled with terror and depravity.

If the real benefits of the Judeo-Christian ethic and influence in secular society were understood, it would be anxiously sought out, even by those who *repudiate* the Christian faith. The influence of the Kingdom of God in the public arena is good for society as a whole.

Notes

1. Walter Shapiro, "Ethics: What's Wrong?" *Time*, 25 May 1987, 14.

2. Ezra Bowen, "Ethics: Looking to Its Roots," *Time*, 25 May 1987, 26.

3. Elwood McQuaid, "Lying as a Lifestyle," *Moody Monthly* (July/August 1987): 8.

4. C. S. Lewis, *The Abolition of Man* (New York: Macmillan, 1974), 35.

5. Richard John Neuhaus, *The Naked Public Square* (Grand Rapids, Mich.: Eerdmans, 1984), 86.

6. Ibid., 89.

7. Ibid., 153.

8. Arthur Schlesinger, *The Vital Center* (New York: Houghton Mifflin, 1962), 188. Quoted in Neuhaus, *The Naked Public Square*, 91.

9. Peter L. Berger, "Religion in Post-Protestant America," *Commentary* 81:5 (May 1986): 44.

10. Russell Kirk, *The Roots of American Order* (LaSalle, Ill.: Open Court, 1974), 81.

11. Will Durant, *Caesar and Christ: A History of Roman Civilization from Its Beginnings to A.D. 337* (New York: Simon and Schuster, 1944), 164.

12. Etienne Gilson, "Foreword," in Augustine, *The City of God* (New York: Image/Doubleday, 1958), 19.

13. Edmund Burke, *Reflections on the Revolution in France.* Quoted in *The Portable Conservative Reader* (New York: Penguin, 1982), 27.

14. A. James Reichley, *Religion in American Public Life* (Washington, D.C.: Brookings Institute, 1986), 9.

15. Kirk, *The Roots of American Order,* 17.

16. Quoted in Sydney E. Ahlstrom, *A Religious History of the American People* (New Haven, Conn.: Yale University Press, 1972), 386.

17. Will Durant and Ariel Durant, *The Lessons of History* (New York: Simon and Schuster, 1968), 50.

18. Boris Rumer, "Soviet Writers Decry Loss of Spiritual Values in Society," *Christian Science Monitor,* 7 October 1986, 1.

19. Ibid.

20. Walter Lippmann, *A Preface to Morals* (New York: Time, 1929), 134.

21. Aleksandr I. Solzhenitsyn, *A World Split Apart: Commencement Address Delivered at Harvard University, June 8, 1978* (New York: Harper & Row, 1978), 49.